MIGRANTS AND MACHINE POLITICS

PRINCETON STUDIES IN
Political Behavior

Tali Mendelberg, Series Editor

Migrants and Machine Politics

HOW INDIA'S URBAN POOR SEEK REPRESENTATION AND RESPONSIVENESS

ADAM MICHAEL AUERBACH

TARIQ THACHIL

PRINCETON UNIVERSITY PRESS

PRINCETON & OXFORD

Published by Princeton University Press
41 William Street, Princeton, New Jersey 08540
99 Banbury Road, Oxford OX2 6JX

press.princeton.edu

All Rights Reserved

ISBN 9780691236087
ISBN (pbk.) 9780691236094
ISBN (e-book) 9780691236100

British Library Cataloging-in-Publication Data is available

Editorial: Bridget Flannery-McCoy and Alena Chekanov
Production Editorial: Nathan Carr
Jacket/Cover Design: Chris Ferrante
Production: Erin Suydam and Lauren Reese
Publicity: Kate Hensley and Charlotte Coyne
Copyeditor: Michelle Garceau Hawkins

Jacket/Cover Credit: Cover illustration by Locopopo Studio.

This book has been composed in Arno

10 9 8 7 6 5 4 3 2 1

For Marcia and Robert Auerbach, for a lifetime of encouragement

For Piyali, for walking and talking through everything

CONTENTS

ACKNOWLEDGMENTS

THIS BOOK is the culmination of eight years of collaborative research. We first began discussing the key questions animating the project in the spring of 2014, and in the years since have been immensely lucky to benefit from the support and encouragement of a wide range of interlocuters. First and foremost, we are grateful to the many residents, local leaders, party workers, elected representatives, and city bureaucrats in Bhopal and Jaipur who took time out of their busy days to speak with us. We thank those who participated in our interviews and surveys, as well as the many people who have engaged with us repeatedly over the years, and generously shared their personal and professional experiences. Without their generosity, there would be no book, and we hope the pages that follow do justice to their rich array of insights.

We are also fortunate to have benefited from the incisive feedback of many colleagues and friends. We would like to express our heartfelt gratitude to participants of our book workshop, held at Vanderbilt University in October 2019: Allen Hicken, Eunji Kim, Isabela Mares, Simeon Nichter, Alison Post, and Elizabeth Zechmeister. Comments and suggestions from the workshop participants proved invaluable in refining and sharpening many facets of the book.

We also thank the following scholars, who provided feedback on small and large pieces of the book, at various stages of our writing: Celeste Arrington, Edward Aspinall, Ameya Balsekar, Pranab Bardhan, Ward Berenschot, Rikhil Bhavnani, Leticia Bode, Aimee Bourassa, Rachel Brulé, Natália Bueno, Ernesto Calvo, Simon Chauchard, Aditya Dasgupta, Alberto Díaz-Cayeros, Jonathan Fox, Siddharth George, Agustina Giraudy, Jessica Gottlieb, Tanushree Goyal, Ken Greene, Erum Haider, Kyle Hanniman, Patrick Heller, Daniel Hidalgo, Wendy Hunter, Niraja Gopal Jayal, Miles Kahler, Devesh Kapur, Mahesh Karra, Kimuli Kasara, Tarun Khanna, Shandana Khan Mohmand, Herbert Kitschelt, Marko Klašnja, Anirudh Krishna, Gabrielle Kruks-Wisner, Tanu

Kumar, Adrienne LeBas, Melissa Lee, Kristen Looney, Xiaobo Lü, Ellen Lust, John McCauley, Mashail Malik, Lucy Martin, Dilip Mookherjee, Sripad Motiram, Noah Nathan, Gareth Nellis, Daniel Nielson, Irfan Nooruddin, David Ohls, Virginia Oliveros, Kelly Rader, Emily Rains, Vijayendra Rao, Danielle Resnick, David Samuels, Mark Schneider, Emily Sellars, Mahvish Shami, Prerna Singh, Aseema Sinha, Neelanjan Sircar, Jeremy Spater, Megan Stewart, Susan Stokes, Pavithra Suryanarayan, Yuhki Tajima, Emmanuel Teitelbaum, Anjali Thomas, Louise Tillin, Lily Tsai, Milan Vaishnav, Ashutosh Varshney, Gilles Verniers, Michael Walton, Rebecca Weitz-Shapiro, Kurt Weyland, Erik Wibbels, Steven Wilkinson, Adam Ziegfeld, and seminar participants at American University, Ashoka University, Boston University, the Carnegie Endowment for International Peace, University of California-Merced, the Centre for Policy Research, University of Chicago, Claremont McKenna College, Columbia University, Duke University, George Washington University, Georgetown University, Harvard University, the Indira Gandhi Institute of Development Research, the International Food Policy Research Institute, King's College, London, the London School of Economics, Massachusetts Institute of Technology, McGill University, the New School, Oxford University, University of Pittsburgh, Princeton University, Queen's University, Texas A&M, University of Gothenburg, University of London, University of Maryland, University of Michigan, University of Minnesota, Northwestern University, University of Pennsylvania, University of Texas-Austin, University of Virginia, University of Washington, University of Wisconsin-Madison, and Yale University.

We gratefully acknowledge generous support from American University, the University of Pennsylvania, Vanderbilt University, and Yale University, without which the fieldwork and data collection for this book would simply not have been possible.

We were very lucky to have worked with outstanding research assistants during our fieldwork in Bhopal and Jaipur. We foremost thank Ved Prakash Sharma, who adroitly—and always empathetically—led the survey teams who carried out most of the data collection efforts for the book—the surveys of residents (2015), slum leaders (2016), and ward councilors (2017/2018). We are deeply grateful to Ved for his supervision, sustained input, and friendship over the last eight years. Research assistants at our home institutions contributed to this book in a myriad of ways, from proofreading to translation work to mapmaking. For these efforts, we thank Shashwat Dhar, Karma Dulal, Shagun Gupta, Sukhmani Khalsa, Julie Radomski, Manaswini Ramkumar, and

Anjali Sah. We are also grateful to several independent researchers who provided valuable assistance, including Akash Bharadwaj, Rashi Chauhan, Prabhat Kumar, Rahul Kumar, Sanjay Joshi, and especially Asgar Qadri.

We are fortunate to have worked with an incredible team at Princeton University Press, including Nathan Carr, Alena Chekanov, Chris Ferrante, and Bridget Flannery-McCoy, each of whom expertly shepherded the book from initial submission to production. Michelle Hawkins skillfully copyedited our book, improving its composition and organization in the process. We are grateful to the three anonymous reviewers for their close readings and valuable feedback, which were enormously helpful in guiding our final revisions. We are also very thankful to Tali Mendelberg for detailed feedback and suggestions on our book, and for including it in the Princeton Studies in Political Behavior Series. Lokesh Karekar and the talented team at Locopopo Studio created the beautiful illustration on the book's cover. We thank them, very much, for such stunning art.

Chapters 2 and 3 of this book are adapted and extended versions of our 2018 articles "How Clients Select Brokers: Competition and Choice in India's Slums" *American Political Science Review* 112(4): 775–91 (published by Cambridge University Press; DOI: https://doi.org/10.1017/S000305541800028X) and "Cultivating Clients: Reputation, Responsiveness, and Ethnic Indifference in India's Slums" *American Journal of Political Science* 64(3): 471–87 (published by Wiley; DOI: https://doi.org/10.1111/ajps.12468). We thank the anonymous reviewers who provided detailed comments on the two articles.

Most importantly, we would like to thank our families and close friends, who have been cheerleaders and providers of much needed refuge, reality checks, food, and laughter. Tariq thanks Jayadev Athreya, Ameya Balsekar, Romit Bhattacharya, Sumita Bhattacharya, Samuel Decanio, Radhika Govindrajan, Adil Hasan, Suvir Kaul, Sandeep Kishore, Ania Loomba, Manjari Mukherjee, Kartik Nair, Amy Scott, Kasturi Sen, Caitlin Stern, and Anshika Varma. Most of all, thanks to Piyali Bhattacharya for her endless patience and boundless enthusiasm in talking through each stage of the project, and for making life full of exploration and adventure. Adam thanks Marcia Auerbach, Robert Auerbach, Daniel Auerbach, Brian Curtis, Jacqueline Demko, Kyle Hanniman, Anthony Lavadera, Sarah Mueller, Nick Mueller, Neil Panchal, Mona Patel, Jyotsna Patel, Ramesh Patel, Hitesh Pathak, and David Ohls. Most importantly, he thanks Prita Patel and little Arjun for daily adventures, laughs, and love.

1

Migrants and Machine Politics

THE ALLEYWAYS OF Tulsi Nagar, a slum settlement in the Indian city of Bhopal, were abuzz in November of 2018. With the state assembly elections just a
few weeks away, campaigning was in full swing. The walls of many *jhuggies*
(shanties) across the slum had been painted with the symbols of the two major
parties fighting the election: the open hand of the Indian National Congress
(Congress), India's centrist party of independence, and the lotus flower of
the ascendant, Hindu nationalist Bharatiya Janata Party (BJP). Posters were
hung throughout Tulsi Nagar featuring headshots of Uma Shankar Gupta,
the incumbent BJP legislator in Bhopal Southwest, the constituency in
which Tulsi Nagar is located. Plastered next to these posters, and in some
instances over them, were posters of the Congress candidate, P.C. Sharma.
Both candidates regularly visited Tulsi Nagar to give speeches and ask residents for their votes.

Beyond Tulsi Nagar, the elections promised to be intensely competitive
across Madhya Pradesh, the central province of which Bhopal serves as the
capital city. Observers believed that there was a good chance that the BJP would
lose its provincial majority in the state after being in power for fifteen straight
years. These same tremors echoed within Bhopal Southwest. Rumors circulated
in the weeks leading up to the election that Gupta, the incumbent, had developed cracks in his base of electoral support. Many voters felt that he had done
little to improve local conditions. Moreover, Sharma was a veteran Congress
politician who was viewed as especially popular. With anti-incumbency in the
air, the vote margin between Gupta and Sharma promised to be razor thin,
requiring the full efforts of both candidates to chase after every last vote.

At the center of this chase for votes were Tulsi Nagar's twenty-four party
workers—eight of whom worked for the Congress and sixteen for the BJP. Far
from being under the thumb of a local don, residents were wooed by these two

dozen workers, who fiercely compete amongst one another for followings, even with other workers of the same party. The most influential BJP worker in Tulsi Nagar at the time of the election was Rajesh, a lifelong resident of the settlement who enjoys a large public following.[1] Rajesh's local political standing had become so prominent in the past decade that he purchased a separate home in Tulsi Nagar just for his *netagiri* (leadership/politicking activities). The fifteen other BJP workers were spread out across the settlement, holding varying ranks in the BJP's organizational hierarchy, each seeking to displace Rajesh in the local pecking order. Congress workers were similarly scattered across the slum, with Prakash being widely regarded as the most influential of the eight.

Party workers do not descend on Tulsi Nagar only during elections. Instead, they are ordinary residents of the slum, living with their families and facing the same threats of eviction and underdevelopment as their neighbors. This embedded status gives them direct, daily access to Tulsi Nagar's several thousand voters. The workers' local influence with residents is built through quiet and sustained efforts to help them between elections, by petitioning bureaucrats and elected representatives to address mounting trash, clogged drains, water shortages, unpaved roads, and difficulties obtaining state-issued documents. Such influence is far from static. During our years of working in Tulsi Nagar we witnessed party workers rise and fall in popularity, as residents continually re-evaluated which was best positioned to assist them.

These oscillations reverberate up to the highest levels of political leadership in the city. Political elites like Gupta and Sharma must continually assess which local leaders in Tulsi Nagar to formally integrate into their party organizations and bestow with limited party positions. A party worker's current level of popularity is of paramount concern as it determines their ability to mobilize support within vote-rich slums. Between the votes, political elites must also decide how to allocate scarce resources in response to the many demands for assistance from slums across their constituencies. Such decisions have consequences for their reputations as responsive patrons, and thus their ability to win intensely competitive urban elections.

In short, party workers like Rajesh and Prakash form the everyday pathways that connect low-income voters in Bhopal's slums to the city's political elites. Thousands of party workers like those in Tulsi Nagar fan out across

1. All names throughout this book have been changed or anonymized to protect respondent privacy unless otherwise noted. The only exceptions are high-level politicians and high-profile public figures, who are easily identified and were interviewed on the record.

Bhopal's 400 slums—informal settlements that house just over a quarter of the city's population.[2] Yet the widespread presence of these party networks belies how recently they took shape. Several decades ago, most slums across Bhopal did not even exist.[3] Once formed, these settlements had no established community leaders in their earliest years. Most residents, including Rajesh and Prakash, were recent arrivals from the countryside, lacking economic and social standing in the city, let alone political clout and connections.

How do slums like Tulsi Nagar transform from clusters of hurriedly constructed shanties into the epicenters of urban elections? How does informal authority emerge within them? How do slum leaders connect to parties and bureaucracies within the city? These related concerns converge into the central question motivating this book: how are poor migrants from the countryside politically incorporated into the growing cities of the Global South?

The rapid formation of political linkages among politicians, community leaders, and poor migrants in India's cities has been nothing short of remarkable. Nearly as remarkable has been the lack of systematic attention to studying how such formative processes have unfolded. In the pages that follow we document how political networks form to connect poor migrants with the heart of urban governments. We show how unraveling these processes yields new and counterintuitive insights about the ability of disadvantaged citizens to secure representation and responsiveness from city authorities, and to demand accountability from those who govern them. In doing so, residents of slums like Tulsi Nagar routinely defy the stereotypes used to portray them, and demand a starring role in the unfolding political drama of urbanization across much of the world.

Politics in the Global South's Expanding Cities

Residents of urban slums are not leading lives that are peripheral to the major political developments of our times. Quite the opposite: they are at the very center of global demographic shifts. Early in the twenty-first century, most humans lived in cities for the first time in recorded history.[4] Between 1950 and

2. Government of India 2015, p. 107.

3. Urban slums like Tulsi Nagar are largely a post-Independence phenomenon in India's cities. UN-Habitat 1982.

4. The United Nations estimated that in 2007 the population of the world became more than 50% urban. United Nations 2018.

2050, the world is projected to transform from seventy-percent rural to seventy-percent urban. Almost all global population growth for the next three decades—roughly 2.5 billion people—is expected to occur in urban areas.[5] And almost all of this growth will happen in Africa and Asia.[6] India alone is expected to add 416 million urban residents during this time frame—the largest projected increase in the world.[7]

The conversion of migrant villagers into urbanites is a big part of this transformation, and has unfolded differently in the Global South than it did in Global North countries during their industrial revolutions.[8] Those earlier periods in the North largely drew farm workers into factory jobs, and often into dense housing constructed in close proximity to manufacturing centers.[9] Poor migrants to cities across the Global South are far more likely to toil in the informal sector, without assured wages or contracts and with little in the way of social protections.[10] These migrants also frequently reside in self-constructed dwellings in informal settlements like Tulsi Nagar.[11] Slums now house almost one billion people worldwide, or one in eight people.[12] These neighborhoods are defined by weak or absent formal property rights, dense and unplanned housing, and severe inadequacies in essential public services. In South Asia, one in three urban residents—over 200 million people—now reside in slums.

These grim statistics trouble assumptions regarding the transformative potential of urbanization for low-income countries.[13] The likelihood of such

---

5. United Nations 2018, p. 11. In contrast, the growth of the world's rural population has been slowing and is expected to peak at 3.4 billion in 2021, after which it is expected to begin a slow decline.

6. In 1950, only four out of every ten city-dwellers lived in low- and middle-income countries. Currently, more than seven out of every ten do.

7. United Nations 2018.

8. While much of the Global South's urbanization has been fueled by natural population growth within cities, roughly forty percent of urban population growth is estimated to come from rural-urban migration and the spatial expansion of cities. Montgomery 2008.

9. Rodden 2019.

10. See Hart 1973, p. 68, who draws on the experiences of migrant slum residents in Accra, Ghana to theorize the key distinguishing feature of informal sector work (a mixture of self-employment and non-wage-earning casual labor) as "whether or not labor is recruited on a permanent and regular basis for fixed rewards." Informal employment characterizes ninety percent of India's labor force. Accountability Initiative 2020, p. 9.

11. On urban informality in the Global South, see Auerbach et al. 2018 and Grossman 2021.

12. See Goal 11 of the United Nations Sustainable Development Goals.

13. Glaeser 2011 sees the expansion of slum settlements as a sign of the desirability of the city—the city as a ladder for socio-economic upward mobility that draws the rural poor. At least

potential being realized requires a fine-grained understanding of how newly urban populations are woven into—or marginalized from—the life of cities. Dilemmas of economic inclusion, specifically inadequate supplies of jobs and housing, rightly inform discussions on urban futures. Yet equally important, and far less studied, are questions of *political* inclusion. To what degree can residents of places like Tulsi Nagar command political responsiveness and meaningful representation? The answers will determine not only their own wellbeing, but the political trajectories of the countries their migrations are transforming.

In the pages that follow, we will show that residents of India's urban slums are unlikely protagonists of city politics. Popular accounts of slums often depict their residents as politically passive, exhausted by dispossession, weakened by exclusion, or subdued within the clenched fists of local dons and venal municipal authorities. Against the grain of such narratives, we show slum residents are embedded in political networks with which they actively engage. This fact itself will not surprise many scholars of urban spaces. Within the field of political science, these networks are often described as *party machines*: pyramidal hierarchies of party workers that mobilize low-income voters during elections.

Yet urban machines, whether in New York and Chicago in the early twentieth century or present-day Accra or Buenos Aires, are almost always studied from the perspective of the elites who sit at their apex. From this vantage point, machine networks are principally understood as expedient conduits for politicians looking to cheaply amass votes. Their key purpose is to enable the disbursement of material handouts, often during campaigns and through intermediaries like Rajesh, in return for electoral support. The material benefits under this arrangement are humble and episodically provided. In return for these offerings, politicians hold citizens "perversely accountable" for delivering their votes.[14] Such depictions lead wealthy residents, middle-class activists, and popular media to regularly lament that slums provide teeming and unthinking "vote banks" to Machiavellian elites.

This book flips the orientation through which urban political networks are studied. Doing so focuses our attention on how these networks are constructed at the grassroots level. Our key argument is that understanding how

---

in the Indian context, however, scholars have demonstrated that the urban poor are often "stuck" in slums, with few prospects for moving to propertied middle-class neighborhoods. Krishna 2013 and Rains and Krishna 2020.

14. Stokes 2005.

urban political networks form reveals who secures representation and accountability within city politics. Our book demonstrates that poor migrants in India do not serve as passive targets of elite machinations. Instead, they take active steps to ensure their place in city politics. Poor migrants build ties to governing authorities, principally through selecting their local community leaders. The latter's powers depend on their popularity among ordinary residents. Far from spaces pinned under the monopolizing thumbs of local strongmen, we find slums to be hotbeds of political competition. Established community leaders jostle among one another while also trying to fend off new upstarts seeking to attract their own followings.

Residents wield this competition for their affections to sow seeds of unexpected representation and responsiveness within the rough-and-tumble world of urban politics. They do not gift their support cheaply in return for election-time treats. Brokers must earn followings through daily efforts to help residents demand and secure a range of services from the state, from water connections to school admissions. The bottom-up construction of local leadership also ensures brokers reflect the qualities that residents value, which we reveal as often diverging from what parochial stereotypes of the urban poor expect.

This overlooked agency of poor migrants reverberates up the hierarchy of urban machines. Local party workers are not simply spigots through which politicians funnel handouts to buy votes, as they are commonly portrayed to be. Instead, these low-level party workers are informal representatives of the communities who have the power to select and replace them. Our bottom-up perspective also reveals the neglected agency and ambitions of party workers themselves. The local leaders we observed do not seek to remain perpetual intermediaries, endlessly content to win elections for others. Instead, they are careerists who aspire to climb up party hierarchies within the city. These unrecognized motivations prompt them to act differently than their images as painted in scholarly and popular accounts. For example, we find slum leaders in India frequently eschew exploiting ethnic divisions within their neighborhood. Instead, they favor more inclusive strategies for mobilizing broad swathes of support inside slums to help to launch political careers outside them.

For their part, political elites must work with the informal leaders that poor migrants select to represent their interests. Political elites cannot simply install their cronies as local leaders and expect residents to fall in line. In fact, we show that political elites prize slum leaders with traits that make them likely to prove effective in helping residents solve everyday problems in the city, thereby ensuring sustained popularity in the settlement.

These insights build on, and offer correctives to, a rich scholarship on urban politics in the Global South. Our study reveals unacknowledged forms of agency among poor migrants in shaping the political networks that govern them. Migrants then use these networks to demand accountability from elected officials. To be clear, we do not suggest slum residents face an inclusive and hospitable government. Indeed, many of the activities we document are catalyzed by systemic acts of state exclusion, eviction, and repression. Instead, we show that the representation and responsiveness that slum residents extract through their efforts is as hard won as it is imperfect, and worthy of acknowledgement and analysis, rather than either celebration or erasure.

How are the Urban Poor Incorporated into City Politics?

The political integration of the urban poor is often described in terms of failure, marginalization in urban governance, and dispossession by city authorities. In one popular account, Davis describes a "planet of slums" in which urban poverty pockets are little more than "living museums of human exploitation."[15] Less apocalyptic accounts still emphasize "differentiated citizenship" regimes which deny slum residents the public services that more privileged urbanites enjoy, while peppering the former with the threat of eviction.[16]

Alternatively, the urban poor are described as subjected to violence and mob rule. Scholars of urban violence have identified slums, particularly in Latin America, as "a hidden continent" of "criminal governance" in which local gangs enforce property rights, provide loans, and tax local businesses.[17] In India, a vision of slums as lawless underworlds has been popularized in films and television, which depict slum residents as ruled by coercive kingpins like Mhatre in the 1998 Bollywood film *Satya*, Mamman in the 2008 Hollywood hit *Slumdog Millionaire*, or Ganesh Gaitonde in Netflix's 2018 show *Sacred Games*.

The deprivations and hostility faced by the slum settlements we worked with are beyond question. Yet accounts focusing on these conditions often render residents as hopelessly docile in the face of repression and dispossession. The events we describe in Tulsi Nagar—and in the more than one

15. Davis 2006.
16. Heller et al. 2015; Bhan 2016.
17. Lessing 2020.

hundred other slum settlements with which we engage in this book—cuts sharply against such depictions. A homogenous view of slums as sites of exclusion prevents us from asking and answering critically important questions about how these settlements elbow their way into city politics.

Perhaps Tulsi Nagar's experiences are better anticipated by studies that argue wily city elites find it more profitable to incorporate the urban poor than to entirely exclude them. Tulsi Nagar's party workers illustrate one important and historically common pathway of inclusion through party machines. A venerable literature documents such machines as marked by three distinctive features. The first is their hierarchical, pyramid-shaped structures that link political elites ("patrons") to voters who support them ("clients"). These linkages are typically facilitated by intermediaries ("brokers") like Rajesh, who are entrenched in neighborhoods and forge face-to-face ties with voters.[18] Second, machines are arranged geographically, with brokers controlling neighborhoods that are nested within the larger electoral domains of their patrons.[19] Third, machines rely on the distribution of material spoils to win support—not lofty ideologies or policy promises.[20] These benefits can range from jobs, electricity connections, and access to hospital beds; to election-time handouts of cash and food; to local public goods like paved roads, sewers, and schools.

Many of the earliest examples of party machines come from cities of the United States, particularly during a period stretching from the Gilded Age (the last quarter of the nineteenth century) through the Second World War. From New York and Philadelphia to Kansas City and Chicago, machine bosses generated electoral support among poor European migrants by doling out jobs

---

18. Cornelius 1975; Fox 1994; Gay 1994; Auyero 2001; Hicken 2011; Szwarcberg 2015; Oliveros 2021.

19. Describing the geography of party machines in American cities, Trounstine 2008, p. 99, notes, "Machine parties were organized in a pyramid with hundreds of precinct workers at the bottom and one or a few party leaders at the top . . . the boss relied on the loyalty and support of many individuals working in the wards, precincts, blocks, and even individual tenements."

20. As Gosnell 1933, p. 21, noted, "When the spoils element is predominant in a political organization, it is called a political machine." Echoing this point, Banfield and Wilson 1963, p. 115, write, "A machine . . . is distinguished from other types of organization by the very heavy emphasis it places upon specific, material inducements and the consequent completeness and reliability of its control over behavior, which, of course, account for the name 'machine.'" And Scott 1969, p. 1143, asserts, "[The machine] relies on what it accomplishes in a concrete way for its supporters, not on what it stands for."

and public services. As the strength of these machines atrophied under institutional reforms and declining poverty rates, scholars observed similar organizations in low-income countries, most prominently in Latin American cities.[21] In these Southern contexts, machines became identified as parties engaging in "clientelism:" a contingent, quid pro quo exchange of goods for support.[22] These transactions revolve around election-time handouts meant to "buy" the poor's votes—exchanges that are enforced by the watchful eyes of local brokers.

Such strategies are expedient for politicians looking to cheaply amass votes, and vulnerable migrant communities are often seen as the most fertile soil for clientelist strategies to take root. The insecurities faced by these "disoriented new arrivals" lead them to "prize instant advantages" and the episodic succor of clientelist handouts.[23] These vulnerabilities allow machines to craft electoral monopolies, thus pushing out competitors on the backs of poor migrant majorities. In doing so, machines invert accountability pressures within electoral politics, holding citizens who accept largesse accountable for their vote.

Party machines are thus described as organizations that callously use poor migrants to stifle competition, deliver paltry benefits, and subvert norms of accountability. Similar concerns underwrite popular ideas of slum politics in India, wherein residents are often understood to either sell their votes for handouts or mechanically assemble behind leaders of their caste or faith. Visiting Tulsi Nagar during elections, when most external observations of slum politics are fleetingly made, might well reinforce such impressions, with party workers like Rajesh distributing *biryani* (a popular meat-and-rice-based dish), liquor, and petty cash.

---

21. Gay 1994; Auyero 2001; Levitsky 2003; Greene 2007; Magaloni 2008; Weitz-Shapiro 2014; Szwarcberg 2015.

22. Stokes 2005; Nichter 2019; Nathan 2019. Gay 1990, p. 648, defines clientelism as "the distribution of resources (or promise of) by political office holders or political candidates in exchange for political support, primarily—although not exclusively—in the form of the vote." Stokes 2011, p. 649, defines it as "the proffering of material goods in return for electoral support, where the criterion of distribution that the patron uses is simply: did you (will you) support me?" Recent studies assert that any material strategy that lacks strict contingent exchange lies outside the realm of clientelistic politics. Nichter 2019, pp. 9–10.

23. Scott 1972, pp. 104–18. The detachment of migrants from the social roots of their villages has long been seen to prevent migrants from advancing their material interests in the city. See Durkheim 1933 [1897]; Wirth 1938; Nelson 1970.

Yet in our decade of observing political life in India's urban slums, we found residents repeatedly defying characterization as the pawns of political elites. They are not helpless, nor are they tricked into trading votes for trinkets. Instead, they engage in everyday forms of political participation, from petitioning elected representatives to protesting in front of government offices. Urban slum residents are not mere kindling for gang violence or exclusionary forms of ethnic politics. Instead, they often cross ethnic lines in seeking help and supporting local leaders. They are not cowering subjects of local kingpins. Far more often, urban slum residents actively select their community leaders, following those they see as best positioned to improve local conditions.

This multi-faceted agency we observed resonates with a literature on urban popular politics in the Global South, rooted in the disciplines of anthropology and geography. In this vein of scholarship, slums are approached as classic examples of "auto-construction," with residents cobbling together their homes and settlements themselves, brick-by-brick and organizing to secure public services and defend their modest gains from the bulldozers.[24] These innumerable acts of squatting, slapdash construction, and political assertion collectively shape the built spaces of cities.

Scholars have documented how such "subaltern urbanization" generates distinct forms of politics.[25] In his study of Tehran, Bayat traces how the poor have "quietly encroached" on the city through small-scale acts of illegal construction.[26] Holston describes a more assertive "insurgent citizenship" among poor migrants in Sao Paolo's periphery, who, over the course of twentieth century, transformed from disoriented squatters into citizens making demands on the state using rights-based language.[27] With reference to India, Chatterjee situates the urban poor within the world of "political society," where access to the state is secured through exertions of political pressure and negotiations with officials.[28]

Due to the informality that pervades everyday life for the urban poor, such exertions and negotiations are understood to lie mostly outside the realm of codified law, and instead exist within a shadowy space that moves to bribery

24. Holston 2008; Roy 2011; Caldeira 2017.

25. See Roy 2011 and Caldeira 2017 for larger conceptual discussions on subaltern urbanization.

26. Bayat 1997.

27. Holston 2008.

28. Chatterjee 2004.

and electoral calculation.[29] A gritty improvisational sense of entrepreneurial-ism can prove critical within political society, as such *jugaad* helps claimants navigate dismissive bureaucracies and muster what political influence they can to get the attention of officials.[30] Also critical to these efforts are brokers like Rajesh, who, armed with their political connections and hard-earned know-how of dealing with public institutions, can smooth access to the state. The widespread use of brokers in India has led scholars to describe India as having a "mediated state," where "blurry" boundaries between state and society are traversed by clever brokers on behalf their clients.[31]

The broad thrust of the literature on urban popular politics thus casts the poor as key actors in expanding cities.[32] Surprisingly, though, scholars have not turned these insights about the political agency of the urban poor towards examining the poor's role in the actual construction of the political networks that connect them to the state. The political brokers operating in political so-ciety are conceptualized as being suspended just above poor neighborhoods, within close enough reach to provide a bridge to the state but too distant to be influenced or held accountable. And these hierarchies are approached as static structures, populated by brokers who perform go-between activities for voters and political elites. Indeed, studies that otherwise stress bottom-up re-sistance and claim-making say little about how the political networks that are so pivotal to these efforts are built and reconstituted over time. In this book, we will show that the poor do not just work through political society to gain access to the state; they play a key role in shaping it, bending political networks through their everyday activities in ways that generate unexpected forms of accountability and representation.

How Political Networks Form During Urbanization

We study the political incorporation of poor migrants within the slums of India's expanding cities, which are estimated to house more than sixty-five million people, a decade-old official figure that is likely an underestimate.[33]

---

29. Gupta 2012.

30. Jeffrey and Young 2014.

31. Berenschot 2014. Gupta 2012.

32. Caldeira 2017, p. 9.

33. Census of India 2011. The Indian census has been conducted every decade since 1881 without delay, but the 2021 census was postponed by the government citing constraints imposed by the coronavirus pandemic. It is important to note that not all poor migrants in India's cities

Of specific empirical focus in our book (as discussed further in Chapter 2) are squatter settlements (*kachi basti*), a pervasive type of slum in India's cities that are defined by their unplanned, haphazard, and unsanctioned construction by residents; crowded living conditions; initial (and for most, continued) lack of formal property rights over the land; and marginalization in the distribution of public services.[34] These are relatively young political environments, predominantly settled by low-income migrants who have moved from elsewhere in the state or country, or more locally from somewhere in the city or its immediate periphery. Residents face a range of vulnerabilities, stemming not only from material poverty but also from informality in employment and housing. Deprivation and newness make slums—and squatter settlements in particular—fertile terrain for the emergence of party machines.[35]

The pervasive and emergent character of political machines in India's slums allows us to closely track how they form in real time. We trace these organizations in two north Indian cities—Jaipur (in Rajasthan) and Bhopal (in Madhya Pradesh). We focused on the BJP and Congress, the two major parties in each city, and also in Indian national politics. Our efforts were premised on ethnographic fieldwork, hundreds of interviews, and large-scale surveys of actors within each major tier of machine anatomy—ordinary residents, neighborhood-level political brokers, and municipal-level political patrons.

---

reside within slum settlements. Poor migrants in urban India who are less rooted-in-place include "pavement dwellers" (groups of people living on sidewalks, under bridges, and in transient tent camps) and a large population of circular migrants, who periodically shift to the city during the year to supplement their rural earnings (see Thachil 2017 on circular migrants). Circular migrants are often more marginalized and politically excluded from city politics than more settled slum residents (Gaikwad and Nellis 2021; Thachil 2020). They are an important urban population beyond the scope of this book and deserving of more systematic scholarly attention.

34. See Auerbach 2020, Chapter 1 for a detailed discussion on squatter settlements and what differentiates them from other urban poverty pockets that are referred to as "slums" in India (for example, dilapidated old city neighborhoods, urban villages, factory housing, and post-eviction resettlement colonies).

35. In this book, we use the broad term "slum" to describe the neighborhoods under study. We do so because squatter settlements are a common type of slum settlement and are colloquially and officially referred to as "slums" in India's cities. We also do so for ease of exposition. Readers should note, however, that squatter settlements are the specific empirical sites of our fieldwork and data collection efforts. Their acute vulnerabilities, migrant populations, and pervasive presence in India's cities make them especially substantively important and theoretically appropriate for our study.

A key insight from our multipronged fieldwork was the abundance of everyday political competition within slums. We observed brokers competing for the support of residents, party elites competing over influential brokers, residents competing for the attention of brokers, and brokers competing for promotion within party organizations. This competition was not restricted to election time. It is a persistent and crucial feature of the cities we study. And it is foundational to the construction of political networks linking slums to city authorities.

Drawing on this insight, we argue that slum residents are politically incorporated into cities via networks that form through interlocking processes of competitive political selection. We identify four major selection decisions—depicted in Figure 1.1—in which residents, brokers, and patrons choose one another. Our book is organized around the sequential analysis of these four selections, each of which is animated by a core question regarding the political incorporation of the urban poor.

First, we ask, *how does political authority emerge within poor migrant communities?* Since this authority takes the form of intermediaries like Rajesh, a different way of putting this question is: how do brokers emerge within their localities? Prior work has either neglected this question entirely or presumed brokers are appointed by political elites, from the top down. Conversely, we draw on ethnographic fieldwork to demonstrate slum residents actively choose their informal brokers (Arena A, Chapter 2). These selections are made through discrete moments like community meetings and informal elections, or via everyday choices over whom to seek help from and follow.

After establishing that residents select their local brokers, we analyze how they make these pivotal choices. We draw on a survey-based experiment with 2,199 slum residents to show how their decisions often deviate from popular assumptions regarding their political preferences. For example, residents do not reflexively assemble behind co-ethnic brokers. Instead, they often prioritize brokers who are most likely to prove competent in petitioning the state, including leaders who have high levels of education, and occupations that connect them to local municipal authorities. We later show that these same traits distinguish ordinary residents from actual brokers operating in slums: the kinds of effective leaders that residents want are often the kinds of leaders they actually get. This simple descriptive fact offers powerful evidence of the bottom-up construction of political authority, and the dynamics of representation within machine politics.

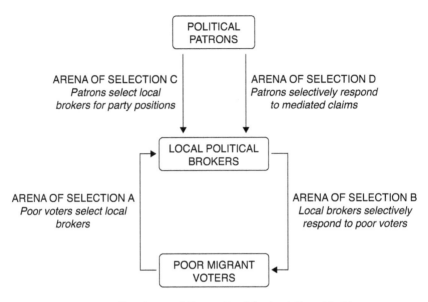

FIGURE 1.1. Four Arenas of Competitive Selection in Party Machines

Second, we ask *which poor migrants are served by these emerging political networks?* The answer depends on a second selection decision: which residents do brokers decide to cultivate as supporters (clients) within their settlements (Arena B, Chapter 3). Past scholarship has narrowly focused on to whom brokers distribute petty benefits during elections, in order to "buy" their votes. In such exchanges, brokers are expected to favor those residents whose votes they can most confidently verify, including members of their own partisan or ethnic community.[36]

Yet we argue that brokers win support through everyday interactions, not election-time transactions. We observed slum leaders receiving a constant stream of requests from residents plagued by informality, poverty, and inhospitable bureaucracies. Residents view such daily assistance as far more important than episodic campaign handouts. At the same time, most brokers have limited time, resources, and political capital, preventing them from addressing every demand placed at their feet.

Which residents do brokers prioritize in evaluating these requests?[37] We find that rather than prioritizing residents they can most easily surveil, slum

36. Stokes 2005; Schaffer 2007; Gonzalez-Ocantos et al. 2012; Hilgers 2012.

37. Scholars increasingly recognize the importance of "request fulfillment" as a central force animating machine politics. Nichter and Peress 2017; Nichter 2019.

leaders favor residents best positioned to boost their own local reputations for problem-solving. Drawing on a unique experiment with 629 slum leaders across our study cities, we argue that brokers prize socially influential residents who can spread word of the former's assistance, and avoid displays of ethnic favoritism that might constrict their followings. These preferences diverge from popular and scholarly portrayals of brokers, suggesting the need to revisit the assumptions behind such depictions. We then draw on evidence from residents themselves to show how their reports of who among them gets help align with the preferences expressed by brokers in our experiment.

These first two selections, underpinned by brokers competing for resident support and residents competing for broker assistance, drive the formation of political networks within poor urban neighborhoods. The next two competitive selection processes drive the formation of networks connecting these neighborhoods to the wider world of city politics.

Our third arena of selection asks *how do patrons select which local brokers to bring into their local party organization* (Arena C, Chapter 4)? Patrons looking to gain a foothold in low-income neighborhoods must decide whom to pluck from the pool of local leaders jostling for positions in their party organizations, and within their own personal factional fold. We draw on an experiment conducted with 343 local urban patrons to demonstrate how their decisions are shaped by the competitive nature of brokerage environments in slums. Intense inter- and intra-party factional competition over brokers leads patrons to prioritize loyalty not only to the broader party, but also to the patron.

Competition for votes also leads patrons to focus on a broker's popularity with residents. Interestingly, this concern leads them to prioritize a broker's everyday effectiveness in fulfilling resident requests for assistance, rather than a broker's election-time ability to mobilize crowds during campaigns, often via petty handouts. We then employ data on the career trajectories of our 629 slum leaders to show that the traits patrons value correlate strongly with actual promotion patterns among brokers within party organizations. The fact that patrons take into account the preferences of slum residents in deciding which brokers to include and promote reveals another important channel of accountability and representation within these political networks.

Fourth and finally, we ask, *given the daily barrage of claims patrons receive from brokers for local public goods, how do party patrons decide which claims to fulfill?* This fourth arena of selection (Arena D, Chapter 5) examines how patrons allocate limited public resources across brokers, and, by extension, the neighborhoods for which the latter speak. While prior scholarship has focused on how politicians target resources to constituencies in a top-down fashion, we focus on how they respond to bottom-up demands from urban neighborhoods. We emphasize that such demands are often made by groups, rather than individuals, and are mediated through a local broker, rather than made directly by voters.

Our framework highlights how in evaluating these collective, brokered requests, patrons must make a three-level consideration. Patrons must bear in mind not only the characteristics of the constituency from which a request emanates, but also of the broker making the request as well as the nature of the good requested. This three-part decision-making process has received little attention in studies of distributive politics. We argue that patrons focus less on how much support their party has traditionally enjoyed in the settlement— the factor perhaps most emphasized by prior studies. Instead, they prioritize requests that best lend themselves to personal credit-claiming, or the ability to cut through the complex assemblage of actors and institutions involved in public service delivery to ensure that beneficiaries know the politician is responsible for the delivered service. Specifically, we show that politicians privilege petitions for local public goods that can be durably tagged, and are more likely to dismiss petitions made by brokers who are likely to be unwilling or ineffectual in facilitating their credit-claiming efforts.

How does our framework emphasizing competitive selection within machine politics advance our understanding of urban politics? Before turning to such contributions, it is important to address a few questions that our discussion so far provokes. First, in highlighting themes of agency and bottom-up accountability within urban political networks, we do not wish to ignore the significant limitations of these networks in improving the lives of slum residents. The competitive choices we study necessarily entail decisions over whom to exclude, not only whom to include. By examining each arena of selection, our book also documents how specific types of individuals and settlements are disfavored, under-represented, or left out of emergent urban political networks. For example, women, religious minorities, and recent arrivals into the slum are all disadvantaged or disfavored in different ways at specific levels of machine organizations.

Finally, in our conclusion, we discuss how machine networks entrench a highly localized, fragmented politics centered around addressing the immediate and ad-hoc demands of residents. We argue this piecemeal politics ensures persistent forms of dependency, inhibits coordinated claim-making across settlements, and fails to deliver systematic policy-based improvements. Yet we caution readers against assuming that the removal of these networks would necessarily yield pro-poor programmatic politics. Even with all their limitations, these structures can equally be seen to provide a bulwark against an even more exclusionary, elitist, and repressive posture towards the urban poor.

Readers may also wonder why we do not analyze certain selection decisions. For example, we study how patrons select brokers, but not how brokers select patrons. This omission should not suggest that brokers are idle participants in the forging of these relationships. Chapter 4 shows brokers often initiate ties with patrons through their claim-making activities. Brokers, however, face more constrained choices over patrons than vice versa. The number of brokers relative to patrons within a local constituency, and the near uniform desires of brokers to obtain scarce party positions, strengthens the control patrons enjoy in these interactions. For this reason, we do not allocate an entire chapter to analyzing the preferences of brokers over patrons.

We also do not allocate an entire chapter to resident selection of patrons. In the distributive politics of India's cities, resident-patron interactions are frequently mediated by brokers, pushing resident efforts to approach patrons through the very networks examined in Chapters 2 and 3. Further, an examination of patron selection by residents shifts toward a more conventional study of electoral behavior, since the patrons we examine are elected representatives or candidates. Though we will touch on aspects of electoral behavior in several parts of the book—for example, the partisan preferences of residents and the partisan composition of settlements—our primary focus remains squarely on what we see as the more important and less studied question of urban politics: how party machines incorporate and respond to the urban poor between elections.

Our final note concerns the terminology of emergence and formation. This language should not suggest a sole focus on the initial origins of party machine networks, that is, during the earliest years of squatting in the communities under study. Instead, our use of this language is deliberate and analytically purposeful, meant to illuminate *ongoing* processes of competition and selection that make questions of emergence and formation of continued importance in understanding the mechanics of party machines. The political machines we study are unsettled, and in constant motion. They bear witness to innumerable stories of individual brokers rising and falling in influence, and the continued construction and reconstruction of linkages among residents, brokers, and patrons.

Tulsi Nagar's history illustrates this constant change, with selection processes dating back to the 1970s. Residents recall choosing Sharma from among several candidates to serve as the president of the settlement's newly formed development committee, the *Tulsi Kalyan Vikas Sangh* (Tulsi Welfare Development Association). While Sharma's selection was a watershed moment in Tulsi Nagar's history, it hardly marked the end of leadership change. Slum leadership does not have fixed term limits, and enterprising upstarts can make a go at slum leadership if they can convince other residents to support them. And other residents did rise up to challenge Sharma, sometimes through community meetings but more often through quieter acts of helping individuals and households, which would attract followers in a more piecemeal manner. At the time of our writing, Rajesh and Prakash still hold sway, but must fend off twenty-two other aspirants, one of whom may well rise to prominence by our next visit. Such perpetual motion demands a theoretical framework that centers on these repeated, every day, multi-level decisions that underpin the ongoing formation of machine networks.

Advancing Scholarship on the Politics of the Urban Poor

How do our arguments and evidence contribute to the venerable and interdisciplinary scholarship on the politics of the urban poor?[38] First, our work emphasizes the importance of studying how political networks form to connect poor migrants with party organizations in cities. Despite substantial research on urban party machines, scholars have yet to provide a systematic account of how those machines form. Early research on American cities provided accounts of machines in cities like Chicago or Kansas City, or biographies of bosses like William Tweed of New York and James Curley of Boston.[39] This literature outlined the aforementioned distinguishing features of machine politics: the targeted distribution of patronage; dense, pyramidal party organizations; and the importance of poor migrants as core support bases.[40]

38. For an important review of the literature on politics in cities of the Global South, see Post 2018.

39. Ostrogorski 1902. Colburn and Pozzetta 1976.

40. In the words of Tom Pendergast, a famous boss of Kansas City, "What's government for if it isn't to help people. They're interested only in local conditions—not about the tariff or the war debts. They've got their own problems. They want consideration for their troubles in their house, across the street, or around the corner . . . They vote for the fellow who gives it to them." As quoted in Larsen and Hulston 1997, p. 72. As Shefter 1978, p. 270, notes, "There is general

Yet, scholars of American machines overlook how such organizations emerged. Biographical accounts of bosses assumed machines grew out of their propulsive charisma.[41] Sociological studies saw machines as an inevitable result of underlying social conditions, in particular the presence of poor immigrants.[42]

The lack of analytical attention to organizational emergence persisted as the study of political machines shifted to the Global South. This contextual transition also prompted a definitional shift. In studies of American politics, machines were seen as organizations providing benefits to generate support among their core constituencies. In studies of Latin America, machines became increasingly identified as parties practicing a more rigidly contingent subset of "spoils-based" strategies: clientelism.[43] Scholars now often use machine politics and clientelism interchangeably.[44]

Recent studies on clientelism have largely focused on how parties enforce these more explicitly quid pro quo exchanges with voters.[45] Various

---

agreement among scholars that political machines were supported disproportionately by the poor and by voters of immigrant stock." Gosnell 1933, p. 26, echoes this argument: "Party machines have been strongest in the rapidly growing urban communities, particularly in the sections inhabited by the poorer immigrant groups."

41. As Trounstine 2008, p. 85, notes, "explanations of party building that rely on the extraordinary leadership qualities or desire for power of individual men are incomplete. They fail to account for the emergence of such leaders and so offer no predictive power."

42. Yet, as Shefter notes, theories of the emergence of a political machine "must focus upon more than the social composition and characteristics of urban electorates; just because residents *can* be politically mobilized in a particular way [doesn't mean] they *will* be." Emphasis in original. Shefter 1978, p. 297. McCaffery 1992, p. 436, notes that scholars have failed to fully account for how political machines and machine bosses emerged in American cities, largely because most analyses have "rest[ed] on a static polar categorization of social groups in American cities."

43. Stokes 2005; Nichter 2019; Nathan 2019.

44. Examples include Stokes 2005, p. 315, "Political machines (or clientelist parties) mobilize electoral support by trading particularistic benefits to voters in exchange for their votes." Gans-Morse et al. 2014, p. 415, similarly note, "During elections in many countries, clientelist parties (or political machines) distribute benefits to citizens in direct exchange for political support." An exception is Szwarcberg 2015, p. 7, who defines machines in a more organizational fashion, "Problem-solving networks are anchored in political machines— informal organizations that link party members with voters. Machines consolidate several problem-solving networks."

45. Stokes influentially articulated this dilemma: "How does the machine keep voters from reneging on the implicit deal whereby the machine distributes goods and the recipient votes for the machine?" Stokes 2005, p. 315.

investigations have explored how this enforcing ability is ameliorated or ex-
acerbated by employing brokers to monitor voters, targeting particular types
of voters, or engaging in iterative rather than spot exchanges.[46] Machines must
not only verify electoral returns from voters but also ensure that their brokers
do not shirk in their canvassing responsibilities.[47]

An overwhelming focus on how machine bosses enforce compliance has
reinforced a particular image of this form of politics. Machine politics is seen
as marked by low competition, passive clients, exploitative brokers, and distributive strategies centered around ethnic favoritism.[48] By focusing instead
on how machines form, we reveal the central role of various forms of competition in continually constructing these networks.[49] These competitive
underpinnings ensure that the political integration of the urban poor is not
simply a process marked by deprivation, exclusion, and control. Instead, they
afford the urban poor an important, if imperfect, degree of representation
and accountability within city politics. Contra "enforcement" studies, our "selection" framework demonstrates how machine politics is marked by high
competition, active clients, entrepreneurial brokers, and a less central role for
ethnic favoritism than commonly assumed.

46. For monitoring voters see, Stokes et al. 2013; Gingerich and Medina 2013; Rueda 2015. For
targeting specific types of voters see, Stokes 2005; Nichter 2008; Schaffer and Baker 2015; Corstange
2016; Chauchard 2018; Cruz 2019. For an examination of iterative exchanges, Nichter 2019.

47. Medina and Stokes 2007; Stokes et al. 2013; Camp 2017.

48. Indeed, formal models of machines often specify a single dominant party, and even a
single dominant broker within a locality. Gingerich and Medina 2013; Camp 2017. Gans-Morse
et al., p. 430, discuss some of the challenges facing formal analysis of what they term "dueling
machines," which underpins some of the neglect of competition within studies of machine
politics. There are numerous reasons behind such assumptions of low competition. Incumbents
can deploy their control of the flow of public resources to ensure voter loyalty in spite of weak
policy performances. Opposition parties who lack access to state benefits will struggle to compete. Such arguments find support from the experiences of dominant incumbents who maintained long reigns despite lackluster policy records. Examples of such parties include the PRI
in Mexico, the Congress Party in India, the Peronists in Argentina, the ANC in South Africa,
and the NDP in Egypt.

49. We build on prior studies that have noted the compatibility of political competition with
machine politics. In the introduction of their influential volume on clientelism, Kitschelt and
Wilkinson 2007, p. 32, note, "From Bangladesh to Jamaica, clientelistic politics has operated
through party competition."

1. "Active Clients": *Competition empowers clients to secure representation and accountability within machine organizations.*

Our framework goes well beyond reiterating the general point that the poor have political agency.[50] We argue that the interlocking selections that constitute machines enable the preferences of poor residents to *shape* the machines that link them to the state. Anthropological work on urban popular politics has rarely taken party organizations seriously as an object of study. Their depictions of the agency of the urban poor, therefore, do not encompass how residents actively construct local brokerage networks. Political scientists largely focus on how party elites select which brokers to work with, not how residents determine who in their communities rise into brokerage positions.[51]

In contrast, our book highlights how political elites cannot impose brokers on slum residents, either by parachuting their own people into settlements or by conferring informal authority on a resident. Instead, politicians looking to extend their reach within slums must choose from within the pool of informal leaders that residents have already chosen. The bottom-up dynamics we uncover generate a degree of representation and accountability within machine organizations, which our multi-layered data allows us to trace. For example, in Chapter 2 we demonstrate how residents value and select brokers who are educated, and hence more likely to prove knowledgeable and effective in procuring benefits from the state. Chapter 3 shows that actual brokers are distinguished from residents by higher levels of education, reflecting resident preferences. And in Chapter 4, we show how party patrons take resident preferences into account in making their selections, and select educated brokers to staff their local organizations.

We also show residents as willing to leave inept, corrupt, or coercive brokers and switch their support to better, more effective alternatives. Take Anil, who once proudly held the title of Congress *pramukh* (chief) in Tulsi Nagar—initially

50. Though, this too is a point worth underscoring, given that several core models of clientelism render poor voters as little more than passive recipients of election-time handouts. Stokes 2005; Nichter 2008; Gonzalez-Ocantos et al. 2012. More recent research has sought to amplify the role of clients in making demands of local machine actors—Szwarcberg 2015, Nichter and Peress 2017—but have not gone so far as to argue clients actively shape machine structures.

51. We re-analyzed 82 recent studies of clientelistic linkages reviewed by Hicken and Nathan 2020 (discussed in Chapter 6). Only 17 studies (21%) discuss mechanisms of broker selection and only 1—Kennedy 2010—discusses selection by clients.

won through acts of courageous leadership to improve local conditions. His standing was taken away in the face of public scrutiny over his escalating *dadagiri*—physically and verbally abusing residents. Sapped of his public support, Anil was thrown out of the Congress, who saw their ties with him as an electoral liability. Congress politicians turned their attention to Laxman and Abdul, who had been building their brands by helping residents with their many problems.

Less dramatic than Anil's example, but with the same ultimate effect, is the story of Ramu, famous for his greased locks of jet-black hair. A group of residents never gathered to pick Ramu as their informal leader. Instead, he slowly built his brand in the late 2000s through a range of local service activities—most prominently, teaching other people how to cut hair (his own vocation) and petitioning the area MLA (member of the legislative assembly) for a community center. Ramu's modest following in Tulsi Nagar yielded a similarly modest position in the BJP's organization. In the few years leading up to the 2018 election, however, we heard reports that Ramu's efforts and efficacy were dwindling. His supporters scattered to other more active party workers in Tulsi Nagar. The examples of Anil and Ramu underscore the fact that resident selection of brokers is an important, ongoing, and often overlooked process that informs representation and accountability within the base layer of machine hierarchies.

2. "Ambitious Brokers": *Brokers seek careers over rents, and to mobilize voters rather than monitor them.*

Our book offers a new understanding of the roles and motivations of political brokers, a set of actors who have been at the center of a proliferating, interdisciplinary scholarship.[52] Yet most of this scholarship has a functionalist flavor, focusing on what these actors do, with far less attention as to why they do it. For example, studies of clientelism in political science emphasize the role of brokers as the spies through which party elites monitor local voters, and the spigots through which they funnel campaign handouts. In such depictions, brokers' motivations are assumed to be little more than siphoning off some of the resources that parties give them during elections.[53]

---

52. On India, see Wiebe 1975; de Wit 1997; Hansen 2001; Jha et al. 2007; Das and Walton 2015; Krishna et al. 2020. Brokerage in poor urban communities has also been documented in Venezuela (Ray 1969), Ecuador (Burgwal 1996), Mexico (Cornelius 1975), Brazil (Gay 1994; Koster and de Vries 2012), Peru (Stokes 1995; Dosh 2010) and Argentina (Auyero 2001).

53. Such assumptions are explicit within some formal models of machines. Larreguy et al. 2016.

Portrayals of brokers as merely spigots and spies underestimate the motivations and ambitions of these actors. The slum leaders we followed were not content to remain perpetual intermediaries, only seeking the chance to skim payments during elections. India's slum leaders enter brokerage in the hopes of moving upward in party hierarchies, and even receiving a party nomination to fight in a local election.

We are not the first to note the "progressive ambition" of brokers.[54] However, past studies have not documented how such ambitions align with actual patterns of broker mobility within party organizations, making little effort to trace their trajectories over time. Our study follows the movement of more than 600 slum leaders within and between parties, and examines the factors driving promotions among them. Broadly, we find that, while upward mobility is difficult, a significant proportion of brokers do rise to positions of prominence within party organizations. Their view of brokerage as a means for a political career cannot be dismissed as simply wishful thinking. Their rise, as locally selected leaders, also reveals another important channel through which poor migrants secure representation within urban politics.

Our research further reveals how careerist ambitions incentivize brokers to mobilize voters rather than to monitor them. Even the few studies that emphasize broker ambitions still argue such impulses are best served by effective monitoring.[55] By contrast, we argue brokers look to craft reputations as inclusive and effective problem-solvers and representatives of local interests. We show that a view of brokers as reputation-seekers better anticipates the kinds of residents they cultivate as clients, and hence the kinds of migrants to whose demands machines will be more or less responsive.

Furthermore, we demonstrate how the progressive ambition of brokers impacts their relationship with party patrons. The conventional view of brokers as rent-seekers highlights shirking or corruption as the major concern

54. We borrow the term "progressive ambition" from Schelesinger's study of US legislators. Schelesinger 1966.

55. The two recent accounts that most clearly note the careerist ambitions of brokers are Camp 2017 and Szwarcberg 2015. For Camp, careerist ambitions drive brokers to bargain with party elites through the threat of exit. However, he views this threat as a tool to extract additional resources from party elites, not to fuel upward mobility within party organizations. Szwarcberg aligns most closely with our account and notes brokers seek political careers to become candidates themselves. However, she retains a view that such mobility is best achieved through effective monitoring. Szwarcberg 2015, p. 63.

patrons face in employing brokers.[56] The latter seek to pocket party resources without expending the requisite effort to win votes. Instead we find that the careerist ambitions of brokers motivate them to work hard on their party's behalf. However, their desire for promotion yields a different dilemma for patrons—how to ensure ambitious brokers do not defect to rival parties, or to rival patrons in the same party. We find that over one in four brokers openly admit to having switched parties, and predominantly do so because they are frustrated by a lack of advancement in their own party, or believe the rival party will promote them more quickly.

Once again, competitive pressures are central to the processes we uncover. Competition between brokers has often been unacknowledged, and such figures are often portrayed as singularly powerful within their communities. The intense competition we observed compels brokers to mobilize large followings in the search for promotion.[57] High levels of inter-party competition and intra-party factionalism compel patrons to pay close attention to a broker's potential for disloyalty.[58]

3. "Multi-ethnic machines": *Machines often avoid ethnic favoritism in diverse cities.*

Our findings question the presumed centrality of ethnicity within machine politics across much of the world. Classical studies of machines within US cities often noted their use of shared ethnic ties in forging relationships with voters.[59] Machines flourished within the enclaves set up by recent immigrants from Italy or Ireland. Local bosses in these neighborhoods built followings by invoking the ethnic status they shared with residents, and channeling benefits along ethnic lines.[60] This strategy was enabled by the clustering of immigrants from a particular country in a given neighborhood.[61]

---

56. Larreguy et al. 2016; Camp 2017; and Van Houten 2009.

57. In our review of prior studies, 55 studies make no mention of competition between brokers, and another 6 specify that individual brokers hold monopolistic control in their localities. Only 9 explicitly mention some form of broker competition, either within (3) or between parties (6).

58. Our focus on loyalty aligns with the work of Novaes 2017 who examines disloyal brokers in Brazil. Again, though, our accounts diverge in that his emphasis remains on how threats of defection are used to extract rents rather than promotions or nominations.

59. We follow Chandra 2006 in defining ethnic identities as descent-based attributes, including race, tribe, caste, and region-of-origin.

60. Luconi 1997.

61. As Bradley and Zald 1965, p. 163, note, "Capitalizing on the neighborhood segregation of their countrymen, and their own ethnic identification, political bosses appeared who were

Similarly, ethnic identities such as race, tribe, and caste have been shown to play a central role in structuring politics across the Global South. The presumed efficacy of ethnicity in structuring clientelist transactions has reinforced its importance. Ethnic identities are seen to provide markers for candidates to use when signaling who they will include in circuits of patronage.[62] Shared ethnic networks can also facilitate trust between politicians and voters, or enable the former to monitor the latter's voting behavior.[63]

India has been invoked as a paradigmatic case of a "patronage democracy" in which ethnicity is a central organizing force.[64] Contrary to these expectations, we find limited evidence that ethnicity plays a central role in the selection decisions that constitute political machines in Indian cities. Indicators of competence in solving everyday problems, notably education, appear more influential than shared ethnicity within resident decision-making about whom to seek help from and whom to follow. Moreover, the high levels of ethnic diversity within slums means that many residents do not even have a leader from their ethnic community available to follow. This constraint is especially apparent for narrowly defined ethnic categories such as caste, which are both the most socially meaningful to residents, and precisely those thought to best facilitate political cooperation and trust within clientelist exchanges.[65]

The importance of shared ethnicity is even more strikingly muted within the calculations of ambitious brokers in cultivating their local clienteles. In fact, the brokers we spoke to actively sought to avoid parochial reputations for favoring members of their own ethnic group. Such reputations constricted their potential support base within diverse slums, in turn hampering their chances for promotion and a political career.[66] Instead, we find slum leaders actively trying to construct multi-ethnic followings. For example, in Tulsi Nagar, Mishra, a high-caste Brahmin, was supported by a range of castes as well as by Muslims—so much so that he insisted the letterhead of Tulsi Nagar's development association include an image of both a temple and a mosque. Ramu, a member of a disadvantaged Dalit caste, attracted a range of followers,

---

supreme in their own bailiwicks." Of course, ethnicity was not always seen as predominant within US machines, e.g., Stevens 2009.

62. Fearon 1999; Chandra 2004; Posner 2005.

63. Habyarimana et al. 2007.

64. Chandra 2004.

65. Corstange 2016.

66. Our account therefore builds on important work on how multi-ethnic coalitions are forged in low-income democracies. Arriola 2012; Ichino and Nathan 2013; Koter 2013.

including high-caste Brahmins; and Abdul, a Muslim, counted hundreds of Hindus among his followers.

Instead of favoring members of their own caste or faith, slum leaders prioritize residents best positioned to boost the former's reputation within the slum's social world, including longtime veterans of the settlement. These findings are especially striking given that prior studies have anticipated political competition to enhance the centrality of ethnic identities in structuring machine politics.[67] The realities we uncover call for a rethinking of the most salient dimensions of inclusion and exclusion within urban machines, even in countries like India which are seen to have highly ethnicized politics.

4. "Politics Beyond Elections": *Urban politics needs to be studied between the vote.*

A focus on how parties verify and enforce electoral quid pro quo has predictably emphasized the study of how machines operate during elections. Our own review of eighty-two recent studies of clientelism, which we discuss in the concluding chapter, found a majority (52%) squarely focus on the election period, while only sixteen percent primarily focus on politics between the votes. This focus has further implications, including amplifying the importance of top-down strategies of mobilization, such as the distribution of campaign handouts in hopes of swaying voters at the polls.

By contrast, an examination centered on how machines form emphasizes the need to study the everyday life of these organizations. Our intensive fieldwork reveals that residents rarely choose which party or broker to support on the basis of petty gifts during campaigns. Even brokers openly confessed that the vast majority of slum residents are unaffected by the handouts they happily receive during elections. Nor is a broker's ability to mobilize attendance at campaign rallies regarded by clients *or* patrons as reliable signals of the broker's electoral influence. Canny voters in Indian slums often attend rallies for multiple parties and candidates, as both performative gestures and also to avail themselves of the small pleasures of food and socializing, while voting their preference in the booth. Instead, we provide evidence that both voters and party elites see a broker's problem-solving abilities between the votes as a more reliable indicator of the former's popularity than their efforts during campaigns.

Our quotidian focus also emphasizes how machines respond to bottom-up requests from residents. Scholars across a range of contexts increasingly recognize

---

67. Kitschelt and Wilkinson 2007, p. 34.

the importance of such citizen-initiated requests for distributive politics.[68] We build on these contributions by providing the first effort to systematically theorize and empirically trace patterns of responsiveness to resident requests up through the multiple layers of machine hierarchies. We study both how brokers decide which resident requests to prioritize (Chapter 3), and then how patrons decide which broker requests to prioritize (Chapter 5).

Situating our Study in the Context of Indian Slums

India's slums are important and theoretically productive spaces in which to situate a study on the formation of political ties between poor migrants and political elites.[69] Most slum residents either fall below the poverty line or teeter on it, with a single illness or injury capable of plunging a family into crisis.[70] Residents work in a bloated informal economy, and are vulnerable to eviction due to weak or absent property rights.[71] In seeking to address these risks, and to secure basic public services, residents face dismissive government institutions that often require the intervention of political elites. These features of slums combine to make them the quintessential "garrisons" of popular politics in India's cities. They are precisely the type of settlements that have animated the literature on machine politics.[72]

Yet a study on political machines within India is unusual. India's parties are often described as organizationally moribund at the local level. Instead of relying on durable and entrenched networks of party workers to mobilize voters, parties cobble together fleeting linkages with local elites. This characterization has been made with respect to our study states (Rajasthan and Madhya Pradesh) and elsewhere in India.[73]

---

68. Nichter and Peress 2017; Kruks-Wisner 2018. Despite such efforts, studies of bottom-up mobilization remain less prevalent than of top-down targeting. Our re-review of 82 recent studies of clientelist linkage found 33 studies (40.2%) focused exclusively on top-down targeting, compared to just 14 (17.1%) that focus on bottom-up requests.

69. Jha et al. 2007; Auerbach 2020.

70. Krishna 2010.

71. For a comparative discussion on informal economies, see La Porta and Shleifer 2014. On India's informal urban economies, see Gill 2012; Anjaria 2016; and Thachil 2017.

72. Chatterjee 2004; Harriss 2005.

73. For Rajasthan and Madhya Pradesh see, Krishna 2007. For elsewhere in India, Kohli 1990; Krishna 2007; Manor 2010; Chhibber et al. 2014; Ziegfeld 2016. Manor 2010, p. 509, for

If India's parties are weakly organized at the local level, they then lack one of the defining features of political machines—hierarchically organized, face-to-face networks of party workers that connect voters and political elites.

Descriptions of weak party organizations, however, have flowed from studies of the countryside, not from cities.[74] With few exceptions, scholars have devoted little attention to studying how party politics works in India's cities.[75] Our book makes descriptive correctives to our understanding of political networks in urban India. Through close studies of Jaipur and Bhopal, we provide fine-grained pictures of local party organization in India's cities. We find that the BJP and INC (Congress) are both well-organized between and during the votes.[76] They have hierarchical structures that connect grassroots party workers to the highest strata of party leadership in the city.

The BJP and INC have nested, geographically defined committees of party workers. At the lowest level of both organizations is the humble polling booth committee, overseeing mobilization activities within areas of roughly 1,000 voters. Above the booth are committees at the levels of the municipal ward, block for Congress/*mandal* for BJP (the latter corresponding to the area of a state assembly electoral constituency), city (*sheher*), and administrative district (*zila*). Each committee is composed of a president (*adhyaksh*) as well as members with the positions of vice-president (*up-adhyaksh*), treasurer (*kosh-adhyaksh*), minister (*mantri*), secretary (*sachiv*), and general member (*sadasya*). In addition to the main party organization, both the BJP and INC have wings (*morcha*) and cells (*prakosht*) to organize specific sections of society. Most

---

example, writes, "Most . . . parties possess only limited organizational strength. In particular, most fail to penetrate effectively downward below intermediate levels to the grassroots."

74. Foundational studies of local politics in India include Bailey 1970, Wade 1988, and Krishna 2002. These studies, and their more contemporary counterparts—Dunning and Nilekani 2013; Kruks-Wisner 2018—fix their analysis on the countryside. What few studies we have on party organization in India's cities mostly focus on Mumbai, and the Shiv Sena Party in particular. Hansen 2001; Bedi 2017.

75. Exceptions include: Jones 1974; Oldenburg 1976; Berenschot 2010, 2011; Auerbach 2020.

76. India's historically dominant party, the Congress Party, was described in machine-like terms: "The Congress' apparatus comprised a series of 'vertical faction chains' that competed for power within the party across the country." Ruparelia 2015, p. 47 citing Kothari 1964, p. 1162. Propertied, high-caste local elites mobilized vote banks and distributed patronage in the districts. The political bosses that ran Pradesh (State) Congress Committees (PCC) elected organizational leaders and influenced the workings of legislative assemblies. The earliest studies of local Congress organization also used the language of machines to describe these networks. For example, Bailey 1970 refers to the Congress party as a rural machine in his study on Orissa.

relevant to our study are the party cells for slum residents (the *Kachi Basti Prakosht* in Jaipur and *Jhuggi Jhopri Prakosht* in Bhopal) and party wings for the Scheduled Castes, Muslims, and women.

We enumerate a staggeringly large number of party workers living across the 110 slums surveyed for this book: 663 party workers, each possessing a distinct position within a committee at one of the party organizational levels just described. These residents have amassed a following within their respective settlements, thus becoming *basti neta*, or slum leaders. Parties recruit slum leaders into their organizations by making them formal position-holders (*padadhikari*). These operatives work at the interface between poor voters and political elites in the city, thus representing classic political brokers. In this book, we use the term "political broker" to describe and refer to slum leaders. Likewise, the term "party worker" refers to a specific and large subset of slum leaders who hold a *pad*, or party position. These actors make up the bottom tier of party machines in India's cities.

The Roots of Competition and Choice in Urban India

Why is there so much political competition in urban India, at all levels of the party machine hierarchy? We argue that several factors underpin the intense, ongoing, and multi-level competition that is so central to our theoretical framework. The first two factors are rooted in the micro social environments of slums: strikingly high levels of ethnic diversity and the recent emergence of these settlements in Indian cities. The third factor is institutional—the high levels of electoral volatility within India's federal, multi-party, political structure. The final factor is the relative absence of coercion and organized violence, which cuts against popular portrayals of slum politics.

Ethnic Diversity in New Urban Spaces

Ethnic heterogeneity and the "newness" of slums converge to make conditions ripe for new forms of informal leadership, and enduring competition. Migration from states throughout India, as well as population movement within cities, produce novel patterns of diversity in slums that are not found in villages. Our sample of 2,199 slum residents across 110 settlements in Bhopal and Jaipur includes over 300 sub-castes (*jati*), stretching across all strata of the Hindu social hierarchy and a wide range of Muslim *zat*. In the average settlement, the *jati* fractionalization score is a remarkable 0.81, meaning that two randomly selected residents have an 81% chance of being from a different *jati*.[77] Not a single settlement in our sample was homogenous in terms of *jati*.

Diversity in India's slums is not limited to the dimension of sub-caste. Only thirty-eight of our 110 settlements yielded a religiously homogenous sample, with most settlements including both Hindu and Muslim residents, and often other religious minorities as well. Residents also hail from a variety of villages, districts, and states. While most sampled residents (79.49%) come from the states in which our study cities are located (Rajasthan and Madhya Pradesh), they have migrated from a range of villages and districts. Other residents migrated from states throughout India, including Bihar, Uttar Pradesh, West Bengal, Maharashtra, Gujarat, and Tamil Nadu. Not only are slums not transplants of villages, but most exhibit some regional and linguistic diversity.

Settlement-level diversity is the result of a scarcity of urban land for squatting and the need to be close to local labor markets, which push poor migrants of different castes, faiths, and regional identities into the same dense settlements.[78] Slums are located on fragmented pieces of land scattered across the city. Squatters tend to settle in areas that are environmentally sensitive—along railway tracks, riverbeds, and mountainsides—where they are less likely to face eviction due to a lack of competing interests over the space.

Squatters squeeze into these nooks in the city through gradual accretion—small, disjointed groups of squatters trickling into the settlement in a drawn-out manner, often over the course of months and years. Squatting in India does not unfold through coordinated, large-scale land invasions, as is sometimes the case in Latin America.[79] Poor migrants do not pre-organize with hundreds of their co-ethnics to capture a vacant area of land and establish an ethnic enclave. Instead, individual migrants and families are guided by pressing concerns over finding shelter and employment, which is sometimes facilitated by a contact in the settlement of arrival.[80] A shortage of land and squatting through accretion all but prevent the formation of ethnic enclaves, and contribute to the rich patterns of ethnic diversity described previously.

77. This measure had a standard deviation of 0.13.

78. For a more detailed discussion on these spatial constraints and reasons for migration, see Auerbach 2020, Chapter 7.

79. Squatting through gradual accretion describes the formation of slum settlements in South Asia and Sub-Saharan Africa more broadly. UN-Habitat 1980.

80. Mitra 2003; Auerbach 2020.

India's slums, and especially its squatter settlements, are several decades old, at most. The average settlement in our sample emerged just after 1980, and the average resident has lived in their settlement for just twenty-three years. Just a quarter (26.53%) of sampled residents were born in their settlement, and the majority (67.29%) of those not born within their settlement were born outside the districts of Bhopal and Jaipur. Because of their recent emergence and ethnic heterogeneity, slums lack the longstanding social hierarchies and forms of customary authority that operate in villages.[81]

Informal slum leadership must be constructed from scratch, among migrants hailing from different villages and states, and belonging to different castes and religions. Our fieldwork demonstrates that informal leadership rapidly emerges in slums to fight eviction and demand public services. Once slum leadership forms in a settlement, however, it does not lock into place, precluding further competition and choice. Just under the surface of current slum leadership are always new cohorts of aspirants seeking to push aside existing leaders and build their own followings. Moreover, migratory churn in slums and more episodic events like evictions, riots, fires, and flooding can destabilize the populations of settlements.[82] These movements of people as well as changes in the built space open possibilities for the competitive formation of new nodes of leadership.[83]

Multi-Level Electoral Environment

Several features of India's multi-party political system further enable sustained competition within urban party machines. Of particular importance is India's three-tiered system of elected government, with directly elected representatives at the levels of the municipal ward, state assembly constituency, and parliamentary constituency. It is common for parties in power at one level of

81. Resnick 2012; Koter 2013. It bears noting that hierarchies in villages also cannot be assumed to be timeless and static. Indeed, recent work highlights transformations such hierarchies have undergone across a range of contexts: Krishna 2003; Shami 2012.

82. Peattie 1978, p. 40, describes a similar social context in the early years of a Venezuelan barrio: "The social world of Barrio La Laja is not that of an insulated village or small community in which everyone knows everyone else. People are always moving in and out; nearly a quarter of the barrio's adults had been there less than a year; and at no time does each person there know all the others personally, or by name."

83. On population turnover destabilizing local slum leadership, see Holzner 2004.

government to be out of power in another. Moreover, India holds non-concurrent elections across these three tiers and exhibits substantial electoral volatility from election to election.[84] That volatility manifests within constituencies as well as governments at the municipal, state, and national levels.

Volatility extends to candidate selection within parties. Politicians who run for office in India are frequently deprived of a party nomination in the subsequent election, even if they won the contest. Sircar, looking at candidates who ran in India's 2009 parliamentary elections and received at least twenty percent of the vote share in their constituency, found that only thirty-five percent were re-nominated in 2014.[85] Jensenius and Suryanarayan, examining state elections between 1986 and 2007, found that only fifty-six percent of incumbent politicians re-ran under the same party label in the following election.[86] At the municipal level, this volatility is especially intense due to seat quotas ("reservations" in the parlance of Indian politics) for women, Scheduled Castes, Scheduled Tribes, and Other Backward Classes, many of which shift from election to election and which restrict who can run within those reserved wards.[87]

Further contributing to this competitive electoral environment is significant fluidity in vote choice. Thirty-four percent of our resident respondents openly reported supporting different parties across the past few elections. Moreover, it is unusual for settlements to be a *garh* (stronghold) for any one party. Across our sample, forty-seven percent of respondents supported the BJP and forty-one percent of respondents supported the Congress. The vast majority (85 of 110) of our sampled settlements had at least twenty percent of respondents supporting each of the two major parties, and in a majority of settlements (58) each party had the support of at least thirty percent of respondents. Many votes are up for grabs in slums, encouraging brokers and political elites to keep on their toes to win local support.

India's multi-party democracy, multi-tiered government, non-concurrent elections, and substantial electoral and candidate volatility collectively generate competition and choice in party machine networks. From within slum

84. Nooruddin and Chhibber 2008; Uppal 2009; Dash and Ferris 2020.

85. Sircar 2018 further found that, "a candidate that was elected in 2009 had a 53% chance of being re-nominated, while a candidate that did not win the election in 2009 had only a 19% chance of being re-nominated."

86. Jensenius and Suryanarayan 2020.

87. On municipal reservations and electoral competition, see Auerbach and Ziegfeld 2020.

settlements, voter autonomy deepens this competitive environment, setting the stage for our four arenas of selection.

These institutional and political factors allow more than one party to have a hand on the gears of the state, intensifying competition within party machine networks.[88] In this environment, most party workers have a co-partisan in power somewhere in the constellation of legislative bodies above them. Take Tulsi Nagar, the settlement discussed in our opening vignette. Following the 2018 state assembly elections in Madhya Pradesh, the residents of Tulsi Nagar had a BJP municipal councilor, a Congress member of the state legislative assembly, a BJP mayor, a Congress chief minister, a BJP member of parliament, and a BJP-controlled central government.[89] Furthermore, within the city, the faces of political patrons are not static over time, especially given the volatility in candidate selections. Such churn deters a calcification of party machine networks, while also preventing a monopoly of political connectivity being bequeathed to brokers of any one party. Instead, most brokers can draw on partisan connections to facilitate the problem-solving activities on which their local support hinges. Of course, they must still compete with other brokers looking to do the very same.

The Limits of Muscle Power

A final key factor underpinning competition within urban slums in Jaipur and Bhopal is the relative lack of coercive violence and criminality. This observation may surprise readers. India's slum leaders are often popularly depicted as gun-slinging *goondas* who maintain their power through brute coercion. Such narratives anticipate little agency and choice among residents. Instead, they expect residents will often be forced to acquiesce to slum leaders, or risk the latter's wrath. Competition among slum leaders, if there even was any, would unfold through displays of muscle power.[90]

---

88. Incumbent resources allow parties to target more benefits to voters than challengers (Hidalgo and Nichter 2016), develop track records of catering to constituents (Chandra and Parmar 1997), and provide credible offers of employment to supporters (Robinson and Verdier 2013).

89. A defection among Congress MLAs to the BJP in Madhya Pradesh in early 2020 dismantled the Kamal Nath Congress government, and subsequently allowed the BJP to reform the government under Shivraj Singh Chouhan.

90. Studies of slums outside of India have also pointed to differences between scholarly observations of slum leaders and popular depictions of these actors. Koster 2012, p. 485, for

We find little evidence that violence underpins slum leadership. Ultimately, slum leaders are residents of the settlement, living with their families and facing the same hardships and dismissive urban authorities as their neighbors. They lack the wealth and dynastic ties that are so often associated with muscle and mafia politics in India.[91] Most of the brokers we surveyed were the first members of their families to be involved in politics in any way (82%) and hence lack prior political connections in the city.[92]

Residents are not shy to openly express disappointment with their slum leaders. In our fieldwork, such expressions of disapproval included spreading rumors of a slum leader's incompetence; using abusive language toward a slum leader; pelting slum leaders with stones; and beating slum leaders with *chappals* (sandals). More commonly, they simply shifted support to another slum leader, in the process reshaping the distribution of public support across slum leaders in a settlement.

Slum leaders rarely monopolize access to land, markets, or employment opportunities. The urban informal sector offers residents few material securities, but is highly decentralized and diverse in ways that evade local dominance. These conditions differ from those in villages, which stimulated much of the foundational scholarship on Indian patronage politics. In rural contexts, local elites—controlling land and access to agricultural markets, and belonging to dominant castes—constrained the political agency of poor, lower-caste villagers. Scholars have also documented the rise of rural mafias capturing natural resources like sand and coal, and relying on muscle power to oppress local populations.[93] Slum leaders in our study setting do not wield such dominating power.

This is not to say that violence and gang activities are absent in slums. In several of our case study settlements gangs of young men harassed residents

---

example, writes, "the leaders I studied in Recife differ from the criminally involved image of community leaders prevalent in studies of Rio de Janeiro . . . In Recife, community leaders often occupy formal positions as presidents of grassroots organizations or representatives on local consultative bodies."

91. Vaishnav 2017; Michelutti et al. 2018.

92. Only 8 percent of our sample were born in their settlement *and* had a family member in politics before them, a combination most likely to indicate prior political ties within the cities in which they worked.

93. Witsoe 2015. It is important to note that various studies have documented important variation in citizen agency and claim-making abilities with respect to their local authority figures across rural South Asia. See Krishna 2002; Shami 2012; and Kruks-Wisner 2018.

and brawled in the streets. In one settlement, a slum leader oversaw the illicit production and sale of *desi daru* (country liquor). Yet, across three combined years of fieldwork in the spaces, not once did we encounter a slum leader whose informal authority was wholly crafted and maintained through violence. We certainly did not see criminality rising to a degree that stifled political competition. We did, however, frequently observe slum leaders falling from grace among residents, and being replaced by new aspirants.

The relative lack of coercion we find may strike readers as anomalous within machine politics. Certainly, scholarship on political machines has documented the myriad ways in which machine patrons use their social and economic power to coerce and intimidate voters.[94] Yet to conclude that such practices centrally define machine politics is an overreach, and does not align with available empirical evidence. Our review of eighty-two prior studies of machine politics found only nine (11%) of them unearthed evidence of coercive strategies, with the majority of these studies focusing on Russia and Eastern Europe.[95] Our account of machine formation through competitive selection is fueled by substantial political competition and choice. Yet, machine politics is often cast in far more rigid terms. A natural question for many readers will be the degree to which the conditions we observe ring true elsewhere in India, and in other cities of the Global South. In the conclusion, we draw on a range of primary and secondary data to show the competition we witness cannot be dismissed as a peculiarity of Indian slums. The equating of machines with uncompetitive politics is largely an artefact of a geographic focus on particular countries within the Americas. What remains striking is the lack of systematic attention to how competition shapes machine politics, given the observed pervasiveness of such competition across the globe.

How We Dissect Machine Anatomy

How did we seek to study political machines in urban India? The two cities under focus in this book are Bhopal, Madhya Pradesh, and Jaipur, Rajasthan. Bhopal and Jaipur are capitals of their respective states. They were both princely states (indirectly ruled by the British) prior to India's Independence in 1947, with large and densely populated old cities at their core and more

94. Baland and Robinson 2012; Berenschot 2018; Frye et al. 2014; Mares and Young 2019.

95. For an important recent statement on coercion within clientelism, see Mares and Young 2019.

recent construction in their peripheries. Like all cities in India, Bhopal and Jaipur have elected municipal governments that are tasked with some responsibilities over public service provision.[96]

We selected these cities for several reasons. First, most slum residents in India do not live in the megacities of Bangalore, Chennai, Delhi, Kolkata, and Mumbai, despite the near exclusive focus on them among studies on India's slums.[97] Instead, they primarily reside in a larger constellation of medium and small cities spread throughout the country. With approximately three million people and two million people, respectively, Jaipur and Bhopal rest in the upper tiers of India's cities but are still considerably smaller than the country's megacities.[98] Second, both cities have large slum populations—26.68 percent of Bhopal's population and 10.62 percent of Jaipur's population, a collective of nearly a million people, reside in the two city's slums.[99] Moreover, both Bhopal and Jaipur are firmly situated in north India's Hindi-speaking belt, which matched our own linguistic competencies. Such alignment was especially important given the centrality of qualitative fieldwork to our empirical approach. Finally, the two cities exhibit two-party competition between India's two major national parties, the INC (Congress) and BJP. In this respect, they reflect the electoral ecosystem of several northern states in India. Furthermore, given the importance of these parties in India's national politics, we wanted to focus our efforts in cities where they were locally dominant.

Our empirical approach was informed by our analytical goals. As noted, there have been precious few attempts to study either the formation of urban political machines across the Global South, or slum-based political networks in India. Consequently, several of the questions we sought to answer were fundamentally descriptive in nature: mapping the demographic characteristics of slum brokers and party patrons, measuring how competitive brokerage in migrant settlements is, and assessing how much agency slum residents have in choosing which local broker to follow. More processual questions included

96. At the height of our fieldwork (2015–2018) Jaipur was divided into 91 municipal wards, with each ward electing a councilor who joins the municipal council. Bhopal had 85 municipal wards.

97. Distributions of urban populations across cities of different sizes may vary. For example, in Argentina, the majority of households living in informal settlements are located in the province of Buenos Aires. TECHO 2016 as quoted in Murillo et al. 2021.

98. Census of India 2011.

99. In absolute terms, the Census of India 2011 records 323,400 people living in Jaipur's slums and 479,669 people living in Bhopal's slums.

tracing how political authority takes shape within slums, how party patrons and slum leaders come into contact with one another, and the trajectory of broker careers within party organizations. Our more explicitly theoretical concerns include assessing how various factors, including ethnicity, partisanship, problem-solving efficacy, and various forms of connectivity shape the selection decisions described in Figure 1.1.

From Ethnography to Experiments

The diversity of these analytical goals compelled a methodologically diverse approach. In the pages to follow, we draw on a combined three years of fieldwork with poor urban communities, and hundreds of interviews with slum residents, party workers, and political elites. We also draw on two waves of original surveys conducted with slum residents in 2012 and 2015 (a combined sample of nearly 4,000 respondents), as well as a 2016 survey of 629 slum leaders, and a 2017 survey of 343 party patrons. These surveys provide rich descriptive data, including hundreds of open-ended audio recordings in which we had respondents narrate their entry into politics, which we subsequently transcribed, translated, and analyzed. These surveys also included choice experiments related to each of the four selection decisions described earlier.

The foundation for this research was our ethnographic fieldwork. Insights from the fieldwork were crucial for addressing the descriptive and theoretical questions at the heart of our study. Our descriptive questions were prompted by the dearth of even basic information regarding the demography and politics of poor urban communities in India. This lack of information reflects the challenges in studying these communities. The poverty, informality, and relative newness of migrant settlements makes them challenging arenas to systematically examine.

Given these challenges, ethnographic research was essential to understanding the daily social and political life of poor migrants. Spending time with ordinary slum residents revealed the highly competitive nature of slum politics, and the tremendous ethnic diversity of migrant communities. Extended interviews with informal leaders helped us learn their motivations in entering brokerage, and the challenges they faced in mobilizing voters. Shadowing party patrons helped reveal the importance of slums as political constituencies, the nature of their dependence on slum leaders, and the threats posed by inter-party competition and intra-party factionalism. Qualitative fieldwork was especially helpful in understanding processual questions, including the varied ways in which brokers emerge through resident selection, and the ways in which slum leaders and parties come into contact. These insights underpin the arguments made in this book.

The second role ethnographic research played was informing our strategies for quantitative data collection. Chapter 2 outlines how this fieldwork was instrumental in devising a strategy for surveying a representative sample of slums, and households within slums. In Chapter 3, we describe how our fieldwork also informed our multi-pronged strategy for surveying slum leaders. To our knowledge, this is the first effort to systematically survey slum leaders anywhere in the world. Qualitative fieldwork also informed our instrument design, helping us to identify questions that would be relevant for our respondents, as well as to word questions in the clearest way.[100]

A final role of our ethnographic fieldwork was in improving the design of the four choice experiments we conducted. Ethnography helped us ground our experimental questions in the lived experiences of our informants; doing so helped improve the contextual congruence between our experiment and the respondent's everyday life.[101] It also enabled us to improve the theoretical precision and intelligibility of these questions. For example, ethnographic insights helped us understand how the choices we sought to understand were actually made.[102] Ethnography additionally helped us operationalize the theoretical concepts we sought to test within these selection decisions. For example, we wanted to assess the degree to which brokers favored residents who were likely to be socially influential within their settlement. Our fieldwork revealed occupation to be an important signal of social influence. We therefore selected occupations that are associated with varying levels of social influence in slums.

100. For a more detailed description of how ethnography can inform and improve survey research, see Thachil 2018.

101. Morton and Williams 2010, p. 265, refer to this congruence as the "ecological validity" of the experiment. In their words, this validity refers to the premise that the environment constructed in the research is similar to that in the target environment.

102. One illustration of this benefit is from Chapter 2, where we discuss how our fieldwork revealed slum development associations to be important and widespread organizations across migrant settlements. We also found the presidents of these associations to be important leaders. To test preferences for local brokers in Chapter 2, we therefore asked slum residents to choose between two hypothetical candidates vying for the presidency of a local development association.

While our quantitative data collection was ethnographically informed, it also allowed us to make contributions beyond our qualitative fieldwork. Most obviously, the observational data we collected allowed us to make a number of descriptive insights at a scale ethnography does not permit. For example, our survey of 629 slum leaders enables us to trace the career trajectories of a representative sample of these brokers across Jaipur and Bhopal. Doing so allows us to assess the degree to which slum brokerage affords opportunities for upward political mobility.

The choice experiments we embed within each of our three surveys are also central components of this study. The advantage of these experiments is their ability to assess the impact of various characteristics of patrons, brokers, and residents undergirding the key selection decisions through which machines form. For example, they help us evaluate how broker responsiveness to requests for assistance was shaped by traits indicating a resident was easy to electorally monitor, as well as those which indicated a resident was well-positioned to boost a broker's local reputation. Similarly, these experiments enable us to test how patrons jointly consider indicators of broker loyalty and efficacy in building their factional networks. However, we are mindful of the limits of such survey-based experiments, which we discuss in Chapter 2. Whenever possible, we also try to assess if the results from these experiments align with observational data about actual patterns of leadership and responsiveness. Our strongest findings are those for which we find repeated evidence across the various empirical strategies deployed in this book.

An important motivation for writing this book was that the architecture of a monograph is best suited for highlighting the complementarities between the different methods we employ, as well as between the findings we obtain from studying different anatomical layers of party machines in our study cities. For example, we use data from our 2012 and 2015 surveys of slum residents regarding their local leadership to help generate the sampling frame of brokers we surveyed in 2016. We also combine descriptive data from our survey of slum leaders with the results of our experiment with residents regarding the types of leaders they prefer. Doing so allows us to explore whether the kinds of leaders residents want are the type they actually get, which helps assess the degree to which clients can shape their local brokerage environment. Similarly, we use descriptive data from our survey of slum residents to see if those getting help match the kinds of clients brokers seek to cultivate in the experiment we conducted with slum leaders. It is the symbiosis between qualitative and quantitative work, and between multiple levels of analysis, that constitutes the book's core empirical contributions.

Plan of the Book

The chapters that follow are organized around the four key processes of selection outlined in Figure 1.1. Chapter 2 provides an account of how brokers emerge within migrant settlements, with a focus on highlighting the agency of poor migrants in actively shaping the machines that govern them. Chapter 3 examines how brokers select which residents to cultivate as clients, with an emphasis on showing how these choices reflect brokers' concerns with building reputations and seeking careers rather than monitoring compliance and seeking rents. Chapter 4 explores how patrons decide which local slum brokers to incorporate within their local machine organizations, emphasizing how patrons balance the need for locally influential brokers with ensuring loyalty within their factional teams.

Chapter 5 examines how local patrons assess which claims brought to them by brokers on behalf of slum residents to prioritize, emphasizing how patrons privilege claims for which they can most readily claim credit. Chapter 6 situates the findings of this book in a broader context. It suggests that several key implications of our arguments are observed outside of Jaipur and Bhopal, both in other parts of India, and in other countries. We also discuss the considerable limits of the machine networks we study in improving the lives of poor urban citizens. Finally, we explore some of the implications of recent political trends in India—notably a centralization of power and rising majoritarianism under the current BJP-led national government—for the ecosystems examined in our book.

Throughout our book, we seek to analyze how migrants and machine actors make key political decisions, as well as how these decisions aggregate to produce the political networks connecting politicians to poor urban voters. In doing so, we show how migrants power the emergence of machines, and how machines fuel the construction of migrant political communities. This interdependence, at once both long acknowledged and under-studied, structures the emergent politics of India's rapidly expanding urban frontier.

2

How Brokers Emerge

PAVAN'S HOME IS SET deep within the serpentine alleyways of Ganpati, one of the largest slums in the north Indian city of Jaipur. With exposed brick walls, chipping paint, and a corrugated steel roof held up by stones, the shanty is almost indistinguishable from others in the settlement. What differentiates it is the inscription on Pavan's front door. The sign displays his name, his position as *adhyaksh* (president) of the settlement, and a lotus flower—the symbol of the Bharatiya Janata Party (BJP). Pavan is an informal slum leader. He helps residents secure government IDs and demand public services from the state. In a handful of folders, Pavan keeps copies of petitions, correspondence with officials, and notes from party meetings, detailing his efforts to improve the slum. He has built a large following through these activities, which he is expected to deliver to the BJP. Pavan, however, cannot rest on his laurels. He must maintain his followers' approval or risk losing them to one of Ganpati's many other slum leaders, who vie to expand their personal following—their source of rents, patronage, and political sway.[1]

How do political brokers like Pavan emerge in the slum settlements proliferating across cities of the Global South? Scholars, focusing on a wide array of countries, have documented the pervasiveness of these types of actors, who "broker" political support from citizens in return for access to goods, services, and protection from politicians.[2] Many such studies even examine the

1. Interview with Pavan, January 29, 2011.
2. On brokers in Latin America, see Nichter 2008; Szwarcberg 2015; Camp 2017; Larreguy et al. 2016. On brokers in Sub-Saharan Africa, see Baldwin 2013; Koter 2013; and Gottlieb 2017. And on brokers in India, see Manor 2000; Krishna 2002; and Auerbach 2020. Stokes et al. 2013 examine brokers across Latin America, India, Great Britain, and the United States.

go-between activities of brokers within urban slums, in India and elsewhere.[3] Scholars, however, have rarely investigated how brokers rise into the positions of informal authority from which they facilitate such exchanges.

This question lacks obvious answers within India's slums. In villages across India and elsewhere, local leaders often surface through longstanding social hierarchies.[4] Even with recent shifts in rural political authority, village leaders still frequently come from socially and economically dominant groups (e.g., local landlords or caste leaders).[5]

Urban slums lack equivalent pre-established forms of customary authority. These populations are almost universally impoverished, and have few connections to city politicians. Leaders like Pavan, who emerge from within these communities, are themselves largely poor, first-generation residents in the settlement. In the slums we studied, only one in ten local leaders enjoyed formal, salaried employment and only one in four had been born in the settlement. Settlement leaders are also almost always the first in their families to be active in politics. They cannot draw on the dynastic ties that many elite politicians rely upon.[6]

How do migrant transplants from the countryside—lacking in wealth, influence, and connections—emerge as leaders of their settlements? Answers to this question usually draw from one of two narratives. The first is pervasive within the popular press and cinema, whose imagination is often captured by the figure of the slum boss. In this narrative, slum leaders are thuggish kingpins who rise through extraordinary acts of violence. For example, a recent Bollywood biopic, *Daddy*, depicts the life of gangster-turned-politician Arun Gawli. He rose to prominence as the boss of Dadgi Chawl, a slum in central Mumbai. His rap sheet includes dozens of criminal cases, and he is currently serving a life sentence for his involvement in the murder of a political rival.

The second narrative is drawn from academic studies of political parties. These accounts see intermediaries like Pavan as little more than interchangeable cogs through which party organizations buy off poor voters. Newspaper

---

3. Ray 1969; Cornelius 1975; Perlman 1976; Auyero 2001; Jha et al. 2007.

4. Bailey 1970; Wade 1988; Pur and Moore 2010; Koter 2013; Baldwin 2016; Khan Mohmand 2019.

5. Recent work on continuities and change in rural political authority in South Asia include Krishna 2002; Shami 2012; Anderson et al. 2015; Kruks-Wisner 2018; Khan Mohmand 2019.

6. Chandra 2017. 81% of slum leaders we surveyed were the first in their family to be involved in politics.

headlines during Indian elections routinely trumpet such nefarious activities, detailing the innovative ways in which parties provide slum residents with cash, liquor, and other freebies.[7] Political scientists have devoted considerable attention to these "vote-buying" strategies, in which brokers play a key role. Party elites provide resources to their preferred intermediaries, who pass them on to voters. By implication, a broker's popularity is largely determined by the resources party superiors decide to bestow upon them.

Neither narrative—of slum leaders as ruthless thugs or as interchangeable cogs—captures the reality we observed in India's slums. In this chapter, we draw on hundreds of interviews with residents, slum leaders, and political elites to advance a different explanation: brokers emerge through fierce competition for resident support. In opposition to popular narratives, we argue slum leaders gain such support by winning residents over, not by intimidating them. Contra conventional scholarly models of brokered politics, we argue slum leaders must *first* win over local residents, not party elites. A survey of over 2,000 slum residents, as well as interviews with residents in two case study settlements, reveal that residents are primarily concerned with a leader's ability to deliver everyday acts of assistance between elections, not in episodic acts of vote-buying during campaigns.

With multiple aspirants vying for resident support, residents have meaningful choices in whom to seek assistance from and whom to follow. We draw on an experiment conducted with a representative sample of slum residents in Jaipur and Bhopal in order to assess how slum residents evaluate local brokers. While shared ethnicity and partisanship do indeed shape such evaluations, in accordance with conventional wisdom, everyday problem-solving efficacy, signaled by a broker's education and occupation, also powerfully shape resident evaluations. Such factors have typically received less attention than ethnicity and partisanship in studies of political selection. Yet our experiment suggests that they can be just as influential. Indeed, our research shows that preferences for education can be even more influential than for shared ethnicity, and can even substitute for a lack of shared ethnicity.

More broadly, our findings cut against conventional portrayals of the urban poor within democratic politics. Privileged urbanites in India often deride slums as bedrocks of corruption in the city. Local slum bosses are seen as predatory figures who sell the votes of "manipulated and exploited" residents

7. Shankar 2018; Sharma 2008; Hiddleston 2011.

to politicians, allowing the latter to avoid being held accountable for their mal-feasance.[8] Political scientists similarly view brokers as enabling parties to hold residents "perversely accountable" with their vote, in return for election time handouts.[9]

Our research demonstrates that the migrants who populate Indian slums are neither passive recipients of election-time handouts, nor cowering victims of local kingpins. In actively selecting their brokers, slum residents powerfully shape who represents their political interests in the city. In choosing their brokers based on their problem-solving abilities, residents ensure a degree of quotidian, performance-based accountability within city politics. As we show in Chapter 4, many of these locally selected brokers go on to hold city-wide positions within parties. Tracing the formation of slum brokerage networks reveals a more substantial, if far from perfect, degree of representation and accountability within political machines than is commonly depicted.

How Leaders Emerged in Saraswati

This chapter was inspired by our qualitative fieldwork in Bhopal and Jaipur's slums, including in Saraswati, a squatter settlement not too far from Ganpati. Saraswati sits along the Aravali mountains, in the eastern part of Jaipur. Migrants first settled the area in the late 1970s to work as miners in nearby stone quarries. The population of the slum now stands at around 2,600 residents, and is diverse in caste and regional terms. Saraswati is located on land administered by the Forest Department. Starting in the mid 2000s, the Forest Department became increasingly vigilant in protecting the forests around Saraswati from encroachment. This culminated in a series of demolitions of shanties that had pushed too deep into the mountains. Officials then turned their attention to reclaiming land lost to earlier waves of squatters, threatening a larger section of the slum. In response, residents planned an informal election in December 2007 to select a slum president to fight the impending eviction. A group of residents first created a list of election rules (Figure 2.1a and Figure 2.1b), which included that the president should be a resident and work for the betterment of the slum; that campaigning would have to stop one day before the election; and that all residents above 18 years of age could cast a vote.

8. Björkman 2014.
9. Stokes 2005.

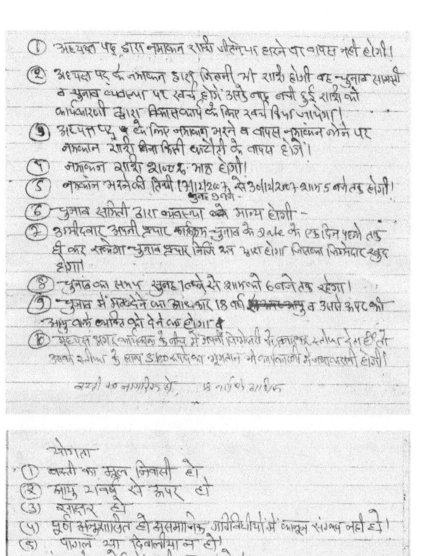

FIGURE 2.1. Slum Leader Election Rules in Saraswati

Three residents stepped forward to fight in the election. Jagdish, the first candidate, was a young private school teacher in his late 20s in 2007. With a high school diploma and an awareness of government programs, Jagdish is one of the most educated residents in Saraswati. He is also a member of the Berwa *jati*, a prominent "Scheduled Caste" community.[10] With a slight frame, quiet confidence, and reputation for honesty, Jagdish strays from the popular image of thuggish slum lords shown in Bollywood films. Prem, the second candidate, had been an informal leader in Saraswati for several years prior to the election. He is a Rajput, one of Rajasthan's dominant upper castes. Prem understood his appeal to residents as flowing from his work as a chauffeur for government officials.[11] This was a valuable outside connection that had yielded a paved road in the mid 2000s. Rahul, the third candidate, was one of the original miners in Saraswati and belongs to the Meena tribal community.

During a public discussion between the candidates and residents, Rahul agreed that Jagdish would be a better president. Residents expressed the need for a leader who was educated and confident in dealing with politicians. Rahul did not fit the bill. After wavering in his decision to run, Rahul dropped out of the race before the election. On January 8, 2008, most adult residents of Saraswati voted in the informal election—almost 800 people in total. Jagdish beat Prem, by 458 to 317 votes. Jagdish was then invited to create a small development committee (the *Saraswati Vikas Samiti*) that could help him in his leadership activities.

Residents collected fees for a modest inauguration event. Jagdish and his appointed committee members took the stage and promised to work hard on behalf of residents. These cannot be cast aside as empty promises—if Jagdish wanted to maintain his public support and keep his position as president, there would be little room for complacency. Indeed, Jagdish's support among residents must be continually re-won through demonstrations of hustle and efficacy in problem-solving. Given the informal nature of the position, there are no fixed term limits. Residents can individually and collectively reject Jagdish whenever they see fit. And they are not shy to do so in public and contentious ways: a little over a year after the election, a group of angry residents (with

10. Scheduled Caste is the official term for members of former "untouchable" castes.
11. Author interview with Prem, May 21, 2011.

rocks in hand) gathered in front of Jagdish's home. Forest department officials had destroyed a few shanties on the edge of Saraswati, and residents demanded to know why Jagdish hadn't stopped them.[12] In another instance, rumors had spread that Jagdish was making money from a ration card distribution drive, and residents were quick to demand answers. While this kind of "rude" accountability is imperfect, it keeps a fire under the feet of slum leaders to perform or risk an erosion of support.[13]

Jagdish not only faces "voice" from residents, but also the threat of "exit," expressed as residents turning to other slum leaders in the settlement.[14] Even after the informal election, Jagdish cannot prevent enterprising upstarts from challenging his authority and poaching some of his supporters. Indeed, just a few years after the 2008 election, another resident—an educated private schoolteacher also belonging to the Berwa *jati*—began to spread word of his own aspirations to become an informal leader in Saraswati. This other resident, Jitendra, took a critical stance on Jagdish's ability to improve local conditions, and was starting to attract a small following in the mid 2010s. Mishra, a storekeeper at the front of Saraswati, also began to pull away some of Jagdish's followers at the same time by helping residents secure ration cards. As we find in many other settlements, slum leaders who emerge through community elections co-exist with those that earn their supporters in more quiet, piecemeal ways.[15] These multiple, overlapping pathways of becoming a slum *neta*—even within the same settlement—reflect the informality of these positions, the intense competition that underpins slum leadership, and the agency of residents in selecting whom they support.

Jagdish's rise exemplifies how competition for the affections of Saraswati's residents affords them meaningful choices in selecting their local leaders. It also begs the question of how such choices are made. Conventional wisdom on Indian politics would suggest one of two factors drive these allegiances: caste or party. Yet both Jagdish and Prem were supporters of the BJP, and so partisan support cannot explain the outcome of their contest. Some of Jagdish's

---

12. Author field notes, January 2011.

13. Hossain 2009.

14. Hirschman 1970.

15. See the eight ethnographic case studies (including one on Saraswati) presented in Auerbach 2020, all of which had histories of informal elections as well as examples of slum leaders who rose by attracting supporters in more decentralized ways.

support stemmed from his ethnic appeal to other Scheduled Caste residents.[16] However, this factor could have only taken him so far within Saraswati, where no one ethnic group is especially large. Indeed, support from members of other communities, including from Tiwari, an influential Brahmin, was crucial to Jagdish's success. Further, residents noted the larger appeal of Jagdish's education and perceived capability.[17] The poor migrants living in Jaipur's settlements demand a more nuanced understanding of their political choices than is commonly afforded them.

Why Do Slum Residents Need Brokers?

Our own understanding of slum politics draws on more than two years of fieldwork conducted in Jaipur and Bhopal between 2010 and 2018. In this chapter, we rely on thirty-six in-depth interviews with residents in two case study settlements conducted in 2018; 262 structured short interviews with slum leaders conducted in 2016; and an original 2015 survey of a large, representative sample of 2,199 slum residents across 110 slums (50 in Jaipur, 60 in Bhopal). We supplement these sources with data from an original 2012 survey of 1,925 residents across 80 of the same 110 settlements.[18]

Our interest lay in a specific and pervasive type of slum: *squatter settlements*, spontaneous areas constructed by migrant residents in an unsanctioned, unplanned fashion.[19] Surveying these communities was no simple task. We

16. Interview with Saraswati residents, January 16 and May 29, 2011.

17. Interviews with Saraswati residents, November 17, 2010; January 16, 2011. Jagdish himself noted (January 9, 2011) that residents demanded a well-educated leader during a pre-election community meeting.

18. This survey was conducted by Auerbach and is discussed in more detail in Auerbach 2020.

19. For a detailed discussion on squatter settlements, and the features that distinguish them from other urban poverty pockets officially and colloquially referred to as "slums," see Auerbach 2020, chapter 1. In this book we use the terms "squatter settlement" and "slum" interchangeably to refer to the neighborhoods under study. We do so for ease of exposition and to resonate with the colloquial and official use of the term "slum" in India, which encompasses squatter settlements. Readers, though, should note that squatter settlements are the specific empirical focus in our book and represent one type of settlement that falls within the larger category of "slums." We estimate that just under half (47%, a plurality) of listed "slums" across Bhopal and Jaipur are squatter settlements. Their widespread presence, intensive vulnerabilities, and significant migrant populations make squatter settlements especially substantively important and theoretically appropriate spaces for our study.

began by collecting recent official slum lists in each city.[20] However, we could not sample directly from these full lists because of the wide array of neighborhoods they classified as "slums." To distinguish squatter settlements from other areas the government classified as slums, we conducted intensive field visits, interviews, and examinations of satellite images. Through this process, we were able to identify the full set of 307 squatter settlements across both cities. From this list we selected 110 settlements to conduct our survey in, using multi-stage random sampling, stratified on population and geographic area.[21]

Next, we had to find a way to systematically select households within each settlement. Standard techniques used in surveys often assume an environment in which houses are arrayed in some kind of planned order, not the haphazard mazes of squatter settlements. To sample households, we first generated Google Earth satellite images for each settlement. A digital drawing program measured pixel widths and lengths of each image. We randomly selected width and length pixel points to mark on each image.[22] We then trained team leaders to navigate the satellite images and place enumerators at the households living at each randomly selected point. If respondents were unavailable or unwilling, enumerators approached an adjacent house. Seventy-three percent of initially selected households were interviewed (only nine percent were refusals). The survey was conducted in the afternoon and early evening to balance access to individuals who stay at home with those working outside the settlement. Enumerators selected individuals within each household based on availability and an eye to ensuring gender balance. To ensure our sampling and interview protocols were followed, at least one of us *and* a team supervisor accompanied the survey teams for the duration of the study. Importantly, we were able to obtain a relatively balanced sample of men (53% of respondents) and women (47%).

Our sample confirms the high proportion of migrants who populate these settlements, with seventy-three percent of respondents reporting moving to

20. In Jaipur, these lists were collected from the municipality, development authority, and PDCOR, a consulting firm. In Bhopal, the primarily list came from the Urban Administration and Development Department, Government of Madhya Pradesh. These lists included recognized and non-recognized slums, avoiding the coverage bias that faces studies limited to sampling from only officially recognized slums.

21. For a detailed discussion on the creation of the sampling frame of squatter settlements in Bhopal and Jaipur, and the stratified random sample of squatter settlements, see Auerbach 2020, chapter 6.

22. New points were selected if a point fell on a vacant area or outside the settlement.

TABLE 2.1. Descriptive Statistics of Survey Respondents

Variables	Sample Mean	Standard Deviation
Age (years)	36.57	13.03
% Women	47	49.91
Education (years)	5.36	5.08
Monthly Per Capita Household Income (INR*)	2,165	2,017
% Born in Slum	27	44.15
% Hindu	74.83	43.41
Time in Slum (years)	22.57	12.69

*At the time of the survey, 1 USD = 65 Indian Rupees (INR).

the settlement during their lifetimes (with the remaining respondents born within the settlement). Among those not born in the settlement, over two-thirds (68%) were born in districts outside of Bhopal and Jaipur.[23] Many respondents retain some connection to their home villages, with over half making at least one annual trip back. As the left panel of Figure 2.2 shows, the average age of settlements is just under thirty-four years, and only a quarter have existed for more than forty years. It is precisely the relative newness of these migrant settlements that makes them productive sites for studying the political integration of the urban poor.

Within slums, the demand for brokers like Jagdish stems from the material precarity residents must endure. Only just over a quarter (26%) of surveyed respondents lived in a fully permanent structure, and less than fifteen percent had a title (*patta*) for their property. Table 2.1 shows average monthly per capita household income reported by sampled residents was a mere INR 2,165, or roughly $1 per day. Importantly, impoverishment was near universal: eighty-seven percent of the sample reported a per capita household income of less than $2 per day. Less than a third of residents had a household toilet connected to a sewer line, and roughly half had no source of water within their home.

Underdevelopment and informality underwrite the need for residents to secure various forms of government assistance: documents to obtain subsidized foods and other welfare schemes; municipal trucks to fill water tanks; staff and trucks to clear debris clogging the gutters that crisscross the settlement;

23. Note that being born in Bhopal or Jaipur *district* does not necessarily mean that the respondent was born within Bhopal or Jaipur *city*. Both districts have large rural areas, with villages that are several-hour drives from the cities. Our figure of 68% is therefore an underestimate of the percentage of first-generation migrants to Bhopal or Jaipur *city*.

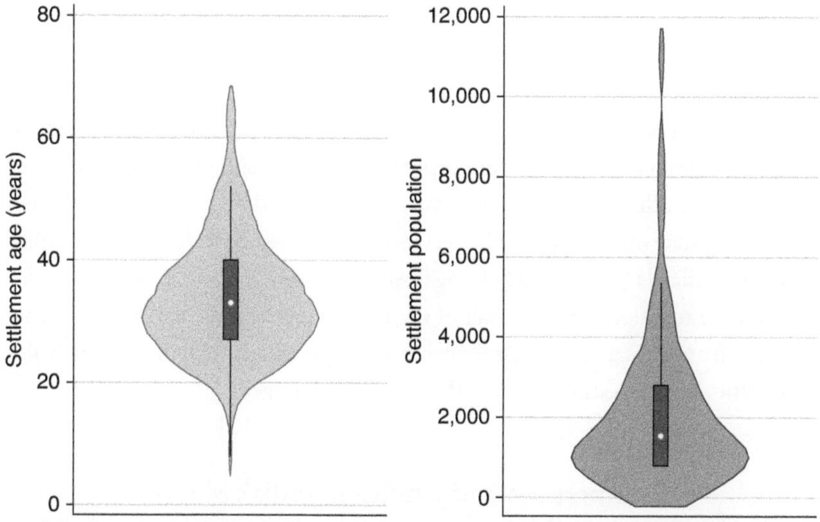

FIGURE 2.2. Age and Size of Sampled Slums

Notes: Each figure represents violin plots in which the white dot represents the median value in the sample; the thick gray bar represents the interquartile range; and the thin bar represents 1.5 times the interquartile range. On each side of the line is a kernel density estimation to show the distribution of the data, with wider sections representing a higher probability that members of the population will take on a given value. The population plot excludes one outlier slum (population = 23,811).

and pumps to drain water from the flooding that immediately follows any heavy rainfall. Yet the public officials responsible for such requests are frequently unresponsive, and themselves stretched thin by scarce resources and spotty staffing. The 2012 survey unearthed a striking pessimism among slum residents, with eighty-five percent saying they expected to be ignored when approaching a government official for assistance, compared to only twelve percent who expected a response.[24]

Consequently, residents must look to other members of their community for assistance in making claims on the state. These demands are supplied by a steady stream of residents who aspire to become community leaders. As we discuss in Chapter 4, these aspirants see local leadership as a platform for launching themselves into city politics. The attractiveness of political careers is enhanced by the paucity of formal jobs for slum residents. More than ninety percent of the combined sample of residents and slum leaders we surveyed lacked formal employment.

24. See Auerbach and Kruks-Wisner 2020.

Precarity thus underwrites both the demand for and the supply of brokers, making them a pervasive presence across Jaipur and Bhopal. Pooling responses from our 2012 and 2015 surveys, we asked 2,543 residents about the activities of brokers in their settlement. Just under three-quarters recognized slum leadership in their settlement. Leaders were reported to help residents with an array of problems, including obtaining state-issued cards (noted by 52% of respondents), petitioning state officials for public services (48%), helping residents meet politicians and officials (41%), and helping residents deal with the police (48%). Our 2015 survey revealed that over half of the respondents (59%) had requested assistance from a local leader. Brokers are widespread and play important roles across the slums we studied. How then do they emerge?

Competition and Choice in India's Slums

He who has not had blisters on his feet, how can he understand the pain of others?

SHIVA, BROKER WITHIN GULAB COLONY[25]

Events within Saraswati show residents defying stereotypes of slum politics. Far from having authority foisted upon them, they shape the nodes of leadership that form within their settlement. Facing eviction, residents recognized the importance of selecting a leader to represent their claims. Their choices determined the pool of people eligible for leadership, even going so far as writing down rules about who could run for the position of settlement president.

While each slum has its own idiosyncrasies, we find such agency to be a remarkably consistent feature of political life across settlements in Jaipur and Bhopal. As a number of residents said:

Slum leaders help us because the residents of the *basti* have chosen them as their leader.[26]

We chose them so that they can help us when there is a problem.[27]

Leaders help the poor people who have no one in the government to go to . . . We have chosen them for a reason.[28]

25. Interview, Bhopal, July 4, 2016. Shiva was quoting a popular couplet poem.
26. Amaltas Colony Respondent 7, August 17, 2017.
27. Jamun Nagar Respondent 3, August 16, 2017.
28. Amaltas Colony, Respondent 9, August 17, 2017.

The *netas* [leaders] live among us so it is their responsibility to help someone who approaches them with a problem. We have chosen them as leaders
for a reason—they have information and knowledge, so they should get our
work done.[29]

In each of these interviews, slum residents repeatedly noted that they actively
select their leaders, and hold expectations for those whom they chose. Party
leaders in our study cities concurred, noting they cannot bestow local authority from above. Nor could they install one of their own cadres as a leader, even
if the worker was a resident of the slum itself.

INTERVIEWER: Could you ever make an outside person a leader in the
slum?

RESPONDENT: No. An outsider would not have any importance
[*mahatva*] within the settlement. A local from the settlement will
know each and every resident, who is good, who is bad, only
someone like that can become a *neta* [leader].[30]

Instead, party seniors have to choose between local leaders who have already
amassed a reputation within their settlements.

RESPONDENT: See, there would always be some leadership in the *bastis*
[slums]; some people who were active and working for people. Our
party needed someone like this in the settlement. It was through such
people that we strengthened our position in the *bastis* . . . These are
the people we would select for a party position.[31]

RESPONDENT: Someone from the community emerges as a strong
leader, has a public following, and has strong influence. In that case,
we must approach him and offer him a position.

AUTHOR: You mean when there is someone the local people already
support, you then approach him and bring him into the party?

RESPONDENT: Yes, somehow we have to make him part of the party.[32]

RESPONDENT: We [the party] can't make someone a *neta* [leader] just
by giving him *neta* clothes and making him stand on the road. In that
case he would just be a statue. They must first have the support of
residents to be a leader.[33]

29. Amaltas Colony Respondent 13, August 19, 2017.
30. Interview, Jaipur, January 15, 2017.
31. Interview with Congress ex–MLA, Bhopal, January 25, 2017.
32. Interview with BJP municipal councilor, Jaipur, February 13, 2017.
33. Interview with Congress municipal councilor, Bhopal, January 23, 2017.

Evidence from our survey of 629 slum leaders provides further corroboration of this sequencing. We asked slum leaders what the biggest reason is for securing a position (*pad*) within a party. Over half (57%) said popularity within the slum, while only a tenth said top-down, pre-existing ties to party leaders.[34] Aware of the limits of closed-ended questions, we also concluded each interview by asking leaders to describe their initial ascent into a leadership position, and their first interactions with parties. 262 leaders (42% of our sample) took the time to respond to these open-ended questions. We recorded, transcribed, and personally read through them to assess pathways of leader emergence.

Poring over these interview transcripts confirmed that most leaders first garner a following within their settlements, which then attracts the attention of party elites. 213 leaders (81% of those who responded) noted that they first built a following in the slum, while only 49 (19%) mentioned the reverse sequence. As one broker described his early ascent:

> If someone would call out my name, I'd join him; if someone's drain would overflow, I'd join him; if someone would get locked up, I'd join him.... Then, new houses kept coming up and I kept helping people in case of water problems or garbage pile ups. I used stones and pebbles to construct roads for people here. I kept doing social work and people got to know my name. When people know you, big leaders also get to know about you. They called me many times. Then, an election campaign rally was going on once near our settlement. They called out my name and asked me to come on the stage. They introduced me to [a local Congress leader] who wanted to give me a post.... Even the senior leaders today, they give the post to someone who does work and is popular.[35]

In other cases, leaders built a following through more sudden, visible activities that brought them to the attention of political elites. Often, local leaders would organize protests as part of their claim-making activities, which would then reach the ears of a local party leader. For example, one leader described how

34. Our observations align with an earlier wave of scholarship on urban politics in Latin America, which described slums as competitive environments in which leaders were locals who had to work to gain resident approval. Ray 1969; Cornelius 1975; Gay 1994; Burgwal 1996. These studies, however, stop short of theorizing and testing the implications of such competition for processes of broker selection by residents.

35. Interview with Broker 2, Settlement 8, Bhopal, July 5, 2016.

a protest they organized in front of a municipal office, demanding land titles for slum residents, brought them to the attention of a local ward councilor.[36] This was a tactic that appeared especially prominently in the narratives of female brokers. As one female leader told us:

> Protest has got me everything. When the councilor refuses to listen to me, I just gather 15–20 women and immediately protest in front of his house. Once we protested for water for three days until even the newspapers had to cover it. Then the councilor had to make sure to send us a tanker.[37]

Indeed, female leaders often draw on the specific grievances of female residents to fuel their initial emergence through such protest activities. Examples we heard included demands for streetlights near the perimeter of the settlement where residents would relieve themselves but where female residents were afraid to go at night,[38] applications for widow pensions,[39] and demands for more regular water supply.[40]

Politics within Saraswati also explodes the myth of slums ruled by omnipotent dons holding local monopolies of power. Instead, we find large amounts of competition, evidenced by significant numbers of brokers, at a variety of levels. In Jaipur and Bhopal, we find party competition extending down to the most local levels, including within slums.[41] Across the 111 slums we worked in, respondents provided names of 1,170 slum leaders, approximately ten leaders in each settlement. Even if we restrict ourselves to slum leaders who officially work for political parties, we find an average of just under six leaders per settlement, and just under two leaders per thousand residents across our study slums.[42] Furthermore, most slums with party workers had leaders with ties to both the Congress and BJP, the city's major parties.[43] Saraswati's own

36. Interview with Broker 3, Settlement 9, Bhopal, July 4, 2016.

37. Interview with Broker 4, Settlement 10, Jaipur, June 21, 2016.

38. Interview with Broker 5, Settlement 11, Jaipur, June 19, 2016.

39. Interview with Broker 6, Settlement 12, Jaipur, June 18, 2016.

40. Interview with Broker 42, Ganpati, Jaipur, June 20, 2016.

41. Even within contexts that a single party dominates, ethnographic studies find evidence of micro-level competition among brokers. Auyero 2001; Zarazaga 2014.

42. The standard deviation across this sample is 1.6 party workers per thousand.

43. 91 of our 111 slums had at least one slum leader who was formally affiliated to a political party. 50 settlements had at least one leader formally affiliated to the Congress and one to the BJP.

experience attests to the intense competition that can occur even between slum leaders affiliated to the same party. India's slums, in short, are hotbeds of competition, not political monopolies.

To gain an understanding of how residents experience such competition, we conducted in-depth interviews about interactions with settlement leaders with thirty-six randomly selected residents from two of our case study settlements. Our intensive fieldwork in these settlements afforded us a prior understanding of leadership patterns and ensured residents had a degree of familiarity with us that enabled more granular discussions of local politics. In these conversations, we asked residents (without prompting) to name leaders they knew about in the settlement, as well as leaders they had personally gone to for help.

Residents were clearly aware they lived in competitive brokerage environments. On average, respondents named 6.5 leaders in the first case study settlement, and 3.9 in the second. Thirty-five out of the thirty-six interviewees named three or more leaders. Further, residents reported availing of the choices offered by such competition. In the first settlement, residents approached 3.31 leaders for help on average, with sixteen of the nineteen interviewees stating they had approached three or more leaders. In the second settlement, residents approached 2.06 leaders for help, and seven of the seventeen interviewees had approached three or more leaders for assistance.

Far from being under one leader's control, residents routinely noted they could abandon one leader in favor of another if they so choose. When asked about why they started seeking help from a different leader, respondents offered answers that reflected a mixture of dissatisfaction with the broker they had originally approached (a "push") or a belief that a new leader might be more effective going forward (a "pull").

> INTERVIEWER: Who was this local leader you met?
> RESPONDENT: Hari.
> INTERVIEWER: When did you meet him?
> RESPONDENT: It has been 3–4 months. Hari heard my problem but did nothing.
> INTERVIEWER: Did you ever approach another leader for help?
> RESPONDENT: Yes. We went to Ravi for a water supply issue. He has a little power.[44]

44. Amaltas Colony Respondent 9, August 17, 2017.

In another interview, a different respondent described how they approached various leaders in attempting to solve an issue.

> INTERVIEWER: Can you tell me the names of the local leaders you met with?
>
> RESPONDENT: Yes, the names that I just told you, I have been to each one of them. Some *lohars* [blacksmiths] have blocked our streets, we are unable to pass through. So, I have met every *neta* here with regards to this. . . . I went to Gopal and Prem for help.[45]

Most often, the process of shifting from one broker to another took the quiet form of discontinuing seeking help from one individual, and beginning to seek help from another. In some cases, the process could be more formal, especially if a broker held some kind of title within the settlement, such as the "president" title Jagdish won in Saraswati. Nearly half (45%) of surveyed residents said they could remove brokers from such leadership positions if they were unhappy with them.

Competition enables residents to choose their own leaders, and to shift allegiances between the many options available. How are such choices exercised? What do residents look for in choosing a leader to support?

Pathways of Selection

Our fieldwork reveals two primary ways in which slum residents chose their leaders. The first consists of discrete events—informal elections and community meetings—such as the 2007 election that Jagdish won in Saraswati. We found evidence of such events across a variety of slums. Over three-quarters (77%) of the 1,925 respondents to a 2012 author survey of slum residents across our two study cities acknowledged informal leadership in their settlement.[46] Remarkably, over half of this subset reported selecting their leaders through informal elections or community meetings. This figure approximates our slum leader survey (detailed in Chapter 3), where over a third (38%) of respondents claimed that they were selected through informal elections or community meetings. Other researchers studying slums in India and Latin America have observed similar selection processes.[47]

---

45. Jamun Nagar Respondent 12, August 18, 2017.
46. Auerbach 2020.
47. Ray 1969; Gay 1994; Burgwald 1996; Jha et al. 2007.

The second pathway of broker selection is through the iterative, everyday choices residents make in whom to seek help from. Over time, these individual choices aggregate to produce a distribution of support for different slum leaders in a settlement. Take the case of Shiva, a leader in Amaltas, another slum in Jaipur.[48] Shiva migrated to Jaipur from his village in Jhunjhunu district in Rajasthan. Initially, he stayed with his in-laws, who lived in the northern part of the city. He struggled to find employment, despite having a college degree, instead working mostly as a part-time mechanic and electrician. He also had difficulty finding a place to live. Then, Shiva heard of a new area being settled where space was still available. He moved there and constructed a makeshift home in which he and his wife settled, along with 150 other families in what became Amaltas settlement.

The new settlement faced a host of problems, chief among them a lack of accessible water. Even as he continued his search for work, Shiva found residents approaching him for help. He noted, "I am an educated person, and I knew how to work keeping in mind the laws here," so residents backed him to spearhead efforts on their behalf. Shiva sensed an opportunity to become a community leader and decided to lead an effort to establish water connections in the settlement. He took a calculated risk, and took loans against his wife's wedding jewelry, while collecting 15 rupees (approximately 18 cents) each from some early supporters who backed his efforts. This sum helped pay for an initial set of connections. Shiva's efforts won him further recognition, which he expanded through continued problem-solving efforts.

Unlike Jagdish, Shiva was not selected in a centralized community election, but rather through more decentralized decisions by individual residents to support him. Like Jagdish, Shiva has felt competitive pressures from three other leaders who have emerged within his settlement, and who jockey with each other for support. Irrespective of the mechanism through which they are selected, brokers in competitive settings rise and fall with resident support. How, then, do residents decide which leaders to support?

How do Residents Choose Leaders?

The rise of Shiva and Jagdish in Amaltas and Saraswati Nagar, respectively, highlights several qualities that slum residents value in their community leaders. Shiva understood his value among residents to flow from his relatively

---

48. Interview with Broker 7, Settlement 13, June 4, 2016.

high level of education. In Saraswati's election, Jagdish (the winner) was the most educated candidate while Prem (the runner-up) had support that stemmed from his connections to local bureaucrats through his job as their chauffeur. The contest also pointed to the limits of ethnic strategies in diverse slums. Jagdish's caste may have helped with other Scheduled Castes, especially his community of Berwas, but his victory also depended on support from residents of other castes.

In our discussions with residents about how they evaluated aspiring leaders in their midst, we found two key concerns animating their decisions. The first was a *distributive* concern: how likely am I (the resident) to receive a portion of the benefits a slum leader distributes within my slum? The second is an *efficacy* concern: how effective will a slum leader be in acquiring benefits to distribute?

A Distributive Concern

It is neither feasible nor efficient for parties to provide benefits to every voter in a neighborhood. Even studies of highly successful political machines, such as the Peronists in Argentina, find these parties actually distribute goods to less than ten percent of voters.[49] Given this constraint, parties often seek the help of local brokers in ensuring benefits reach those voters the party most strongly wishes to cultivate as supporters. Brokers must therefore decide which residents to favor.

Such targeting feeds voter concern that their support may not be duly rewarded. Parties similarly worry that voters may not hold up their end of the bargain. In the face of these mutual concerns, risk-averse parties and brokers are expected to favor those whose reciprocity they are most confident of receiving. Such voters may include their own partisan supporters.[50] These voters are most likely to offer support at the polls, since they ideologically favor the party anyway. Furthermore, politicians are most likely to be embedded in shared social networks with their own partisans, and hence best able to verify whether the latter are upholding their end of the deal.

Studies of clientelist politics in South Asia and Africa similarly emphasize the utility of shared ethnic networks—those based on race, language group, caste, religion, or tribe. Since parties in these regions often lack clear policy agendas or ideological positions, their connections to voters are often forged

49. Stokes 2005.
50. Cox and McCubbins 1986; Dunning and Nilekani 2013; Stokes et al. 2013.

along ethnic lines. Voters anticipate that politicians from their own ethnic group will be more likely to give them benefits.[51] For their part, politicians are more confident of being able to hold co-ethnic voters accountable for holding up their end of the bargain.[52]

In India, these and related arguments have primarily been made with regard to the relationship between voters and formal political candidates.[53] This logic can be extended to how residents choose informal local brokers. If parties favor their own, residents will hold higher expectations of getting benefits from those brokers with whom they share a partisan or ethnic affiliation.[54] Accordingly, they should be most likely to support those local leaders who are from their own group, and/or who affiliate with their preferred party.

An Efficacy Concern

The distributive issues of trust and inclusion are often viewed as the central problem of machine politics. A tremendous amount of energy has gone into studying how parties and voters evaluate each other in the shadow of such concerns. A second concern voiced by slum residents has received far less attention: how effective will brokers like Jagdish and Pavan be in securing resources for their followers? Unless they can secure such resources, the question of whom brokers distribute benefits to is moot.

Why has this fairly obvious concern received so little scholarly attention? One reason is that prior studies have mostly focused on broker activities *during* elections, in particular their efforts to buy votes. In standard accounts of vote-buying, parties deliver campaign handouts to brokers, who pass them on to poor residents. The benefits involved in this process—petty cash, sacks of grain, liquor—are modest. Further, their allocation is often managed by campaign operatives, and is either assumed to be a fixed amount or to be distributed according to local demographics.[55] In these accounts, a broker's individual skill plays little-to-no role in determining the benefits they have to distribute to their supporters.[56]

---

51. Chandra 2004; Posner 2005.

52. Besley et al. 1993; Fershtman and Gneezy 2001.

53. Chauchard 2016.

54. Calvo and Murillo 2013. 85% of our 629 surveyed slum leaders had partisan affiliations.

55. Gans-Morse et al. 2014.

56. Gonzalez-Ocantos et al. 2012. Recent models of vote-buying even explicitly assume "all brokers are equally effective," attributing any variation in their efficacy (again conceptualized

Yet everyday life in India's slums paints a different picture. Slum leaders primarily forge relationships with residents through everyday acts of problem solving in response to the latter's demands, not petty handouts. We asked a random sample of residents in two case study settlements the circumstances around which they first made contact with a leader. *None* of the thirty-six residents we interviewed at length mentioned such contact being established during elections. Instead, they spoke of approaching a leader with a problem between elections, such as having a road paved,[57] cleaning gutters,[58] getting information on the possibility of securing property titles,[59] and ration cards.[60]

The primacy of daily problem-solving activities highlights a broker's individual capabilities in securing the resources to address resident requests. As one leader told us:

> See, you need two things to become a leader—*jagruktaa* [awareness] and *jaankari* [information]. And these qualities are needed to solve problems. You need awareness to see what the problem is. Most people go to work, come home, eat, and go to sleep. There is little time to do anything else in the settlement. But people like me notice—that road has not been built; ok, how can we fix it? That is awareness. Then you need information—what government scheme might be available for a given problem. Nothing is given to us.[61]

We are hardly the first to acknowledge the significance of routine problem solving in brokerage.[62] Yet prior studies fall short of examining how brokers vary in their problem-solving efficacy, how residents evaluate such variation, and how these evaluations impact their choice to support one broker over another.[63]

---

from the party's perspective) as shaped by the extent to which party superiors can monitor and punish them, rather than any individual ability. Larreguy et al. 2016, p. 165.

57. Jamun Nagar respondent 4, August 16, 2017.

58. Amaltas Colony respondent 9, August 18, 2017; Jamun Nagar respondent 5, August 16, 2017.

59. Jamun Nagar respondent 15, August 20, 2017; Amaltas Colony respondent 17, August 19, 2017.

60. Amaltas Colony respondent 5, August 17, 2017.

61. Rajesh, BJP party worker, Tulsi Nagar, Bhopal, January 17, 2017.

62. Ray 1969; Cornelius 1975; Auyero 2001; Krishna 2002.

63. More recent studies of Argentine brokers do note broker popularity partially hinges on their individual abilities to secure resources. Zarazaga 2014; Camp 2017; Szwarcberg 2015. But

Existing scholarship tends to assume that residents rely on a broker's past performance in determining their future efficacy.[64] We certainly saw established slum leaders relying on prior successes to recruit supporters. However, a sole focus on past performances is analytically problematic for two reasons. First, it rests on a tautology—the perceived efficacy of a slum leader is a function of their past efficacy as a slum leader. This circular logic provides no answer to the question as to how residents are initially drawn to leaders, before the latter have had a chance to accumulate a record. Second, if residents exclusively privilege past accomplishments, aspiring new leaders with no record will find it hard to poach support from even minimally competent existing leaders with a proven record.[65] Yet we observe precisely the opposite in our field sites, where new leaders routinely surface to compete against—and often displace—existing *netas*.

Entrants were able to break into the current structure of leadership if they could signal the potential to get things done better than established leaders. Take Praveen, who told us about how he displaced several older leaders to become the preeminent leader in his settlement:

> When I was just starting out, I asked the older leaders of the slum why there was no development. I told them that they were the leaders of the slum. I asked them if they had development committees. They said, they didn't. They didn't even know what registration meant.
>
> Then I put forward a proposal to them about the establishment of a committee and got its registration number issued [from the municipality]. Afterwards, we printed a letterhead. And on that we wrote down all our problems. Water supply, electricity, and roads were our main problems.
>
> People started recognizing me. They'd say, "he is a knowledgeable man," "he's a very active man." Then the people of the party also got to know about me. They wanted to know who has the strongest hold over this place. So, everyone came to me—leaders of the Congress, BJP, and other parties, as well as many independent leaders.[66]

---

even this recognition has not generated insights into how residents go about assessing the efficacy of brokers in their locality, and the degree to which such evaluations guide their decision over which broker to follow.

64. Stokes et al. 2013.

65. Szwarcberg 2015, p. 3.

66. Interview with Praveen, Sitaram Nagar, Jaipur, June 4, 2016.

The fluid and competitive nature of slum leadership thus affords residents ongoing choices as to which slum leader they view as most efficacious.[67] Our survey of slum leaders found evidence of several generational cohorts of leaders, and that, over time, leaders consistently faced competition upon entry into the brokerage environment.[68]

Slum residents continually evaluate the efficacy of informal leaders in their settlement, and frequently compare a mixture of existing leaders and new arrivals with no past record. The question is, what serves as the basis for such comparative evaluations? We argue that, in such fluid and competitive environments, residents often draw on observable traits of local aspirants to help assess, project, and compare their likely efficacy.

One important set of observable traits indicates how *connected* a potential leader is likely to be to the municipal government. We can imagine such connectivity in several ways. *Partisan connectivity* refers to when a leader is affiliated with the incumbent party. Such leaders are perhaps more likely to get their supporters' requests heard. Voters might also prefer brokers with *bureaucratic connectivity* to government departments responsible for public service delivery.

The second set of attributes residents consider relates to a leader's *capabilities* in effectively making claims on the state. For example, studies have noted that successful local brokers in India and elsewhere are often well-educated.[69] Yet these accounts have not assessed whether residents actively support better-educated leaders.

We have outlined two key concerns that motivate resident evaluations of slum leaders: which leader is most likely to *distribute* benefits, and which leader is most likely to be *effective* in securing benefits to distribute. We argue

---

67. This assertion also holds for those settlements that emerge through large-scale, pre-planned land invasions in which informal leadership is initially present—a type of settlement formation most often documented in Latin America. Collier 1976; Gilbert 1998. Scholars describe these settlements as competitive brokerage environments, where new challengers emerge to compete with established slum leaders, affording residents ongoing choice over leader selection. Ray 1969; Gay 1994; Burgwal 1996.

68. Respondents had varying tenure lengths as slum leaders, attesting to the openness of the brokerage environment. The mean tenure length was 20 years, with a standard deviation of just over 10 years. We asked respondents how many slum leaders were in operation when they began slum leadership. Responses indicated a stably competitive environment, with an average of 10.18 competitors for leaders who began more than 25 years ago, and 9.5 competitors for those who began within the past 5 years.

69. Auyero 2001; Jha et al. 2007; Krishna 2002; Manor 2000; Ray 1969; Stokes 1995.

each concern should encourage residents to focus on certain observable attributes of local leaders. Distributive concerns should lead them to support leaders from their ethnic and partisan background. Efficacy concerns should lead residents to support leaders with connections to local government actors, and the capabilities to make claims on the city government. But how is slum resident support shaped by whether they share the same ethnic group or party as a slum leader? And how impactful are the latter's capability and connectivity in shaping resident evaluations?

Who Do Residents Want to Lead? An Experiment

To better understand how residents evaluate brokers within slums, we conducted an experiment with our survey respondents. We presented respondents with two hypothetical slum leaders, and provided information about each leader. We then asked respondents which of the two leaders they preferred. This design, called a forced-choice conjoint experiment, was developed within the field of marketing research to study consumer preferences. It has proven helpful in assessing the importance of different pieces of information consumers are asked to simultaneously consider in making a purchase.[70] In the case of political research, this technique is often used to assess which traits influence citizens' choices between political candidates, or in our case slum leaders.

While such experiments are analytically helpful, we were concerned that they might be overly complex or artificial. To allay these fears, we looked to ground our experiment in a process of leadership selection eminently familiar to slum residents. To find this example, we drew on our ethnographic fieldwork. We presented respondents with two hypothetical slum residents running to be president of a *vikas samiti* (development committee). These neighborhood associations, typically headed by a president, are widespread across slums, where residents use them as vehicles through which to make public claims.[71] Figure 2.3 provides example letterhead used by *vikas samitis*, with the name of the settlement on the top, and the list of council members (headed by the president) on the left.[72]

---

70. Hainmueller and Hopkins 2015. These designs can also help disentangle the effects of attributes that are correlated in real life (such as caste and partisan preference). Furthermore, conjoint experiments have the potential to reduce social desirability concerns because they offer respondents the confidentiality of several potential justifications for a decision.

71. See Auerbach 2017 on development committees in India's slums. Slum associations have also been documented in Brazil (Gay 1994), Mexico (Cornelius 1975), and Venezuela (Ray 1969).

72. We deliberately selected a letterhead from a development committee that has been disbanded. The displayed letterhead is no longer in use.

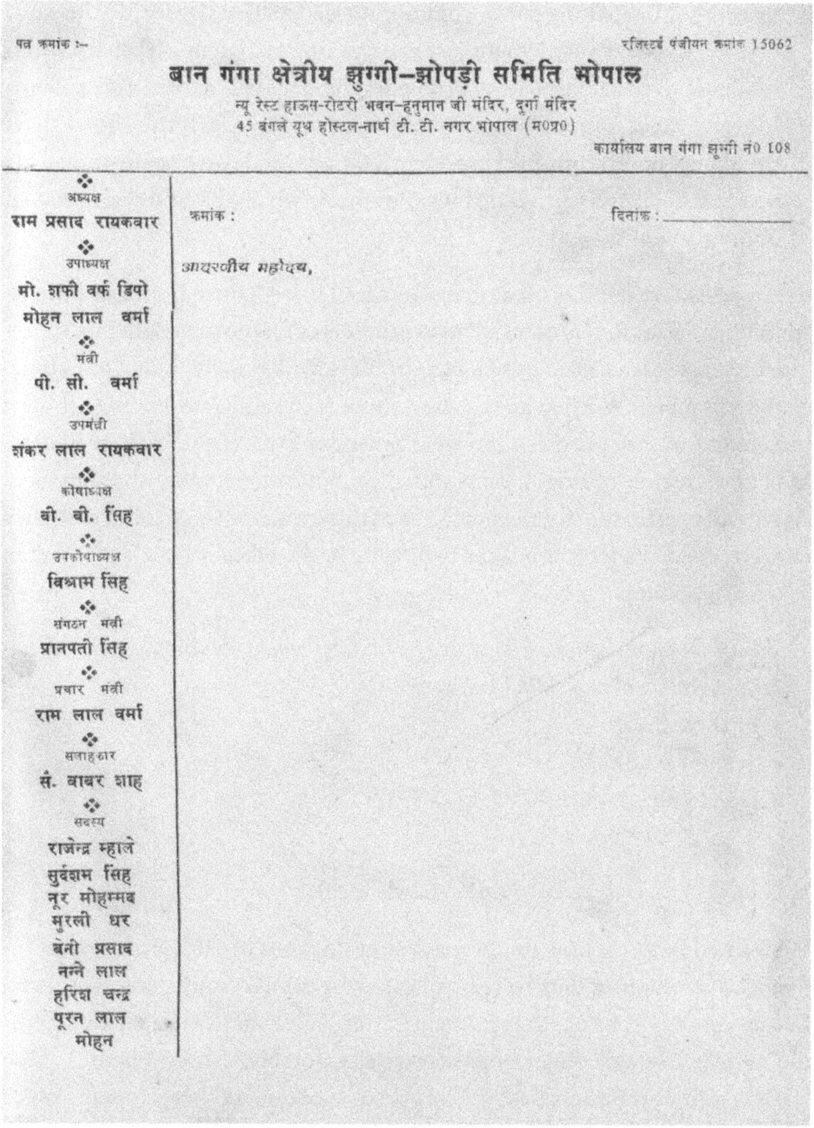

पत्र क्रमांक :—   रजिस्टर्ड पंजीयन क्रमांक 15062

बान गंगा क्षेत्रीय झुग्गी–झोपड़ी समिति भोपाल

न्यू रेस्ट हाऊस-रोटरी भवन–हनुमान जी मंदिर, दुर्गा मंदिर
45 बंगले यूथ होस्टल-नार्थ टी. टी. नगर भोपाल (म0प्र0)

कार्यालय बान गंगा झुग्गी नं0 108

अध्यक्ष
राम प्रसाद रायकवार

उपाध्यक्ष
मो. शफी वर्क डिपो
मोहन लाल वर्मा

मंत्री
पी. सी. वर्मा

उपमंत्री
शंकर लाल रायकवार

कोषाध्यक्ष
बी. बी. सिंह

उपकोषाध्यक्ष
विश्राम सिंह

संगठन मंत्री
प्रानपती सिंह

प्रचार मंत्री
राम लाल वर्मा

सलाहकार
सं. बाबर शाह

सदस्य
राजेन्द्र म्हाले
सुबंशम सिंह
नूर मोहम्मद
मुरली धर
बेनी प्रसाद
नन्ने लाल
हरिश चन्द्र
पूरन लाल
मोहन

क्रमांक :

आदरणीय महोदय,

दिनांक :____

FIGURE 2.3. Example Slum Development Council Letterhead Stationery

The process of selecting a president of the *vikas samiti* is something our survey respondents were familiar and comfortable with, as events in Saraswati slum illustrated. Our experimental question read as follows:

In some slums there are people that do *netagiri* [politicking]. I'm not talking about the ward councilor or MLA [member of the state legislative assembly]. I'm talking about community leaders that live inside the slum. I recently visited a settlement just like this one in [Jaipur/ Bhopal], where residents were having a lot of problems and decided to form a *vikas samiti* [development committee] to improve development in the slum. There could only be one *adyaksh* [president], though, and two people wanted the position. I will tell you a little bit about these two people and then ask your opinion about them.

After reading out this preamble, we placed two pictures in front of the respondent, meant to represent the two candidates for the president position.[73] The pictures served as cognitive placeholders, which we included to help respondents retain the listed information about each candidate. Pointing to each picture in turn, we provided information about five traits of each candidate: their caste, region-of-origin, party affiliation, education level, and occupation. As we will explain shortly, the first three of these traits relate to the distributive concern residents face; the latter two relate to the efficacy concern. We then asked respondents:

> *In your opinion, which of these two candidates would you prefer to support as council president in a slum like yours?*
> - First candidate
> - Second candidate
> - Don't know[74]

Trait 1: Caste identity

We wanted to assess how much resident evaluations of slum leaders were influenced by whether they were from the same ethnic group. However, India houses several forms of ethnic categorization. Prior studies use the term "ethnic" to refer to single dimensions of ethnicity, notably caste or religion).[75] We felt it was important to assess the importance of each of these dimensions of ethnicity in slum leader selection.

---

73. These pictures were identical other than the color of their shirt. We made this decision in order to ensure differences in the candidate's image did not drive respondent choices.

74. Interviewers were instructed not to read out "don't know" in order to minimize such responses by residents.

75. For the use of "ethnic" to refer to caste see Chandra 2004. For its use referring to religion see, Wilkinson 2004.

In order to assess the various ethnic dimensions, we varied a leader's name, which indicates their *jati* (sub-caste), as well as their religion.[76] Slum leaders were randomly assigned to come from the respondent's own *jati*, one of three well-known upper caste Hindu *jatis*, one of three well-known disadvantaged Dalit caste Hindu *jatis*, or one of three well-known Muslim *zats*.[77] By providing this information, we could assess how the probability of a leader profile being preferred was changed in going from their being of a different *jati* to the same *jati* as the respondent. We were also able to do the same for faith.[78]

These ethnic categories also vertically partition society into groups of unequal social and economic status. Dalits and Muslims are disadvantaged relative to upper caste Hindus.[79] Our experiment's design thus allows us to assess the effect of shifts in ethnic status categories.

Trait 2: Regional identity

Scholars of Indian politics have typically thought of ethnicity solely in terms of caste and religion.[80] Yet urban slums also house migrants from a wide array of regions. Our survey respondents hailed from fourteen of India's twenty-eight states, and included states from the north, south, east, and western parts of the country. This multi-regional demography stands in sharp contrast with largely mono-regional village populations, and raises the question of whether regional differences inform political preferences. To examine this possibility, we varied each leader's home state in the experiment. Slum leaders were randomly assigned to come from the survey respondent's home state, the state of the study city (Rajasthan or Madhya Pradesh), another prominent source state in north India's "Hindi belt" (Uttar Pradesh or Bihar), or a prominent source state from a different linguistic region of India (West Bengal or Maharashtra).

76. Indian *jatis* are endogamous sub-castes that denote traditional occupations, are highly localized, and number in the hundreds across India. *Jatis* are ranked and nested within broader caste status groups, indicating whether a *jati* is considered high or disadvantaged caste. *Zats* denote caste-like stratification among South Asian Muslims.

77. We include several *jatis*/*zats* within each status level to ensure estimated effects were not driven by comparisons with any one particular *jati*/*zat*.

78. 98% of slum residents and 98% of slum leaders we surveyed were Hindu or Muslim.

79. According to the Sachar Committee 2006, p. 159, the poverty rate among Muslims in urban India was 38.4%, comparable to the rate among Scheduled Castes and Scheduled Tribes (36.4%), both much higher than among upper castes (8.3%).

80. The scholarship on nativist violence is a notable exception. e.g., Weiner 1978; Bhavnani and Lacina 2019.

Trait 3: Partisanship

We randomly assigned our hypothetical leaders as either affiliated with one of the two major parties in our study cities—the Indian National Congress (INC) and Bharatiya Janata Party (BJP)—or to be non-partisan independents. Doing so allows us to assess the impact of shared partisan affiliation.[81] It also allows us to see the effect of broker affiliation with the local incumbent party. Leaders affiliated with the ruling party might find it easier to have requests met by local government actors, for example.

Trait 4: Education

Our fieldwork revealed that slum residents were concerned with whether a broker possessed the raw capability to lobby public officials. As one respondent put it:

> We have chosen them as leaders for a reason—they have information and knowledge, and perhaps connections, so they should get our work done.[82]

The slum leaders we interviewed concurred, noting that their success as leaders hinged crucially on key abilities that distinguished them from other residents.

The key question then, is how do residents assess the capabilities of leaders in their midst? In interviews, slum leaders underscored how their educational qualifications often serve as one important indicator:

> See, here in the slum, we have only poor people. Most people are uneducated. So, when there is an issue, they need help in writing applications. They began coming to me, saying, "brother, fill out this application for me." . . . slowly people told others [I do] this kind of work . . . that's how I built my early support base.[83]

---

81. It is worth noting that while caste can often inform partisan affiliation in India, the two are distinct categories, especially so in our study cities. Among Hindu voters, upper castes are more likely to support the BJP, yet both parties draw support from across the caste spectrum. Conversely, while Muslim voters are more likely to support the Congress, 21% of Muslim surveyed slum residents identified the BJP as their preferred party.

82. Amaltas Colony Respondent 13, August 2017.

83. Broker 48, Ganpati, June 1, 2016.

Especially striking was how often leaders referenced their own education as a trait that attracted supporters. Sixty-eight of our 262 interviewees (26%) made unprompted and direct references to their education in explaining their rise to prominence:

> In the beginning, not a lot of residents were educated. They needed help with anything that needed literacy skills, such as filling forms for ration cards, ID cards, or petitions. Since I am literate, I helped them with these things, and as word spread, more people started approaching me for help regarding issues that required reading and writing skills.[84]

> The way they say: in a blind world, the one-eyed man is the king. The same way here, I was a little educated. I used to consider myself capable, that I can help the workers and the poor. There are ration card forms and other kinds of government forms; I kept doing them, and kept getting people's attention. So, they made me a leader.[85]

Education is especially important within urban slums because of the centrality of written claim-making. Unlike Indian villages, slums do not have substantial fixed allocations of government funds. Slum leaders are not like local political leaders in villages, such as *sarpanches* (the heads of *panchayats*—village councils). Not only are those village leaders elected into formal positions, but the bodies they preside over are given funds to spend on local public services.[86] The informal conditions of slum environments compel leaders to have to fight and claw for every scrap they are given. Such fighting often requires the ability to make written claims and to keep "informal archives" of correspondence with bureaucracies.[87] Our fieldwork unearthed hundreds of examples of claims made through such written applications and petitions.[88]

84. Broker 46, Settlement 40, Jaipur, June 23, 2016.

85. Broker 47, Settlement 41, Bhopal, June 27, 2016.

86. The funds available for local village councils has significantly increased following the 73rd amendment to the Indian constitution, which institutionalized *panchayats* as the basic units of rural administration. Kruks-Wisner 2018.

87. See Auerbach 2018 on the collections of paper petitions, correspondence with officials, committee meeting notes, and political ephemera that slum leaders keep within the settlement.

88. One typical letter read, "Since last year we have been suffering from water scarcity. At times, we have to go to the factories or the cremation grounds for water . . . We are in trouble and request that you take action." Slum petition letter, Jaipur, late 2000s.

Education enables these efforts.[89] Consequently, we decided to use education as an indicator of a slum leader's claim-making capabilities in our experiment. Leaders were randomly assigned to have no schooling, an eighth-grade education ("secondary school" in India), or a college B.A. Our survey confirmed that each of these education levels were realistic for a slum resident to have. Forty percent of surveyed residents had at least an eighth-grade education and nearly nine percent (8.9%) had at least some college education.[90]

Trait 5: Occupation

We have outlined already how a slum leader's efficacy hinges not only on their capabilities in making claims, but also on their degree of connectedness to local bureaucracies. However modest the connection, bureaucratically connected brokers may be regarded as more likely to be aware of the dizzying array of government benefits residents might be eligible for, be better informed about the specific requirements to be eligible and apply for such benefits, and be better able to compel municipal personnel into actually providing those benefits.

We indicated a leader's connectivity in our experiment through their occupation. Our fieldwork reveals occupations to be a useful indicator of bureaucratic connectivity. First, we find most slum leaders hold jobs outside their leadership activities (83.3% of our surveyed brokers held jobs outside brokerage), as the latter are rarely lucrative enough to be a full-time occupation. Second, certain occupations place a leader in particular proximity to local bureaucracies.

---

89. Scholars disagree about the usefulness of education as an indicator of leader competence, with some calling it a "compelling indicator of a leader's quality" (Besley et al. 2011, p.55), and others seeing it as simply reflecting elite membership (Dal Bó et al. 2017). These debates typically focus on formal elected politicians operating in far wealthier environments than ours. For reasons we articulated previously, we view education as an especially important signal of efficacy within the specific context of claim-making and leadership in informal slums. Furthermore, education does not correlate with privilege within slums for two reasons. First, no slum resident can be considered privileged by national, or even local, standards. Even slum residents with over an eighth-grade education have an average monthly per capita household income of $36. Second, education does not even mark a relatively privileged micro-elite within the slum. The average monthly per capita income for those with less than an eighth-grade education is $30, not substantially different from that of more educated residents.

90. 23.06% of urban Indians have finished high school, and 13.2% have finished college. Census of India 2011.

Take the example of Prem in Saraswati, whose appeal derived from his job as a government chauffeur.

Residents might view leaders like Prem who work within municipal offices as having greater access to bureaucrats. As one slum resident told us:

> Even if a man is just a *chowkidar* [security guard] at the municipal office, his bosses will be important people he sees every day. So, if he asks them to make sure the municipality sends sweepers to clean our gutters, won't it be more likely they listen to him?[91]

While poor slum residents are unlikely to hold significant positions within municipal government, they can work in low-level jobs within these offices. Such positions can prove significant, as several leaders explained to us:

> When I first began my rise as a leader, I worked as a local clerk in a government hospital. I used to give massages to the sick invalids [*mariz*] in the wards. That is also how my work started, in a way. Because I used to take the sick when they were discharged, and take them to see *adhikaris* [government officials] to see if there was some scheme from which they could benefit. Between the slum and the hospital I was constantly going to visit *adhikaris*, so these officials got to know of me.[92]

> I was in administrative service, a central government employee. That's why people trusted me. I would go to any department without any hesitation. I would go as a complainant along with other complainants, be it [to] the collector's office or the municipal office. I had the support of everyone. They would put me in the front as their representative.[93]

> Once I started working for the government, people felt that because [I work] in the Secretariat, [I can help them]. Slowly, like a chain reaction, everyone got to know that I'd helped resolve an issue. Then I undertook the work involving ration cards.[94]

Our short interviews with a larger sample of 262 slum leaders further reinforce the importance of occupation. Fifty-nine leaders (22.5%) explicitly mentioned

91. Field notes, Jaipur, June 27, 2015.
92. Laxman, Tulsi Nagar, January 16, 2017.
93. Interview with Broker 10, Settlement 15, July 3, 2016.
94. Interview with Broker 11, Settlement 16, June 4, 2016.

the connectivity afforded by their occupation in narrating their rise within the slum.

Drawing on this insight, we assigned a third of the leaders in our experiment to have one of three "highly connected" municipal jobs: clerk (*chaprasi*), sweeper (*safai karamchari*), or security guard (*chowkidar*) in the municipal office. We assigned another third of leaders to jobs that were entirely contained within the slum, which provide little scope for external connections. Ubiquitous examples of such "low-connectivity" jobs are owners of informal shops within the settlement catering to residents. We included three such jobs: corner shop owner, tea stall owner, and cigarette-*paan* stand owner.[95]

The final third of leaders in our experiment were assigned occupations that fell in between highly connected municipal jobs and less-connected slum jobs. This "medium-connectivity" category included three professions: street vendor, auto rickshaw driver, and unskilled house painter. Each of these professions require residents to circulate outside the slum, providing greater opportunities to gather information about developments within the city than "internal" slum professions. However, the medium-connectivity jobs do not place the holder in direct contact with municipal authorities.

How Do Residents Evaluate Brokers?

Our experiment allows us to assess how much shifts in the five traits outlined in the prior section impact resident evaluations of the broker profiles with which they were presented.[96] The dots with whiskers in Figure 2.4 depict the Average Marginal Component Effect (AMCE) for each broker attribute. These quantities tell us how much better or worse on average a randomly selected candidate would fare against another randomly selected candidate, if that attribute changed to a given value from the baseline value (indicated by the dot without a line). These results are estimated using OLS regressions with the

95. *Paan* is a popular stimulant combining betel leaves and areca nuts.

96. Auerbach and Thachil 2018 outlines a series of robustness checks to guard against particular design effects, including a randomization balance check, and experiment, profile, and attribute order effects. Overall, our diagnostics find no evidence of systematic design effects. We specified attribute options that were plausible in any combination. While all combinations are not equally typical, this is not a requirement for effective conjoint analysis. Hainmueller et al. 2014. We also find our results are robust to excluding decisions featuring potentially implausible brokers.

rated profile as the unit of analysis, and the outcome coded 1 for preferred profiles within a pair, and 0 for those that were not preferred.[97] The independent variables are binary indicators for each attribute value. Since each respondent evaluated two candidate profiles in making their choice, our full sample has 4,350 rated profiles.[98]

Let us begin by examining the three traits we argue residents use as signals of their likely inclusion in a broker's network of beneficiaries. We first find that shared caste and faith do register a positive average causal impact of six and seven percentage points (pp), respectively. This means a randomly selected candidate would on average earn six (seven) percentage points more support against another randomly selected candidate if their caste (faith) shifted from one that differed from the respondent to one that matched the respondent.[99] This result aligns with conventional thinking in Indian politics. Perhaps less expected is our finding of a corresponding causal impact of going from a different region-of-origin to one that matched the respondent's region to be nine percentage points. Since villages are usually regionally homogeneous, such

97. Since our attributes were randomized independently, we estimate the average marginal component effect (AMCE) for all included attributes simultaneously through a simple linear regression. Hainmueller et al. 2014. We cluster standard errors by respondent also following Hainmueller. Clustering standard errors may not be necessary or advisable for certain experimental designs (Abadie et al. 2017), including conjoint experiments (Schuessler and Freitag 2020). We also estimate each of our main models without clustered errors and find our results to be substantively unchanged in those specifications.

98. Many conjoint experiments in wealthier settings are administered in a written format to highly educated respondents, who are asked to rate multiple profile pairs. However, in our setting, the conjoint question was administered orally using cognitive placeholder images, given our low-literacy respondent pool (average education level was 5 years, with a third of the sample having no formal schooling). We prioritized a detailed oral procedure to ensure intelligibility, which led us to decide against having respondents rate more than one pair of profiles.

99. We use the cjpowR package developed by Schuessler and Freitag 2020 to establish the minimum detectable effect (MDE) for our sample size (N = 4,350), with 80% power and 95% significance. The MDE for 2-level variables is 4.25 pp, and for 3-level variables 5.2 pp. These MDEs are comparable to the average AMCEs across all conjoint experiments in this book (5.6 pp). Each of our significant AMCEs for *jati*, religion, state, Muslim leaders, co-partisanship, secondary and college education are greater than the MDE (the only exception is high status jobs). Our non-significant AMCEs for Dalits (2.6 pp), medium-connectivity leaders (2.5 pp), partisan alignment with incumbent (1.3 pp), and opposition (0.8 pp) are all substantively small. Obtaining MDEs equal to these coefficients would have required far larger samples (17,392–183,934 rated profiles), which were not feasible in our setting.

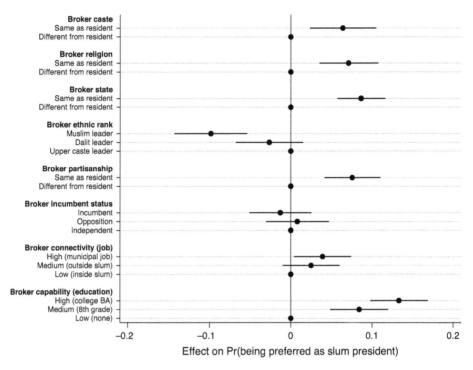

FIGURE 2.4. Effects of Broker Attributes on Preferences for Slum Leader
Notes: This plot shows estimates for the effects of the randomly assigned slum leader attribute values on the probability of being preferred for president of the slum development council. Estimates are based on an OLS model with standard errors clustered by respondent; bars represent 95% confidence intervals. The points without horizontal bars denote the attribute value that is the reference category for each attribute.

identities do not typically structure rural politics. The fact that regional origins matter in the political decisions of migrants suggests important potential shifts in the relevant forms of ethnic political attachments in the city, compared to the countryside.[100]

Beyond shared ethnicity, we also find evidence that the status of a slum leader's ethnic group has an impact on resident preferences. Shifting a candidate's ethnicity from high-status upper caste Hindu to Muslim results in an average decrease of ten percentage points in their probability of selection. Further analysis suggests that this divergence between upper caste and Muslim brokers is specifically driven by low support for Muslim brokers among

100. All p-values reported here are for two-sided tests.

Hindu residents.[101] By comparison, the penalty against Dalit leaders appears to be less pronounced. Going from an upper caste to Dalit status decreases the chance of selection, but by a much smaller margin (2.6 pp) that is not statistically significant.

We also find shifting a candidate's partisan status to match that of the respondents increases the candidate's chance of selection by eight percentage points.[102] However, we do not find a similar positive impact in shifting from a non-partisan independent status to being affiliated with the local incumbent party. This lack of impact may reflect India's highly volatile electoral system, where incumbency can be fleeting, and thus may not serve as a solid basis for shaping evaluations. Alternatively, our results may reflect the difficulty in disentangling the effects of incumbency from partisanship in a setting where the same party (BJP) was incumbent at the local level at the time of our survey.[103]

Our results thus show slum residents do take into account whether brokers share their ethnic and partisan backgrounds, which have traditionally been seen as helping assuage the distributive concern as to whether they will be included in a given broker's network of beneficiaries. More strikingly, our analysis reveals the importance of traits we see as indicative of a broker's problem-solving efficacy; such traits have received far less attention than distribution-related attributes of shared ethnicity and partisanship.

Perhaps most arresting is the large influence of leader education, which was included as an indicator of their claim-making capability. Shifting a leader's education from no schooling to an eighth-grade level corresponds with an eight percentage point increase in their likelihood of selection, and going from no education to college education yields a thirteen percentage point increase.[104]

---

101. Figure S2.7 in the Online Supplement presents marginal means partitioned by respondent religion. While Hindu and Muslim respondents on average favor upper caste Hindu slum leaders at broadly comparable rates, the former support Muslim brokers at far lower average rates than the latter.

102. The reference category includes all combinations that are not a co-partisan match, including unaffiliated brokers and residents.

103. In separate analyses, we remove the co-partisanship measure, and separately run the analysis for respondents who are BJP supporters, and those who are not. We find that, among BJP supporters, incumbents are preferred over independents, while for all other voters, they are disfavored. We therefore cautious in over-interpreting our incumbency finding.

104. The effects we interpret as large compare to the largest effects recovered in other conjoint candidate experiments in wealthy (Carnes and Lupu 2016) and poor (Carlson 2015) settings.

The difference in going from an uneducated to college-educated status is the single largest effect found in our analysis, significantly greater than the comparable impact of shared ethnicity and partisanship.[105] Further analyses finds that the positive and significant effects for college and secondary education manifest within several different subgroups of slum residents (partitioned across age, faith, and partisan lines).[106]

Our analysis also reveals evidence related to the importance of occupation, included as an indicator of connectivity to urban bureaucracies. Switching a broker's occupation from a low-connectivity "inside slum" job to a high-connectivity municipal job results in an average four percentage point increase in their being favored.[107] However, we do not find a significant effect for medium-connectivity occupations outside the settlement.

We also examine whether the importance of leader attributes depends on the good or service a resident seeks help with, rather than their overall evaluation for a development council presidency position. However, we find no systematic differences between our original results, and results from asking residents to select the leader within the pair who they believe would be more likely to provide them with a household-level private good (a voter ID card), or more likely to provide them with a slum-wide collective good (piped water for the whole settlement) (see Figure S2.1 in the Online Supplement).

These results suggest that the political choices of slum residents cannot be reduced to any single consideration, including ethnicity. It is more fruitful to examine the interplay between considerations of ethnicity and those of efficacy. For example, we find some evidence that suggests a candidate's effectiveness can substitute for a lack of shared ethnicity, at least within the framework of our experiment. The top panel of Figure 2.5 shows the average probabilities of selection for candidates with specific characteristics. Candidate A is from the same *jati* as a respondent, holds a high-connectivity municipal job, and is college educated. Candidates with this desirable mix are preferred within a

---

105. Two-tailed equality of coefficients tests show the AMCE for college education is significantly greater than that of co-ethnicity and partisanship at the 94% level, and all other attributes at the 95% level.

106. See Figure S.11 in the Online Supplement.

107. While significant, the AMCE here (3.9 pp) is below our MDE with a 3-level variable of 5.2 pp. We may therefore especially worry that this result is susceptible to Type S (wrong sign) or Type M (exaggerated effect) errors. Gelman and Carlin 2014. However, using the cjpowR package developed by Schuessler and Freitag 2020, we find less than a 0.004% chance of a wrong sign, and an exaggeration ratio of only 1.335, indicating slight overestimation.

pair over seventy-one percent (71.7%) of the time in our sample. At the opposite end of the spectrum is candidate D, who is from a different *jati*, is uneducated, and works in the slum. This candidate is preferred only thirty-eight percent of the time.

Now consider the two candidates in the middle (B and C). Candidate C is from the respondent's *jati*, but is uneducated and works within the confines of the slum. Respondents prefer candidates with this mixture of traits on average just under fifty-three percent (52.9%) of the time. This is statistically indistinguishable from how frequently they prefer a college-educated, municipality-employed leader from a different *jati* (54.5% of the time, Candidate B). In other words, respondents exhibit indifference between a "low-efficacy" slum leader from their own *jati* (C) and a "high-efficacy" leader from a different *jati* (B).

These findings are especially interesting when read alongside evidence we present in the Chapter 3 which demonstrates that capable leaders are far more plentiful in our study slums than leaders from a resident's own narrow *jati*. The high diversity of settlements ensures most residents do not have a leader from their own caste to support. Consequently, supply-side factors may strengthen the ability of residents to act on their preferences for efficacious leaders, while constraining their ability to act on their preferences for leaders from their caste. The bottom panel of Figure 2.5 shows that capability and connectivity can similarly mitigate penalties against Dalit and Muslim leaders, compared to upper caste leaders. Thus, while the latter do face discrimination relative to upper caste aspirants, acquiring markers of competence and efficacy, to some extent, can help ameliorate such biases.

In presenting these results (and those in subsequent chapters), we are mindful of the need to interpret findings from conjoint experiments with care. First, we can only speak to respondent preferences for the bundle of attributes that we chose to manipulate in the experiment, and cannot speak to how other attributes might matter or shape the importance of traits we did include in the experiment. We deliberately avoided including large numbers of attributes that might overwhelm respondents, many of whom had little or no schooling.

Second, the AMCEs we report in Figure 2.4 represent the *average* of individual-level causal effects of a given attribute, and thereby incorporate both the direction and intensity of preferences. For some respondents the impact is larger than for others, and indeed for some the impact might be in the opposite direction of the AMCE. Consequently, the AMCE does not provide information on the fraction of respondents who preferred a given attribute level (say, college education) over another (for example, no education)

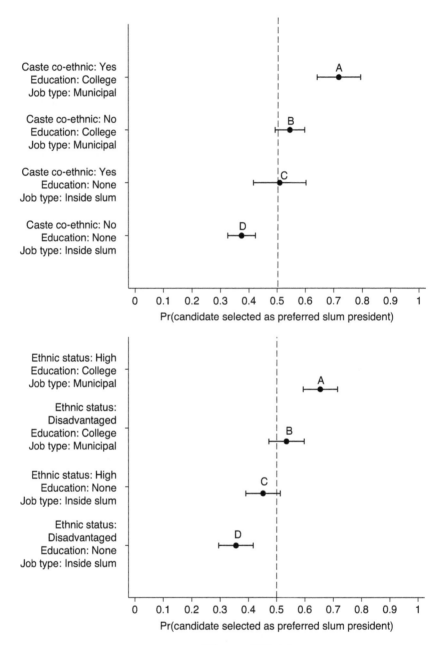

FIGURE 2.5. Efficacy and Ethnicity

Notes: The plot shows the average probability of being preferred for selection as a president of the slum development council. The estimates are shown for profiles with traits specified on the vertical axis. Bars represent 95% confidence intervals. Due to asking each respondent to choose one of the two profiles, the baseline probability of choosing a randomly drawn slum leader profile is 0.5 (depicted by the dashed line).

and cannot be read as necessarily indicating the direction of preference for a majority of respondents.[108] This is not unique to AMCEs, and "is no different from most of the commonly used causal estimands in any other experiment, such as the ATE or local ATE."[109] Finally, our results do not identify the proportion of residents who strictly preferred a given attribute value (college education) over another (no education). We are more interested in how shifts in a given trait impact a broker's probability of being preferred (e.g., if they go from having no education to college education).[110]

Perhaps most importantly, we make considerable efforts in the chapters that follow to assess whether our experimental findings align with other forms of qualitative and quantitative evidence. For example, we assess if actual slum leaders are distinguished by the attributes that we find to be most influential in resident evaluations of hypothetical leaders. The alignment we find across different forms of data deployed in this book strengthens the credibility of our experiments and offers support for the link between our experimentally measured preferences and the patterns of selection that we argue these preferences underpin.

Some readers may be interested in seeing our results disaggregated across key resident attributes. In the Online Supplement, we present conditional marginal means and AMCEs partitioned by respondent gender, partisan support, religion, age, education, and time in the settlement, as well as by settlement population, ethnic diversity, and age.[111] We do not find much evidence of variation

108. Abramson et al. 2020. For example, the positive AMCE for college education we observe could indicate a strong preference for college education (relative to no education) among a minority of residents and a weaker reverse preference for the remaining majority. It could also indicate the reverse situation in which a majority of residents hold a weaker preference for college-educated leaders. Yet for our purposes, either scenario could drive the emergence of a college-educated leader.

109. Bansak et al. 2020.

110. Note that we do not seek to link preferences to predictions of winners of formal elections, and instead focus on informal selections in settings marked by multiple active brokers. The concern about the need to identify the direction of preference for a given attribute among a majority of respondents has been argued to be important when seeking to estimate the probability of a candidate winning a formal election. Abramson et al. 2020. However, Bansak et al. 2020 note that even in formal electoral settings, multi-dimensional choices hinge on both the intensity and direction of preferences, and that AMCEs derived from forced-choice conjoint experiments still represent a key quantity of interest, namely the causal effect of a particular attribute on a candidate's expected vote *share*.

111. The choice of reference category can complicate the use of AMCEs for comparing preferences across different subsets of voters. Leeper et al. 2020. We show conditional marginal means,

in preferences across the majority of these different factors.[112] However, we cannot interpret these results as strong evidence of stable preferences given our limited statistical power to discern differences across subgroups.[113] We therefore provide these analyses merely for descriptive interest.

Good Leaders, Good Neighbors

Two important concerns linger. First, our experiments examine how residents evaluate whom they would prefer as slum leaders, not who they actually get. We argue the two are linked because slum residents actively choose their leaders, and so their preferences drive who actually becomes a leader. But our experiment cannot directly demonstrate this link. To do so requires data on the characteristics of actual slum leaders, which we will turn to in Chapter 3.

For now, we focus on a second concern. Specifically, how confident can we be that the experiment measures how various traits specifically impact *political* preferences for slum leaders, as we claim? Could it be that we are simply assessing the impact of these traits on a resident's *social* preferences for another slum resident? For example, perhaps our finding regarding education simply indicates that higher-level schooling boosts how respondents evaluate another resident of their settlement? To refute this possibility, we require a benchmark of social preferences to compare our results against.

To that end, we conducted a second experiment with our survey respondents. We asked them to evaluate two people looking to move into the slum with their families. Respondents were asked to indicate which person they would prefer as a neighbor.[114] The attributes manipulated in this experiment perfectly matched those on the slum leader question (see Online Supplement

---

which allows us to assess differences in preferences in a manner robust to reference category choice. We also provide conditional AMCEs, which show the causal impact of slum leader features for each subgroup.

112. Drawing on Leeper et al. 2020, we formally tested for group differences in preferences through an omnibus F-test comparing a regression with interaction terms between the sub-grouping variable and all feature levels with an equation without the interactions. In six of the eight cases, this F-test fails to reject the null hypothesis of no overall differences across subgroups at the 95% level.

113. Schuessler and Freitag 2020.

114. We randomize the ordering of the neighbor and leader experiments on the instrument. We find no evidence of systematic experiment order effects.

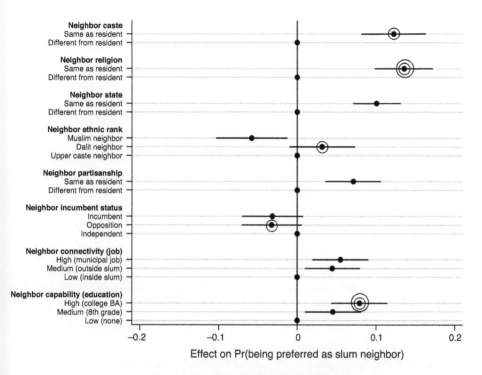

FIGURE 2.6. Comparing Brokers and Neighbors

Notes: The figure shows estimates for the effects of the randomly assigned slum neighbor attribute values on the probability of being preferred as a neighbor. Estimates for both panels are
based on an OLS model with standard errors clustered by respondent; bars represent 95%
confidence intervals. The points without horizontal bars denote the attribute value that is the
reference category for each attribute. Rings indicate significant differences between the AMCEs
in the leader and neighbor models (1 ring = p < 0.1; 2 rings = p < 0.05).

Figures 2.12–2.13). This experiment allows us to compare the impact of a given
attribute when selecting a neighbor compared to a leader. If the results across
both experiments are identical, it would reinforce doubts that our leader experiment was not capturing specifically political preferences.

Instead, the results reported in Figure 2.6 reveal clear differences between
the significance of various traits in evaluations of neighbors versus leaders.
Rings in the figure indicate significant differences with the leader results. First,
we find that the average impact of shared ethnicity (specifically caste and faith)
on the probability of selection is significantly *higher* when evaluating potential
neighbors than when evaluating leaders. For example, the impact of shared *jati*
on selecting a neighbor is nearly twice as large (12 percentage points) as for a

leader (just over 6 percentage points). By contrast, the impact of going from no education to college education is significantly *lower* when selecting neighbors (8 percentage points) than slum leaders (13 percentage points).[115] Figure 2.6 also illustrates that shifting a neighbor's ethnicity from upper caste Hindu to Muslim results in an average decrease of six percentage points. This evidence of social prejudice suggests one possible root for the observed penalty against Muslim leaders in our first experiment.

Overall, the divergences in the effect of key resident characteristics on preferences between our neighbor and leader experiments improve our confidence that results in the latter are not simply reflecting general social evaluations.

Roots of Representation

This chapter sets the foundation for showing how greater attention to the formation of political networks during urbanization can revise our understanding of how the poor are integrated into growing cities. We focused on tracing the emergence of political authority figures within slums, who connect settlements to the wider world of city politics. Our findings cut against conventional narratives depicting these political brokers as thuggish goons or mechanical cogs controlled by party elites. Both views missed what we find to be the key force driving the production of informal authority in urban slums: poor residents themselves.

Residents are far from passive targets of political elites or trembling victims of kingpins. They actively organize and select their leaders. Their agency stems from the fierce competition between brokers for their support. Experimental evidence suggests residents will not simply assemble behind members of their own ethnic group, as is commonly assumed. Residents greatly value brokers whom they see as well positioned to effectively solve their everyday problems. Qualitative and survey evidence also reveal that residents are free to abandon underperforming brokers in favor of others they anticipate can serve them better.

These findings reorient how we think about representation and accountability within urban machine politics. Brokers are not simply top-down enforcers of elite directives, but rather are selected by residents to serve as

---

115. Overall, an F-test reveals the differences in the 11 AMCEs across the neighbor and leader experiments are jointly distinguishable from zero (p = 0.048).

bottom-up representatives of the latter's interests. This simple fact explodes stereotypes of slums as unthinking and desperate "vote banks" that politicians can cheaply buy off with campaign freebies.[116] Instead, poor migrants actively construct the networks that connect them to parties and the state.

However, in showing migrants actively choose their local leaders, this chapter does not suggest that the forms of representation produced by such choices are necessarily egalitarian or inclusive. Indeed, the very nature of the competitive selection decisions we study implies that if residents with certain traits are favored for leadership positions, residents without those traits will be underrepresented in those same positions. In certain cases, such preferences can potentially inform larger patterns of exclusion, such as the bias we find against brokers from India's Muslim minority.

Indeed, even the privileging of markers of efficacy by residents has potentially complicated, and sometimes conflicting, implications. On the one hand, the prioritization of problem-solving abilities underscores a promising feature of these emergent machines with respect to their responsiveness and accountability towards residents. On the other hand, this same prioritization means slum residents who lack education, or who toil in unconnected professions, are likely to be underrepresented within local socio-political hierarchies.

Furthermore, this brokered claim-making remains well short of a policy-driven programmatic politics. The narratives slum leaders provided of their own rise to prominence that we presented in this chapter are especially instructive on this point. These leader narratives repeatedly emphasized the centrality of everyday problem-solving for highly localized issues within the household or settlement. Nowhere did leaders emphasize the importance of wider mobilizations for particular policies that would benefit the urban poor or slum communities specifically.

Yet the system we describe is also not one in which accountability is "perversely" inverted. The ability to choose these local, albeit informal, representatives affords a channel of bottom-up accountability that several slum residents themselves articulated:

> The leader belongs to the settlement; he is one of us so he should help. This way we are able to solve each other's problems. When the elections happen and the big leaders visit, then these local *basti neta* goes to sit next to them,

116. Björkman in Piliavsky 2014 discusses these stereotypes (p. 177).

so that is why they help in the *basti*. The slum leaders listen to us and in turn, the big leaders listen to them.[117]

Why have they become *netas* in the first place? It is like a links in a chain—we are connected to the *basti* leader who is connected to a bigger leader who in turn is connected to an even bigger leader. When we complain to the local leaders, they complain to the higher officials on our behalf and that's how work gets done.[118]

In Chapter 3, we go even further to show how the preferences of slum residents correspond to the distinguishing features of actual slum leaders. The kinds of brokers residents want are the types they get. This simple descriptive finding is a powerful testament to often-ignored, yet meaningful, forms of representation within machine politics.

Of course, a fuller understanding of how political network formation impacts accountability and representation requires answering further questions. Which residents do brokers serve? Who is included and excluded from their claim-making efforts? And do political party elites align with, or differ from, residents in the qualities they most prize in the brokers who connect them? We take up these questions in Chapters 3 and 4.

117. Jamun Nagar Respondent 1, August 16, 2017.
118. Jamun Nagar Respondent 19, August 20, 2017.

3

How Brokers Cultivate Clients

KISHORE HAS LIVED IN Jamun Nagar *basti* for over three decades. He moved to Jaipur in his mid-thirties to find work, all the way from Thane district in the state of Maharashtra. Initially, life in Jaipur was no easier. Struggling to find employment, Kishore joined some other residents who scavenged in the city's periphery for coal that they would then sell to shopkeepers. He then worked as a street vendor, selling fruits and vegetables from a rickety *thela* (pushcart) that he had rented from a friend. It was during this period that other residents began coming to him because he was educated and could help with applications for government schemes.[1] Kishore realized he needed to capitalize on this advantage and began working to cultivate a following. From his humble origins, Kishore has emerged as one of the main brokers in the slum, fueling his affiliation with the BJP.

A number of residents we interviewed mentioned how responsive Kishore had been when they approached him with requests for assistance. One noted, "Kishore *neta* was helpful when we asked for help with a ration card. He filled the form for us, and secured the card."[2] Another noted that he had approached Kishore because his neighbors were not letting him spread gravel in front of his house. Kishore quickly resolved the dispute. "He is always helping residents. When he needs our help and support, we are there for him."[3]

Yet other residents of Jamun Nagar reported very different experiences with Kishore. One resident told us that the open drain next to their house has been jammed with filth for weeks. He decided to approach Kishore for the first time

---

1. Interview with Kishore, Jamun Nagar, Jaipur, June 18, 2016.
2. Jamun Nagar, Jaipur, Respondent 4, August 16, 2019.
3. Jamun Nagar, Jaipur Respondent 18, August 20, 2019.

for help with getting the drain covered. The results were disappointing: "We met with him, and he said he would come to help but he never did. It has been 2–3 months already."[4] Another resident of Jamun Nagar complained that brokers like Kishore had never helped him fill out the form for a ration card, which he still did not have. "They cannot get the work done . . . Even if they can, they purposely don't do it. . . . Nobody in the *basti* cares about them, we don't give them any importance."[5]

Such conflicting reports regarding slum brokers are hardly specific to residents of Jamun Nagar. We heard similarly divergent reports from residents of another settlement, Amaltas Colony, in a different part of the city. For example, many residents described Hari, a prominent BJP *neta* in Amaltas Colony, as helpful:

> I needed help for an electricity connection for my house. The women from the electricity department said I couldn't get one. But Hari made a phone call, and the electricity poles arrived.[6]

> If I have a problem, I let Hari know and he takes care of it.[7]

Yet other residents of Amaltas Colony complained of Hari's unresponsiveness:

> Hari heard my problem but did nothing.[8]

> We went to Hari for help with getting a road paved. He heard us out but did nothing.[9]

That Kishore and Hari cannot address every resident request should not be especially surprising. The poverty and daily insecurity that plagues residents of Jamun Nagar and Amaltas Colony ensure a constant need for assistance.[10] With limited time and resources at their disposal, these brokers would be hard-pressed to address each and every concern. Like all slum brokers, they have to make difficult daily decisions about which requests to prioritize.

4. Jamun Nagar, Jaipur Respondent 9, August 18, 2019.

5. Jamun Nagar, Jaipur, Respondent 13, August 18, 2019.

6. Amaltas Colony, Jaipur, Respondent 11, August 19, 2019.

7. Amaltas Colony, Jaipur, Respondent 14, August 19, 2019.

8. Amaltas Colony, Jaipur, Respondent 9, August 17, 2019.

9. Amaltas Colony, Jaipur, Respondent 10, August 17, 2019.

10. Underscoring this point, Stokes 2005, p. 315, argues, "Limited resources force political machines to choose among poor voters."

In Chapter 2 we examined how poor slum residents actively select their local leaders from the many aspirants competing for such positions. Equally important to the formation of political networks within slums are the decisions leaders must make in selecting which residents to assist among the many vying for their attention. Why do Kishore and Hari decide to help certain residents, while ignoring others?

We argue these small, daily choices are squarely political in nature, and aggregate into important outcomes for city politics. For brokers, these decisions are important to get right given the competitive conditions in which they operate. Helping residents is a key way in which brokers cultivate their supporters, or "clients." In competitive environments, those residents who are ignored are likely to turn to other brokers. Kishore and Hari know they must choose whom to help wisely, and in ways that best position them to fend off their rivals. Kishore worries about Vikram and Ashok, brokers affiliated with the BJP and INC, respectively, who both have large followings that they hope to expand at Kishore's (and each other's) expense. Hari faces fierce competition from Meena and Mukhtar, both of whom are affiliated with the INC.

In this chapter, we draw on fieldwork and an experiment embedded in a unique survey of 629 slum leaders across Jaipur and Bhopal to study how brokers choose which residents to assist. In contrast to conventional wisdom, we do not find brokers to singularly focus on residents whose electoral behavior they can most confidently verify, including those from their own caste or faith. Indeed, we find that these ethnic identities play a strikingly muted role in broker decisions. In fact, we observe brokers prioritizing residents best positioned to amplify their reputations for effective problem-solving within the settlement, including longtime residents and those who are arguably central to the settlement's social community. We argue these priorities reveal the frequently overlooked, careerist ambitions of brokers seeking upward mobility within party organizations.

The local decisions slum brokers make regarding whom to help also aggregate into larger distributional patterns of inclusion and exclusion. In doing so, these intensely local decisions determine citywide patterns of responsiveness and representation towards the urban poor: who is heard and helped, and who is not. Understanding how such decisions are made is thus crucial not only to understanding how political networks form within urban poor communities, but also in understanding whom they do and do not serve.

Finding Slum Brokers

We begin by addressing a simple, yet key descriptive question: who are India's slum brokers? It is difficult to analyze how these brokers act, without an appropriate understanding of who they are. Unfortunately, there are no publicly available lists of informal slum leaders. To our knowledge, there has been no prior effort to systematically survey slum brokers in urban India, or indeed in any other city across the Global South. This chapter outlines our efforts to survey slum leaders across our study cities.

Constructing a sample of slum brokers was a laborious, multi-phase procedure. The first step was assembling a comprehensive sampling frame of squatter settlements in Jaipur and Bhopal, which we detailed in Chapter 2. We selected a combined total of 110 squatter settlements from our full list of 307 such settlements in the two cities.

Next, we had to generate a reliable list of slum brokers within these sampled settlements. We drew on our 2015 survey of 2,199 slum residents across all 110 settlements, along with an earlier 2012 resident survey conducted in eighty of these settlements.[11] Both surveys asked residents to provide the names of informal brokers in their settlement. Next, we created a census of official party workers of the Congress and BJP across all 110 slums through exhaustive settlement visits, interviews with party workers, and by collecting available party membership rosters.

We then drew on these two data sources—resident surveys and party organization data—to compile our list of slum brokers. To reduce frivolously named individuals while casting a broad net, we set a modest bar for inclusion in the final sampling frame. First, we only included individuals named by more than one respondent on the resident surveys. Second, we automatically included any confirmed party worker, each of whose status we verified personally. This procedure balanced high inclusiveness with reducing frivolous names that would bog down enumerators in interviewing individuals who were not actual brokers. The final sampling frame totaled 914 informal brokers.

We conducted our leader survey in the summer of 2016. Enumerators were extensively trained with the instrument and protocol for finding slum brokers. To ensure our sampling and interview protocols were followed, both authors and a team supervisor accompanied the survey teams for most of the survey duration. We attempted to interview all 914 informal brokers, and successfully

11. See Auerbach 2020.

interviewed 629—an impressive response rate of 68.16%. Most non-responses were due to death, sickness, or moving out of the settlement, while only twenty-four were refusals. Our exhaustive listing process, combined with this high response rate, allows us to regard our sample as plausibly representative of slum brokers in Jaipur and Bhopal.

We are confident that this high number of brokers—on average, eight per settlement—is not an artifact of our bar for entry into the sample. All of the individuals populating our sample frame were explicitly described by residents as slum brokers (*basti neta, mukhiya, pradhan, rajnaitik karyakarta*) following a detailed script.[12] Furthermore, survey enumerators would have had a difficult time finding slum brokers if they had not been, in fact, prominent members of the settlement engaged in informal leadership. Instead, the high number of slum brokers we found underscores the highly competitive nature of slum leadership. Importantly, Jaipur and Bhopal are far from idiosyncratic. Scholars have documented competitive, multi-focal slum leadership in other Indian cities, as well as in slums across a number of other countries.[13]

Who Are India's Slum Brokers?

Our survey reveals several striking facts about slum brokers in our study cities. First, slum brokers are ordinary residents of humble means who assume positions of leadership by virtue of their own efforts. Nearly three in four brokers were first-generation residents of the settlement. Over four in five were the first in their families to be active in politics. Unlike higher-level politicians, who often rely on dynastic ties, slum brokers are self-made political entrepreneurs.

Second, India's slum brokers represent a remarkable diversity of castes and religions. 160 distinct *jati* populate our broker sample, representing all strata of the Hindu caste hierarchy and a number of Scheduled Tribes and Muslim

12. The full question on the survey asked residents, "In some slums, there are people that do leadership activities (*netagiri*). I'm not talking about the ward councilor or MLA. I'm talking about community brokers that live inside the slum. These brokers go by several names, like slum leader, slum president, slum headman, or a party worker in the slum. They are prominent people in the community. Are there brokers like this in your settlement?"

13. On India, see Wiebe 1975; de Wit 1997; Hansen 2001; Jha et al. 2007; Das and Walton 2015. Competitive leadership in poor urban communities has also been documented in Venezuela (Ray 1969), Ecuador (Burgwal 1996), Mexico (Cornelius 1975), Brazil (Gay 1994; Koster and de Vries 2012), Peru (Stokes 1995; Dosh 2010) and Argentina (Auyero 2001).

zat. Just over seventy percent (70.75%) of our broker sample was Hindu, while the remainder was mostly Muslim (26.87%). Most brokers were originally from Rajasthan (58.19%) and Madhya Pradesh (26.71%), the states in which our study cities are located. Others migrated from various parts of the country, including the eastern states of Bihar and Chhattisgarh; the northern states of Delhi, Haryana, and Uttar Pradesh; the western states of Gujarat and Maharashtra; and the southern state of Tamil Nadu.

Third, the vast majority (86.49%) of slum brokers in our sample have a connection to a political party. Of these 544 sampled brokers with a party affiliation, 215 (34.18%) expressed support for the INC and 321 (51.03%) for the BJP. Of our full sample of brokers, 415 (65.98%) were party *padadhikari*, or formal position holders.

Importantly, we find brokers of all castes and faiths within *both* parties. For example, while the majority of our 169 Muslim brokers were tied to the Congress, forty-six (27%) were affiliated with the Hindu nationalist BJP. This is especially striking given that many Muslims are alienated by the BJP's rhetoric, and victimized by violence wrought by its grassroots affiliates within the Hindu nationalist movement. Furthermore, there is considerable underrepresentation of Muslims within current or recent BJP-led state governments, including in Rajasthan and Madhya Pradesh, the states in which our study centered.[14] Even more striking, as we report in Chapter 4, Muslim slum brokers do not appear to be discriminated against in promotion patterns within internal local party organizations.[15] At the highly localized level of slums, and even at the level of urban municipal wards, the BJP appears willing to include Muslims within its ranks, and Muslim brokers appear willing to join the BJP.[16]

14. For example, in the most recent state elections held in Madhya Pradesh and Rajasthan (in 2018), the BJP fielded a total of two Muslim candidates across 430 seats.

15. This pattern does not extend to elected legislators for the party. In the 2014 national elections, only 7 of the BJP's 428 candidates (1.6%) were Muslim, compared to 27 out of 462 (5.6%) for the INC (Jaffrelot 2019b).

16. Our data cannot provide a clear explanation for this phenomenon. We suspect the BJP's inclusiveness is motivated by bottom-up pressures. Despite the biases against Muslim leaders among some slum residents we document in Chapter 2, other residents do support effective Muslim brokers in some settlements. Winning these slums, therefore, requires the BJP to incorporate such brokers. Muslim brokers, for their part, face strategic incentives to join the BJP. The supply of brokers outstrips available party positions, precluding all Muslim brokers from finding a place within the Congress. Second, the BJP has been increasingly successful in Jaipur

In Chapter 6, we discuss the possible implications of rising Hindu majoritarianism across India in recent years for these patterns of representation.

Fourth, we examine the self-reported political activities of our sampled slum brokers. Prior studies have traditionally focused on the election-time activities of such brokers; we certainly see evidence of that. The vast majority of brokers reported mobilizing residents for rallies (84.74%), canvassing door-to-door during elections (94.30%), and bringing residents to the polls (91.18%). A majority also reported distributing campaign gifts to voters (52.15%). Less emphasized in prior works, but as frequently mentioned by brokers, were their efforts to spearhead local claim-making between elections.[17] Over sixty-five percent (66.45%) reported having organized protests for public services, eighty-six percent (86.17%) claimed to have filed a petition, and over ninety-three percent (93.20%) had organized community meetings to discuss local problems. Among their most common activities were helping residents secure ration cards and government IDs (93.80%), making claims for public services (93.32%), and resolving disputes (97.62%).

Fifth, nearly eighty-eight percent (87.76%) of the slum brokers in our sample were men. The fact that twelve percent of our sample were women is not trivial. Female representation in city governments in Jaipur and Bhopal is aided by mandatory quotas for elected representatives, which are unavailable for the informal position of slum leader. The more appropriate comparison may be with women in state and national legislatures, where quotas for women are absent. A recent analysis found that between 1980 and 2014, roughly five percent of candidates to these elite positions were women.[18] In comparison to these figures, the prevalence of female slum brokers in our survey is impressive.

Do Slum Brokers Reflect Resident Preferences?

Do slum residents get the brokers they want? In Chapter 2 we argued that brokers emerge through a process of bottom-up selection by clients. This implies that there should be some correspondence between the traits that most influenced resident preferences when selecting brokers with the traits of actual

---

and Bhopal, and in recent years dominated the Congress in local elections. This success further compels slum brokers to consider seeking a position within the party.

17. Exceptions include Krishna 2002; Kruks-Wisner 2018; Auerbach 2020.

18. Vaishnav and Hintson 2019.

slum brokers who have emerged through such selection processes. We assessed such correspondence along three fronts: educational attainment, occupational differences, and the role of ethnicity in linking residents to slum brokers.

These tests address a first-order concern: what if the factors shaping resident preferences have *no* correspondence with actual slum leader characteristics? This possibility is anticipated by top-down theories of machine politics, which assume the desires of residents have little impact in determining local authority. Party elites, rather than poor slum residents, determine who will become a leader in these theories. This possibility is also anticipated by critics who claim results in hypothetical choice experiments such as ours reflect the types of brokers residents idealize, but not whom they realistically expect to get. Against these expectations, we demonstrate that the traits that proved significant in shaping resident preferences also distinguish actual brokers from the larger pool of residents from which they emerge. Such alignment improves confidence in our claim that brokers are selected by residents.

Educational Differences

The average slum broker in our sample was educated for just over eight (specifically, 8.37) years. This exceeds the average education of sampled residents by three years (a 60% increase).[19] Ninety percent of sampled slum brokers were literate, compared to just over sixty percent (61.85%) of slum residents.[20] Figure 3.1 illustrates how slum brokers are also significantly less likely to be uneducated than residents, and significantly more likely to have had at least an eighth-grade education. Brokers are also twice as likely to be college-educated.[21]

Occupational Differences

Recall that among surveyed residents discussed in Chapter 2, we noted an advantage for brokers with "high-connectivity" jobs that were more likely to put them in proximity to the circuits of city officialdom than those without such employment.[22] Consistent with this evidence, we find slum brokers to

19. This difference is equal to 60% of a standard deviation in resident education, and statistically significant (Welch two-tailed t-test, p < 0.00).
20. 49.13% and 73.09% of female and male survey respondents were literate, respectively.
21. All of these tests were statistically significant (Welch two-tailed t-test, p < 0.00).
22. See Online Supplement Tables S3.1–S3.4 for the breakdown of how we categorized jobs.

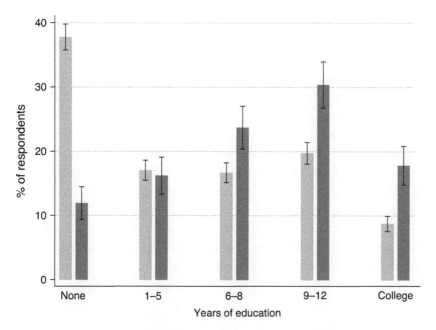

FIGURE 3.1. Comparing Slum Leader and Slum Resident Education
Notes: The figure indicates the percentages of our sample of surveyed slum residents (light gray, N = 2,199) and slum brokers (dark gray, N = 629) who attained a certain level of education. The capped bars indicate 95% confidence intervals.

be roughly four times more likely to have been in such highly connected jobs than ordinary residents (12.72% versus 3.27%). These jobs included government jobs, professional jobs (lawyers, doctors, accountants, and engineers), and educators.[23]

Slum brokers are also more likely than everyday residents to have medium-status small businesses that are typically run outside the slum, such as owners of mechanic or barber shops, and small electronic and auto part stores. Almost fifteen percent (14.47%) of our sampled slum brokers had such businesses, compared to only four percent (4.32%) of residents, a significant difference (p < 0.00). Such small businesses are "medium-connectivity" jobs that provide less exposure to officials than small-time government positions and

23. 6.68% of slum brokers held government jobs, 3.50% held professional jobs and, another 2.07% were educators. In contrast, only 1.77% of ordinary residents held government jobs, 0.50% were professionals, and 1% were educators. These differences are also statistically significant at conventional levels: government jobs (p < 0.00), professional jobs (p < 0.00), and educators (p = 0.08).

professional jobs, but nevertheless afford a greater likelihood of generating ties with city elites than unskilled laborers or jobs contained within the settlement.

Few slum brokers toil in the most precarious and least connected jobs. The most common profession among slum residents is that of unskilled manual laborers. Thirty percent (30.71%) of sampled residents worked in this humble, low-connectivity profession compared to seven percent (7.15%) of slum brokers.[24] Slum brokers are thus more than four times *less* likely to hold jobs as unskilled laborers. We see similar discrepancies among women. The largest occupational category of sampled female residents was homemaker (52%), yet not a single female slum leader fell into this category. Homemakers are particularly deprived of opportunities to foster connections with bureaucrats and local politicians. By contrast, female brokers were more likely to be in government jobs (10.39% to 4.09%) and small businesses (6.49% to 2.23%) than female residents.

Ethnicity

As discussed in Chapter 2, changing a broker's caste from one that differed to one that matched the respondent's caste increases the broker's probability of selection, although we noted this effect was not as dominant among the traits examined as conventional wisdom might have anticipated. Our survey of slum brokers revealed another factor constraining the importance of shared caste: the limited supply of brokers from a resident's caste group. Seventy percent of residents (1,519 respondents) acknowledged leadership in their settlement. Among those who acknowledged slum leadership, only thirty percent had a slum leader from their own *jati* available in their settlement. In other words, most residents cannot support a leader from their caste, even if they want to. This shortage stems from the high diversity of settlements, where most castes comprise a small percentage of the slum's population.[25]

Interestingly, residents are not deterred from seeking help when slum brokers from their caste are not available. Among respondents who acknowledged leadership, sixty percent who had a leader from their own *jati* in the slum reported visiting a slum leader for help. This figure is highly comparable to the

24. This difference is statistically significant (p < 0.00).

25. The average *jati*-based fractionalization index across our sample of slums is 0.81. This figure indicates that if two residents were selected at random from the slum, the chance they would be from different castes is 81%.

fifty-eight percent of residents without a local leader from their own *jati*, who nevertheless reported meeting a leader.[26]

The fact that slum residents overcome the limited supply of brokers from their own *jati* and still seek help at high rates resonates with other findings in Chapter 2. In particular, Chapter 2's Figure 2.5 suggests that a slum leader's capability and connectivity can substitute for a lack of shared ethnicity. The ability of a leader's competence to compensate for a lack of shared ethnicity may help explain why so many residents seek out help from brokers of other castes.

Gender

Our empirical analyses uncover some interesting features of female slum leaders. First, female brokers are widely dispersed across Jaipur and Bhopal, with at least one present in roughly half of our sampled slums. Significantly, women brokers are figures of genuine political authority. Three-quarters of them hold formal positions (*pads*) within a major party. Their success is especially impressive given the specific hurdles they face. For example, while female leaders are on average significantly more educated (6.1 years) than female residents (4 years), they are significantly *less* educated than male leaders (8.7 years).[27] Female leaders are also significantly less likely to have high- or medium-connectivity jobs (16% to 28.26%).

In Chapter 2 we drew on narratives of individual female leaders to show how they appear to circumvent these constraints of education and connectivity by drawing on specific strategies to mobilize support. For example, female leaders especially rely on organizing other female residents to engage in collective protests in order to pressure government officials. Such tactics afford them a way to generate pressure without the advantages conferred by education or occupational connectivity that their male counterparts enjoyed. Our survey corroborated these narratives; just over eighty percent (81%) of female

26. The difference of 2% is not statistically significant at the 90% confidence level. Most settlements have multiple slum brokers, and so this is a conservative test, given that some of the respondents with leaders from their own *jati* may have still approached a leader from a different *jati*, but residents without brokers from their *jati* necessarily had to approach a leader who was not a co-ethnic for help.

27. Women leaders are also less likely than male leaders to be college-educated (15.5% to 27.8%).

leaders reported their use of protest to secure services for residents, compared to sixty-four percent of male leaders.[28]

Finally, our survey uncovers a unique aspect of female leaders regarding their marital status. Specifically, we find widows to be overrepresented among female leaders (21%) relative to female residents (6.6%); widows are also over-represented relative to the proportion of widowers among male leaders (1.8%). It is plausible that widows have both increased imperatives to seek careers (including via brokerage), and also that they experience fewer constraints from male gatekeepers in entering leadership positions. However, we cannot provide systematic evidence explaining this aspect of female leadership, which remains a subject for future research.

Distinguishing Residents from Brokers

Finally, we assess which characteristics systematically distinguish brokers from residents through simple Ordinary Least Squares (OLS) regressions using a pooled sample of residents and brokers. Our dependent variable is an indicator variable identifying brokers (coded 1) from residents (coded 0). We code several explanatory variables to match key attributes manipulated on our experiment as closely as possible. We include variables identifying survey respondents with college education, and an eighth-grade education (defined as between 8–11 years of schooling). We also include variables identifying respondents with high or medium-connectivity jobs.[29] With respect to ethnic variables, we code indicators of upper caste Hindu, disadvantaged caste Hindu, and Muslim status. We also code a variable indicating whether a respondent comes from the largest caste within the settlement. Our intuition here was that if residents mechanically support co-caste brokers, we should see successful brokers disproportionately coming from the settlement's largest caste. Finally, we include some simple demographic controls for respondent gender, age, income, and whether they were born in the city.

Figure 3.2 displays the results of this validation check. Coefficients indicate the impact of a given attribute on distinguishing brokers from residents within

28. This difference was statistically significant at the 95% level.

29. As listed in Table S3.1 in the Online Supplement, high-connectivity jobs are those falling in the categories of government jobs, professional jobs, and educator jobs. Medium-connectivity jobs are those falling into the category of medium status small business jobs.

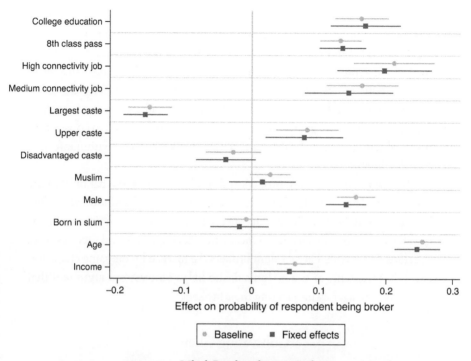

FIGURE 3.2. Which Residents become Brokers?

Notes: The figure reports results from OLS regressions in which the outcome variable identifies slum brokers (1) from slum residents (0). Explanatory variables include key attributes manipulated on our broker selection experiment reported in Chapter 2, and some demographic controls. All explanatory variables displayed in the figure are binary indicators except age and household income, which have been divided by two standard deviations for comparability. See, Gelman 2007. Dots indicate coefficients recovered from the regression analysis, and bars indicate 95% confidence intervals.

the pooled sample.[30] Overall, we find considerable alignment between this observational analysis and our experimental findings. Brokers are positively selected for college education, eighth-grade education, and high and medium-connectivity jobs. They are also positively selected for upper caste status. All of these effects are significant and in the direction of our experimental results. We also find brokers are negatively selected for lower caste status, which also

30. The dark grey squares in Figure 3.2 show the results of a model that includes settlement-level fixed effects. In this specification, coefficients indicate the impact of a given attribute on distinguishing brokers from residents within the same settlement.

mirrors our experimental results.[31] In contrast, we find no observational support for the bias against Muslims revealed in our experiment. Interestingly, we find members of the largest caste within the settlement to be relatively underrepresented within the ranks of established brokers.[32] This result further cautions us against assuming residents mechanically assemble behind their co-ethnics. Such behavior should lead us to expect brokers from the largest caste gaining an initial advantage from which to consolidate their influence, not to be underrepresented in relative terms within informal slum leadership.

Our comparison of slum brokers and residents thus finds that brokers are distinguished by higher levels of education, and a greater likelihood of holding high-connectivity jobs. These traits are precisely those we find slum residents to value as markers of a leader's efficacy in securing goods and services from the state. The fact that actual slum brokers are marked by the same characteristics that residents of those slums desire helps buttress our argument that residents have agency in selecting their brokers.

Cultivating Clients

We now turn to examining the question that began this chapter: which residents do brokers cultivate as supporters? Scholars have often focused on how brokers choose which residents to target with handouts during elections.[33] Studies of top-down "vote-buying" often portray brokers as motivated by spot payments they receive from parties during this transactional window.[34] Consequently, slum brokers are expected to prioritize those residents whose support they can verify most effectively and cheaply. Doing so allows brokers to deliver on their promises to their political superiors, while pocketing a greater share of the resources given to them by parties.

Yet the importance of campaign handouts in cementing the ties between brokers and their clients is overstated. Far more important are the cacophony of daily requests poor voters make on their local brokers to help them with

31. This result is significant at the 90% level.

32. We note our measure of "largest caste" is imperfect (also used in the analysis for Figure 3.6), since we lack official demographic caste data at the settlement level. We code this variable on the basis of our survey sample.

33. Stokes 2005; Schaffer 2007; Nichter 2008.

34. Stokes et al. 2013; Larreguy et al. 2016.

quotidian problems: obtaining a needed document, applying for a benefit, or lobbying for repairs or public service delivery. Such requests have been found to be the predominant form through which residents and brokers interact in many parts of the world.[35] Residents in our study slums value such everyday assistance far more highly than episodic gifts around elections. Slum brokers concurred, and viewed election-day gift-giving as unimportant and ineffective. A majority (55.29%) even said less than ten percent of residents would have their vote affected in any way by such gifts.

Recognizing the importance of everyday problem-solving over campaign handouts reorients our attention to a question that has received no systematic empirical scrutiny: which resident requests for assistance do brokers prioritize?[36] Examining this question provides a richer understanding of the motivation of brokers. We certainly saw evidence of the election-time payments highlighted by vote-buying studies. One prominent slum leader told us that influential brokers in his settlement received roughly Rs. 20,000 ($300) from parties in a recent municipal election—four months of income for many of their neighbors.[37]

Yet we also found that election-time payments were hardly the only motivation for brokers. Instead, many local slum leaders enter brokerage in the hopes of launching a broader political career, one beyond the settlement. These aspirations include acquiring a formal position (*pad*) within parties, obtaining promotions to more senior positions, and even garnering tickets to serve as political candidates in municipal elections. Eighty-eight percent of leaders either already held a party position, or said they wished to hold such a position.

We discuss the dynamics of slum leaders joining parties in more detail in Chapter 4. Our main point here is to note that these careerist ambitions lead brokers to prioritize residents who are best positioned to boost their local reputations as effective problem-solvers, not simply those residents whom brokers can monitor most easily. In our analysis we contrast the expectations of our "reputational model" with prior "monitoring models" regarding the kinds of residents that slum brokers should prioritize. We then test these expectations through an experiment embedded within our slum leader survey.

35. Auyero 2001; Krishna 2002; Szwarcberg 2015.

36. Nichter and Peress 2017 highlight the importance of requests for assistance, but their theoretical focus is on requests for campaign handouts, not every day problem-solving.

37. Author interview with Leader 49, Ganpati, February 2011.

Monitoring Voters

Machine politics across the Global South is widely understood as creating a central concern for parties: how can they ensure that the voters they distribute benefits to return the favor at the polls? This problem compels parties to deploy armies of local brokers to monitor voters during elections. Indeed, this concern is understood to be a primary reason parties employ brokers in the first place. Accordingly, such arguments expect parties to evaluate brokers in terms of their ability to verify whether a resident has actually voted for the party, or at the very least verify if they turned out to vote.[38]

If brokers are primarily interested in effectively monitoring voters, which residents should they prioritize? For our study, the key implication of monitoring models is that they anticipate brokers to prioritize residents whose vote choices they can efficiently observe or verify. After all, monitoring how citizens vote is challenging in contexts like India with its secret ballots and dense and diverse electorates.

Prior studies have suggested one means through which brokers can strengthen their ability to monitor voters are shared social and political networks.[39] For example, brokers in Latin America are found to be tightly linked to voters who are "co-partisans."[40] Consequently, Latin American brokers often prioritize residents who are embedded in these shared party networks. Scholars of politics in South Asia and Africa have found shared ethnic networks can play a similar role.[41] Residents who are of the same ethnic group as a broker will often be embedded within the same dense social networks, facilitating cooperation and trust.[42] As such, brokers may be better able to monitor such "co-ethnics" and hence more likely to prioritize them.

---

38. Nichter 2008; Stokes et al. 2013; Larreguy et al. 2016.

39. Stokes et al. 2013.

40. Calvo and Murillo 2012. This logic aligns with theories arguing risk-averse political actors will favor loyal "core" over persuadable "swing" voters. Cox and McCubbins 1986. While Cox and McCubbins 1986, p. 379, do not explicitly focus on monitoring, they do argue risk-averse political actors target core voters because they are "in frequent and intensive contact with them and [have] relatively precise and accurate ideas about how they will react." Nichter 2008 argues parties focus on buying turnout, which is easier to monitor than vote choice, prompting them to target co-partisan *non*-voters over swing voters.

41. Chandra 2004; Posner 2005.

42. Habyarimana et al. 2007.

A broker's preference for co-ethnic residents might be further conditioned by the size of the ethnic group they share. For example, members of a small, narrowly defined ethnic identity might be especially close-knit (such as *jati* in India), relative to a larger, more diffuse identity (such as religion or region). Monitoring through shared social ties is likely more effective for *jati* than for religion or region.

In sum, scholars have argued that parties seek brokers who can verify voter behavior. Brokers, in turn, are compelled to favor residents whom they can most closely monitor. Such "monitoring models" therefore expect brokers to prioritize requests from residents who are from the same party, relative to requests from independent voters or residents affiliated with a rival party. Brokers are also be expected to prioritize requests from residents from the same ethnic group, especially if that ethnic group is relatively small and tight-knit.

Building a Personal Reputation

A preoccupation with party efforts to buy votes during elections has circumscribed our understanding of the role brokers play. Voter support is seen as a function of whether they receive a handout, not the result of the skill, knowledge, or personal appeal of a local broker. Indeed, in many accounts of vote-buying, brokers are little more than localized spigots through which handouts flow, and local spies monitoring whether voters repay the favor. However, recent work has questioned the degree to which brokers can or will monitor electoral behavior, noting that "systematic evidence of the monitoring of vote choices is surprisingly rare."[43] In India, Schneider found that even within close-knit village communities, brokers were not especially proficient at correctly knowing how residents voted.[44]

Such skepticism compels a more multi-faceted understanding of what brokers do and why they do it. The slum brokers we followed proved far more than spigots and spies for their parties. This broader value is especially apparent if we shift focus from election-time transactions to everyday requests for assistance. Brokers who establish reputations for handling such requests attract large personal followings to deliver to their parties.

43. Hicken and Nathan 2020.
44. Schneider 2019.

Consequently, the daily efforts of brokers are often motivated by the need to craft local *personal* reputations for competence. As one broker described it:

> People come up with various issues like they are not getting water or their pipe lines have been damaged. So, my job is to write letters to the water department and councilor, and also to send a letter to the MLA on the councilor's recommendation. It is summer now and electricity goes away very often. People don't have contacts in the electricity department. People would come running to me to call the electricity department. Even if takes 2 rupees, I am the one who calls. If the electricity comes, people come to recognize me.[45]

Or as other brokers stated:

> I wanted to work for people so that I become popular. People bless you then. I used to live with my brother. I would participate in the public events of the slum. Slowly I started making my name in public. Whenever people came with their problems, I would go along with them to solve their problems without thinking where it will take me to. The work ranged from getting a child admission into a school, work in a police station, and going to the electricity department.[46]

> My reputation grew because of my work. As you know, when we first start out, for doing anything, it's a slow process. So, I used to organize all-night prayer vigils . . . today this entire block gets involved. Then, I used to organize cricket matches, and through them I reached out to the entire slum . . . So because of that people started associating with me, and the public supported me.[47]

Such reputation-seeking is also compelled by the longer, careerist aspirations brokers have for climbing up their party ranks. The slum brokers we interviewed repeatedly noted their reputation with residents as being central to their own upward mobility:

> I was first a party supporter. But when I went to party meetings, and brought 10–20 people with me, party brokers saw that I was helping make the party popular. They were impressed and made me [Ward] Vice President.[48]

45. Interview with Broker 43, Ganpati, Jaipur, June 4, 2016.
46. Interview with Broker 44, Ganpati, Jaipur, June 4, 2016.
47. Interview with Broker 13, Settlement 17, Jaipur June 9, 2016.
48. Interview with Broker 14, Settlement 18, Jaipur, June 16, 2016.

Let us say that I rise with public support—if the party gives me a task and I do it well, I get a higher *pad* [formal position], and this will help me get problems solved faster and this gets me more public support. So, in this way the public support and party *pads* are connected to one another.[49]

I hold a meeting every 15 days or once a month. I listen to their problems and find a solution to those problems. When I organize an event at the community level, I also invite senior leaders. The leaders notice that this person is active and should be a member of BJP. That's why they took me. And when the work is done under my leadership, the credit goes to me. They get to know about it. They get to know [that I am] capable of becoming a leader and work for BJP.[50]

Scholars have increasingly recognized the importance of reputations for careerist brokers both within India and in other settings.[51] However, prior accounts have not theorized or tested how broker responsiveness to residents is shaped by the formers' need to craft such reputations.[52] Below, we argue that brokers prefer those residents best poised to deliver the biggest boost to the brokers' own reputations of competence. We highlight two kinds of client attributes that make certain residents especially attractive to reputation-seeking brokers: attributes that signal a broker's *inclusivity*, and attributes that signal that a resident is *socially central* within the slum.

49. Interview with Rajesh, BJP party worker, Tulsi Nagar Bhopal, January 17, 2017.
50. Interview with Broker 16, Settlement 19, Bhopal, July 3, 2016.
51. Manor 2000; Krishna 2002; Szwarcberg 2015; Nichter 2019.
52. In their seminal study, Stokes et al. 2013 note that clients prefer brokers with reputations for competence, but do not theorize or test how such reputations are forged. Camp 2015 acknowledges variable broker reputations in Argentina, but focuses on how the strength of broker reputations impact upward intra-party bargaining with party superiors. He does not examine how reputation-seeking shapes downward broker responsiveness towards residents. Szwarcberg's study of Argentina 2015, pp. 60–1, notes that brokers must structure their responsiveness toward potential clients in ways that maximize reputational returns. Yet her account does not theorize or test how such maximization is achieved, especially with reference to client characteristics. Nichter and Peress 2017 examine reputational considerations for elected *politicians* rather than brokers. Principally they find that politicians will favor small requests by co-partisan supporters. Nichter 2019 argues reputation-seeking compels politicians to work to fulfill requests, and that citizens screen against politicians with poor reputations of responsiveness.

Building an Inclusive Reputation

How many residents do brokers want to win the support of? Some observers might expect that brokers seek narrow pluralities within the slum. In other words, brokers want a vote bank that just exceeds the support base of any other slum leader. In essence brokers should seek to assemble a "minimum winning coalition," much as politicians have been argued to do.[53] Such a strategy ensures victory, but also minimizes the number of followers with whom a victor must share the spoils.

The slum brokers we spoke to did not target such a narrow plurality. Rather, they hope to assemble the largest possible support base within their settlements. There are two reasons for this. First, slums are not electoral constituencies. As such, parties want to carry as many votes as possible from the slum, not simply a narrow plurality within them. Indeed, the average population of one of our sampled slums is 2,400 people, which is roughly ten percent of the population of an average municipal ward in Bhopal and Jaipur—the smallest electoral constituency in Indian cities.[54] Consequently, parties search for brokers with the largest possible base. Secondly, brokers themselves have ambitions that grow beyond their settlements. As we detail in Chapter 4, brokers must compete not only with other leaders in their settlement, but with leaders of other settlements for positions and promotions within party organizations. Consequently, slum brokers seek to assemble the heftiest vote-bank possible within their settlements, from which to launch their careers outside them.

These proclivities compel brokers to look for residents whose support helps them project an inclusive image, rather than a parochial reputation of serving narrow subgroups of voters. We focus on two resident characteristics that facilitate such inclusive reputations. The first is a resident's ethnic identity: their caste, religious, and regional affiliation. Slum brokers may wish to avoid a reputation for exclusively serving their own ethnic group because doing so will limit their ability to assemble broad followings. A Brahmin slum leader, for instance, told us that he would never favor Brahmins over lower castes because he could not afford a reputation as a "Brahmin leader."[55]

---

53. Posner 2005.

54. The average population of a municipal ward in Jaipur and Bhopal, as per the Census of India 2011, is 39,557 and 25,689, respectively.

55. Author field notes May 31, 2016.

Other brokers echoed similar sentiments, emphasizing the importance of appealing to residents of all castes and faiths:

BROKER: I go with residents to hospital, and have shared their pain in times of trouble. If they had a case registered against them in relation to their house, I would go with them to the police station. In such situations, if you support people, you are like their brother. It doesn't matter to me if the person belongs to another caste . . . I help in whatever way I can . . . and that's why they started recognizing me as a leader.

INTERVIEWER: There must be other people working in the slum? Why did people come to you?

BROKER: They used to come to me because I always stood behind them. No matter whether the person is a Hindu or Muslim.[56]

The adverse consequences of ethnic favoritism are amplified by the highly diverse nature of slum populations, especially with respect to caste. Figure 3.3 presents a simple descriptive violin plot of the distribution of ethnic fractionalization (a measure of diversity) across our 110 settlements. It shows extremely high levels of caste-based diversity, alongside nontrivial rates of regional and religious diversity in our sampled slums. Such diversity reduces the strategic value of shared caste as the basis for coalition-building, since a broker will have relatively few residents from their own caste in the settlement.

The reputational penalty for favoring members of one's own ethnic group might be especially harsh for smaller ethnic categories. For example, a reputation for favoring co-ethnics along the narrow dimension of *jati* is more constraining than a reputation for favoring co-ethnics along the broader dimensions of religion and region-of-origin, simply because a slum leader has far fewer residents from their own *jati* than their faith or region in the settlement.

With respect to the ethnicity of residents, the compulsions of reputation-seeking are in stark tension with those of monitoring. Recall monitoring concerns are anticipated to lead brokers to exhibit ethnic favoritism. Such favoritism should be most pronounced for residents who share a narrow ethnic identity such as *jati*, and least for residents who share a broader identity such as region or religion. In contrast, reputational concerns should lead brokers to exhibit ethnic indifference (defined as a lack of pronounced favoritism towards co-ethnics) when considering resident requests. Furthermore, brokers should

56. Interview with Broker 17, Settlement 20, Jaipur, June 16, 2016.

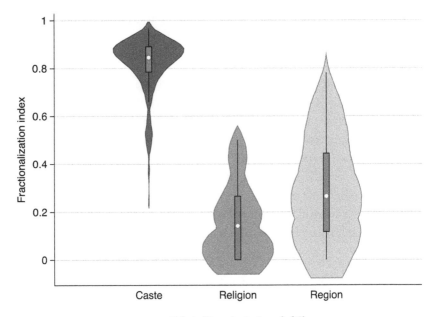

FIGURE 3.3. Ethnic Diversity in Sampled Slums
Notes: Each figure represents violin plots in which the white dot represents the median value in the sample; the thick gray bar represents the interquartile range; and the thin bar represents 1.5 times the interquartile range. On each side of the line is a kernel density estimation to show the distribution of the data, with wider sections representing a higher probability that members of the population will take on a given value.

most want to project such indifference for narrow *jati* identities, in order to avoid constraining the size of their potential base of support.

A second type of resident that reputation-seeking brokers might covet are those who are relatively disadvantaged within the settlement. It has long been argued that political machines across the world target the "poor," whose support is relatively cheap.[57] Yet in the slums we studied, practically all residents are poor relative to national averages.[58] Accordingly, existing theories would predict machines will be responsive to every slum resident, and cannot explain who brokers will target *within* slums.

57. See Calvo and Murillo 2004; Kitschelt and Wilkinson 2007; Stokes et al. 2013; Murillo et al. 2021.

58. The average per capita income in our settlements was only $1.09 per day, and 87% of households earned less than $2 per capita, less than half the national average. The unadjusted per capita income in India for the year of our resident survey (2015) was $4.40 per day. World Bank 2015.

Yet even within a broadly impoverished setting, some residents are worse off than others. In Jaipur and Bhopal, most slum residents engage in low-income work, but a large number toil in jobs that are also plagued by informality, irregular pay, and social stigma. We find brokers prioritizing residents from these relatively underprivileged categories because doing so helped burnish their local reputations. Prioritizing the occupational "elite" in slums is more easily perceived as exclusionary by larger, relatively disadvantaged professions than vice versa. One leader explained:

> I will help the *mazdoor* [laborer] before the *karamchari* [clerk]. If I am known to help the *mazdoor*, everyone will come to me. If I am known to help the *karamchari*, *mazdoors* may not see me as their man, or worse still may see me as in the pockets of the *karamcharis*.[59]

Furthermore, even if more privileged residents resented the targeting of disadvantaged residents, the former outnumbered the latter. Finally, brokers could use their assistance of especially marginalized residents to project an image as selfless social workers, rather than cunning and self-serving operatives. As one broker explained:

> I kept helping people; for example, I helped them get BPL [Below Poverty Line] cards, ration cards and identity cards. Or if someone had a water supply problem or sewer problem or electricity problem, I would help resolve those. How could a daily-wage laborer be expected to run around offices for solving these problems? They would then say that I help them.[60]

Broadcasting A Reputation

Reputational concerns drive brokers to prioritize a second type of resident: those who are socially central within their communities.[61] Such residents are more likely to spread positive information stemming from a broker's assistance than residents who are socially peripheral.[62] Brokers are very aware of how

---

59. Author field notes June 2, 2016.

60. Interview with Broker 45, Ganpati, Jaipur, June 4, 2016.

61. Our argument here differs from studies that note brokers themselves are likely to be central figures in social and political networks. Ravanilla et al. 2020.

62. Schaeffer and Baker 2015.

such beneficial gossip can ensure a widespread reputation for problem-solving within the slum.[63] As several different brokers explained:

> If you work for one person, they will tell four other people about it. They will spread the news that this leader helped me in this work. And gradually everyone in the slum will come to know about it that this person helps in both good and bad times. So, you don't need anyone to campaign for you. If you do good work people join you. People are always ready to help if you are a helpful person.[64]

> If you help one person, he will certainly tell 10 others about it. He will say "so-and-so is very helpful" . . . your reputation will automatically take care of itself.[65]

Recall that unlike higher-level politicians, brokers lack financial resources and dynastic ties. They are typically first-generation residents of their settlement and of humble means, and without any family in politics. These constraints make free public relations from clients especially crucial for ensuring a widespread personal reputation.

Measuring Broker Responsiveness

To better understand how different resident traits affect broker evaluations of potential clients, we conducted an experiment with the slum brokers we surveyed. To our knowledge, this is the first such effort to experimentally assess broker responsiveness to everyday client requests. This experiment was designed to mirror the one presented in Chapter 2, in which we presented

---

63. Nichter 2019 distinguishes between a politician's specific reputation with an individual voter, and a broader "collective element" of their reputation, spread through networks of families and friends. Schaeffer and Baker 2015 focus on the targeting of campaign handouts, rather than request fulfilment. In their model, election handouts function as spot payments for residents to engage in electoral persuasion, essentially acting as temporary brokers. Full-time brokers play little role in this process beyond identifying those influential residents. Our model places greater emphasis on the independent incentives of careerist brokers, and the iterative relationship between brokers and clients. In doing so, our argument demands far less of socially central citizens than Schaeffer and Baker's model. In our model, rather than win votes for the party, targeted residents are merely expected to spread word of a broker's assistance, widening the net of people who approach the latter for help.

64. Interview with Broker 19, Settlement 21, Jaipur, June 4, 2016.

65. Interview with Broker 12, Settlement 16, Jaipur, June 4, 2016.

residents with two hypothetical slum brokers and asked which one they preferred. Here, we presented brokers with a scenario in which another slum leader, in a settlement like theirs, was approached by two residents asking for help accessing a public service for residents in their alley.

Our experimental question read as follows:

> Slums suffer from low development and slum residents often do not have basic necessities. Brokers like you help secure important goods and services for residents. But you have limited time, and government funds allocated for slums are also limited. Fulfilling each resident's demand is difficult, and brokers like you must make difficult decisions each day over which residents you will help. I was recently in another slum like this in [City: Jaipur/ Bhopal], talking to a leader like you. They were facing the following problem: two residents from different parts of the slum had come to them asking for help with [PROBLEM]. But government funds are limited and so the leader could only help one of them at this time. I will give you some information about these two residents, and then I would like to know your opinion about who you think the leader should help.

It is important to note that our interest is in how the attributes of *residents*, not the nature of their *requests*, shape broker responsiveness. To ensure slum leader evaluations were not impacted by differences in perceived effort or cost between the requests made by residents, our experiment ensured both clients make identical demands. This premise was believable, as slum brokers frequently receive identical requests for basic necessities. To guard against our results being specific to any one particular demand, we randomized the goods being requested across pairs of respondents. We also ensured that requests, while identical, were understood as separate and mutually excludable. To do so, each request was for the resident's specific alley within the slum, and our preamble specified each resident came from a different part of the settlement.[66]

After reading this preamble, we placed two pictures in front of the leader, meant to represent the two residents requesting assistance. Pointing to each

66. The six goods were: building a gutter, installing a streetlight, paving an alley, installing a community water tap, extending a sewer line, and cleaning a gutter. All were specified to be for the requesting resident's alley. We prefer "alley-level" goods because slum-level public goods benefit all residents and violate the premise of choosing between clients. Household-level private goods (e.g., voter IDs) can be sufficiently low cost for brokers to fulfill both requests simultaneously. Our results are robust to dropping all requests for a particular good from the sample (for each of the six goods).

in turn, we then provided information about five traits of each candidate: their caste, region-of-origin, party affiliation, occupation, and how long they had lived in the settlement. Finally, we asked brokers:

> *In your opinion, which of these two residents would you choose to help first?*
> - First resident
> - Second resident
> - Don't know[67]

The treatments for the first three traits (caste, region, and party) replicate those used in our experiment in Chapter 2. These traits are especially relevant as indicators of how effectively a broker might be able to verify a resident's voting behavior.

The remaining traits should affect brokers focused on how to craft widespread reputations of competence. First, we varied each resident's occupation. One-third of residents were randomly assigned to hold jobs indicating relative privilege. For this category, we selected low-level jobs within the municipality: municipal sweeper, security guard, and clerk. These occupations have modest earnings as we intended them to be realistic for slum residents to hold. Yet the stability of government work is still coveted, compared to private contract work or self-employment.

A third of residents were assigned to hold jobs indicating relative disadvantage: unskilled house painters, street vendors, and autorickshaw drivers. Each of these jobs was beset by some combination of erratic earnings, short-term contracts, and risks of injury. Forty-three percent of surveyed residents held such "disadvantaged" jobs—the largest employment category in our sample.[68] We can thus examine whether slum brokers prioritize relatively disadvantaged residents by comparing how their evaluations change when shifting a resident's occupation from a high-status municipal job to these low-status jobs.

A final third of residents were assigned to jobs that place a resident centrally within the slum's social environment. Specifically, we assigned these residents jobs as shopkeepers running stores within the slum itself. We found shopkeepers to be an important and constant presence within the slum, not only because they worked within the settlement, but also because their stores were popular spaces for residents to socialize. In our field visits, we would often find

---

67. Enumerators were instructed not to read out this answer to minimize the number of responses of "don't know."

68. This figure includes all laborers and painters, drivers, and street vendors.

residents clustering and chatting at these shops, and indeed we often had our own conversations at these venues. During our broker survey, ever-present shopkeepers were often our most reliable sources for finding out where brokers resided in the settlement. Our experiences were confirmed by data from our 2015 survey of residents, in which we found shopkeepers were more likely than other residents to say they socialized with other residents.[69]

We included three types of shopkeepers: corner shop (*kirana*) owner, tea stall owner, and cigarette-*paan* stand owner. This enables us to examine whether shifting a resident's occupation from municipal employees to socially central shopkeepers increases their probability of being preferred by the broker. We chose municipal jobholders as the baseline category for this comparison because, like shopkeepers, they are considered privileged occupations relative to our "disadvantaged" category.[70] However, unlike shopkeepers, municipal jobholders have occupations that take them outside the settlement. From a broker's perspective, we argue that the main difference between these two relatively secure job types is their degree of social centrality, and attendant consequences for reputation building.[71]

Note that the occupational connectivity we emphasize differs here from in our previous experiment regarding how residents select brokers. Residents seeking effective brokers value vertical connectivity to municipal authorities. Brokers seeking reputations within the slum value clients with horizontal connectivity to other slum residents.

Finally, we varied the length of time each resident was said to have spent in the slum. Our intuition here was that slum brokers would regard residents who

69. Storekeepers were 9.4 percentage points more likely than other residents to say they socialized with neighbors in their settlement (74.7% to 65.3%, p < 0.08, two-tailed).

70. This is not to say both categories are identical. Municipal jobholders enjoy a degree of wage security not enjoyed by most shopkeepers. Still, small storeowners are considerably more secure in their day-to-day earnings in comparison with their neighbors who are unskilled laborers and painters, street vendors, and auto rickshaw drivers.

71. We preferred this subtle treatment to more overt alternatives. We were especially reluctant to specify a level of social centrality (Resident A has as many/some/no friends in the settlement). Such evaluative statements provide an ordering of clients and carry strong normative connotations that one trait (and resident) is more desirable than another, exacerbating social desirability concerns. Such treatments are also abstract, raising the construct validity concerns we seek to avoid. Brokers cannot directly observe a resident's social connections, and must infer this quality from more easily observable traits. We therefore prefer a non-evaluative and directly observable measure of centrality, such as occupation.

had spent many years within the settlement as more likely than new arrivals to wield social influence and have connections to other residents. We find support for this in our survey of slum residents. Residents who had lived in the slum for over ten years were eight percentage points more likely to socialize with their neighbors than residents who arrived less than three years before the time of the survey.[72] Veteran residents thus will be more attractive as potential clients to reputation-seeking brokers. Our baseline category is a resident who had only been in the settlement for a few months. The other half of residents were said to have lived in the settlement for ten years.[73]

Our expectation here contrasts with certain theories of machine politics, which expects these formations to favor "disoriented new arrivals."[74] These arguments anticipate that new arrivals will be especially economically and socially vulnerable, and therefore particularly attracted to the inducements offered by machines as well as easier for machines to exert political control over.

How Do Brokers Evaluate Resident Requests?

In the experiment we conducted, each of our 629 slum brokers evaluated three pairs of residents.[75] Note that our unit of analysis is the evaluated resident profile. Since each of our 629 slum brokers evaluated three pairs of residents (six profiles), this yielded a total of 3,538 rated profiles.[76]

72. This difference, 68% to 60%, is also statistically significant (p < 0.01, two-tailed).

73. The average sampled resident had lived in their settlement for 22 years. Yet we found rates of socializing to be similar for residents with tenures between 10 and 22 years (67%) and those with tenures longer than 22 years (68.4%). Thus, for an indicator of social centrality, we preferred the lower value as a conservative treatment. At the other end, two–three months unambiguously signals a newcomer.

74. Scott 1972, pp. 104–18; Colburn and Pozzetta 1976.

75. To account for the non-independence of ratings from the same respondent, we cluster standard errors by slum leader, as suggested by Hainmueller et al. 2014. Recent work has suggested clustering may not be necessary or advisable for certain experimental designs (Abadie et al. 2017), including conjoint experiments (Schuessler and Freitag 2020). We also estimate each of our main models without clustered errors, and find our results to be substantively unchanged in those specifications.

76. Recall our protocol required attempting to contact every eligible slum leader in our sampling frame. Accordingly, our sampled respondents represent an upper bound for the number of subjects who could have been interviewed for this study. Using the cjpowR package developed by Schuessler and Freitag 2020, we calculate that our sample size is powered to obtain a minimum detectable effect of 4.7 pp for the five 2-level attributes, and 5.75 pp for the single

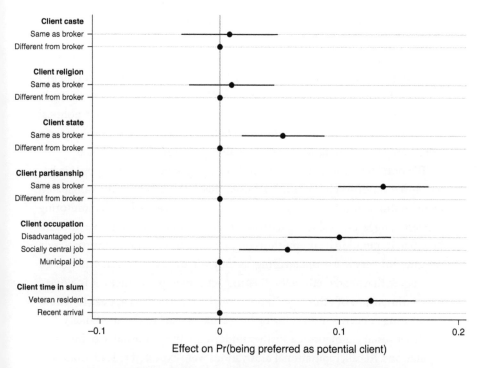

FIGURE 3.4. How Do Resident Traits Impact Broker Responsiveness?
Notes: This plot shows estimates for the effects of the randomly assigned slum resident attribute values on the probability of having a request prioritized by a slum leader. Estimates are
based on an OLS model with standard errors clustered by respondent; bars represent 95%
confidence intervals. The points without horizontal bars denote the reference category for
each attribute.

Once again, we estimate Average Marginal Component Effects (AMCEs,
see Chapter 2). Recall AMCEs indicate how much the probability of a given
resident profile being selected over another randomly selected profile
changes when we shift an attribute from its baseline to a given value. The main
results are presented in Figure 3.4.[77] The dots with bars in the figure indicate

---

3-level attribute of occupation status (with 80% power and 95% significance). These MDEs are
comparable to the average AMCEs across all conjoint experiments in this book (5.6 pp).

77. These results were estimated using an Ordinary Least Squares model in which the binary
(0–1) outcome variable indicated selected profiles within a pair. The independent variables are
all binary variables measuring whether a resident had a given attribute (1) or not (0).

the AMCEs.[78] The dots without bars indicate the baseline category used for these comparisons.

The first finding to note is the lack of impact on the probability of a resident's request being selected in shifting their caste (0.8 pp) or faith (0.9 pp) from one that differs to one which matches that of the broker. These are striking results, as shared *jati* and religion are seen as central in structuring political life in India.[79] This ethnic indifference better aligns with a view of brokers prioritizing their reputations over their ability to monitor vote choice.

The only dimension of shared ethnicity along which we see a positive impact is region-of-origin (5 pp).[80] Yet even this favoritism is better anticipated by reputational motivations than by monitoring concerns. Recall monitoring concerns suggest that sharing narrow ethnic identities should prove most influential. Reputational compulsions predict narrower ethnicities are precisely the ones brokers will avoid favoring, as they will be the most constricting. To the degree that shared ethnicity does impact broker preferences, it is along a broad dimension of ethnicity. Reputational concerns thus appear to trump monitoring concerns in structuring how brokers react to client ethnicity.

Other results in Figure 3.4 further underscore the importance of inclusive reputations. Recall, reputational motivations were expected to lead brokers to prioritize residents in relatively low-status jobs, compared to more privileged municipal employees. Both types of jobs take place outside the slum, and hence are equally socially peripheral. Yet being known to serve disadvantaged residents is helpful in projecting reputations for inclusivity, and expedient given such residents constitute a larger share of the slum's votes. We find that shifting a resident's profession from a privileged municipal job to a relatively disadvantaged job results in a ten percentage point average increase in their probability of selection.[81]

We expect reputational concerns to attract slum brokers to more socially central residents. In line with this expectation, we find shifting a resident from

---

78. We conducted a number of robustness checks to test for potential design effects reported in Auerbach and Thachil 2020. First, we conduct a randomization balance check by regressing important respondent attributes on indicator variables for all client profile attributes. Next, we examine experiment order effects, carryover effects, profile order effects, and even attribute order effects. We find little evidence of systematic design effects.

79. Srinivas and Shah 2007; Chandra 2004.

80. This result was significant at the 99% confidence level.

81. This result was significant at the 99% confidence level.

being a new arrival to a veteran of the settlement—the latter having had more time to develop local friendships and acquaintances—yielded a thirteen percentage point increase in their probability of selection.[82] Recall our resident survey found longer tenured residents were more likely to socialize with their neighbors. Reflecting a similar difference in local social rootedness, those residents who had lived in the slum for more than ten years averaged 1.17 fewer visits a year to their home village than those residents who had lived in the slum for less than three years (3.42 visits per year to 2.25).[83]

Figure 3.4 also illustrates how changing a resident's occupation from an out-of-settlement municipal job to a local shopkeeper yields a six percentage point increase in their probability of selection.[84] Recall slum shopkeepers were chosen as jobs with comparable economic security to municipal jobholders, yet more firmly embedded within slum social life. This result is also striking when comparing slum leader preferences for clients with slum resident preferences for brokers (examined in Chapter 2). Recall that when clients evaluated brokers, a shift from a slum storekeeper to a municipal job conferred an advantage, while here the results are reversed. This divergence is consistent with our expectations regarding the kinds of connectivity that brokers value in clients, and clients value in brokers. In the former case, reputation-seeking brokers value clients with horizontal connectivity inside the slum. In the latter case, residents value brokers with vertical connectivity to municipal authorities outside the settlement.

Overall, Figure 3.4 strongly supports a view that brokers are most affected by client traits that signal the latter's potential to boost the former's local reputations.[85] The importance of reputational concerns, however, does not preclude the importance of all monitoring-related attributes. For example,

82. This result was significant at the 99% confidence level.
83. Both of these differences were significant at the 99% confidence level.
84. This result was significant at the 99% confidence level.
85. All significant AMCEs (for region, co-partisanship, disadvantaged jobs, and time in the settlement) are larger or almost equal to the relevant MDE. The only exception is the coefficient for "Socially Central Job" which is powered at just under the conventional 80% threshold (79%). As per the *cjpower* package, the chance of a wrongly signed coefficient (Type S error) is negligible (0.0001%), and the exaggeration ratio (Type M error) is a modest 1.13. Gelman and Carlin 2014. Our two non-significant AMCEs for shared caste and faith were extremely small (< 1 pp). Obtaining an MDE lower than this threshold would have required an infeasibly large number of rated profiles (> 122,000) to obtain from our sample (see footnote 76).

changing a resident's partisan status to match the broker's results in a fourteen percentage point increase in the resident's probability of selection.[86]

The stronger impact of shared partisanship over shared ethnicity goes against India's conventional portrayal as a democracy with weak parties and strong ethnic attachments. Our theory and empirical analysis cannot provide conclusive explanations for this preference. However, our findings do align with recent studies that emphasize political actors must knit together partisan coalitions of diverse ethnicities, even at the local level.[87] Furthermore, unlike ethnicity, partisanship is not a sticky identity in our study setting. Excluding a resident along partisan lines does not forever foreclose the possibility of a future relationship, especially given that many residents (34%) reported voting for different parties across recent elections.[88]

Readers may be interested in seeing our results disaggregated for different types of brokers. In the online supplement, we present conditional marginal means and AMCEs partitioned by respondent gender, partisan support, leadership experience, and education, as well as by settlement population, ethnic diversity, and age.[89] As with residents, we did not find substantial evidence of variation in preferences across the majority of these different factors.[90]

---

86. This result was significant at the 99% confidence level. This result aligns with theories of core-voter (Cox and McCubbins 1986; Nichter 2008) rather than swing-voter targeting (Stokes 2005). The baseline category for this comparison includes all combinations that are not a co-partisan match, including unaffiliated brokers and residents.

87. Dunning and Nilekani 2013.

88. Conjoint analysis does not require all attribute combinations to be equally likely. Hainmueller et al. 2014. Yet we might worry if certain combinations are so unrealistic that they threaten ecological validity. Perhaps Muslim clients never support the BJP, or higher caste residents never work in disadvantaged jobs. We drew on our resident survey to ensure this was not the case when designing our experiment. For example, 21% of Muslim respondents identified as BJP supporters. We also found all caste groups to be represented within each major occupation group (for example, 19% of elite Brahmins were manual laborers). Our results are also robust to dropping seemingly "unlikely" attribute combinations such as Muslim residents who support the BJP.

89. The choice of reference category can complicate the use of AMCEs for comparing preferences across different subsets of voters. Leeper et al. 2020. We show conditional marginal means, which allow us to assess differences in preferences in a manner robust to reference category choice. We also do provide conditional AMCEs, which show the causal impact of slum leader features relative to the baseline for each subgroup.

90. Drawing on Leeper et al. 2020, we formally tested for group differences in preferences through an omnibus F-test comparing a regression with interaction terms between the sub-grouping variable and all feature levels with an equation without the interactions. In all seven

However, we provide these results for descriptive interest, and cannot interpret them as strong evidence of stable preferences, given our limited statistical power to discern differences across subgroups.[91]

In the remainder of Chapter 3, we address three important questions that our results prompt. First, how do we know that our findings in Figure 3.4 reflect a slum leader's specific *political* evaluations of potential clients to cultivate? Perhaps, instead the findings reflect a leader's *social* evaluations of other residents in their settlement. Second, do we have any evidence that the traits that most influenced slum brokers in our experiment reflect the actual slum residents who reported getting assistance? If not, we might worry that slum brokers are merely telling us what they think we want to hear. Finally, even if we feel confident broker responsiveness is shaped by particular resident traits, are we confident they do so for the reasons we argue? For example, do brokers target disadvantaged and socially central residents because doing so is helpful for their reputations? Or are there other possible motivations?

Are Brokers Being Honest?

An important concern for any survey-based study such as ours is that respondents may give us the answers they think we want to hear, otherwise known as social desirability bias. Perhaps the lack of ethnic favoritism we observe, or the favoring of veteran residents, reflect that such answers are more acceptable, and portray leaders in the best light. Next, we discuss three checks for such social desirability bias.

Do Good Clients Make Good Neighbors?

First, our survey included a second experiment. We asked respondents to evaluate two people looking to move into the slum with their families. Brokers were asked to indicate which person they would prefer to have as a *neighbor*. The characteristics of each resident manipulated in this experiment replicated those on our original experiment, with one exception. Since our neighbor

---

cases, this F-test failed to reject the null hypothesis of no overall differences across subgroups at the 95% level, although we note again this analysis is hampered by limited statistical power.

91. Schuessler and Freitag 2020.

experiment focused on a family looking to move into the settlement, we could not vary time in the settlement.[92]

This experiment helps address two concerns. First, it helps check our assumption that slum brokers viewed the residents we presented them on the original experiment through a distinctly political lens. In other words, it allows us to better differentiate how resident traits shape a leader's *political* evaluations of potential clients, from their *social* evaluations of potential neighbors. If the two are largely indistinguishable, we might worry that our original experiment is not capturing what we intended. And if the impact of resident traits on preferences for neighbors and clients are distinct, we can be more confident that our original experiment worked as intended.

Second, observed differences across our neighbor and client experiments would also help assuage concerns of desirability bias in the latter. For example, if we find a clear positive impact of shared ethnicity in evaluating neighbors, we might be less worried that the lack of a corresponding impact on our client experiment is simply driven by brokers being unwilling to express parochial preferences to survey enumerators.

Figure 3.5 demonstrates clear differences in attribute AMCEs across our two experiments. First, switching a resident's ethnicity (both *jati* and faith) from one that is different from the broker to one that is the same increased the resident's average probability of being preferred as a neighbor by six-to-ten percentage points. By contrast, we found no equivalent impact when evaluating potential clients (Figure 3.4).[93]

The results for partisanship are also sharply distinct, but in the opposite direction. Changing a resident's partisan affiliation to match a broker's increased the resident's probability of being selected as a *client* by nearly fourteen percentage points. The corresponding impact when the brokers evaluated potential *neighbors*, however, while significant, is less than half that size (just over six percentage points).[94] Similarly, the result of changing a resident's occupation

92. To equalize the number of attributes across neighbor and client experiments, we randomized the potential neighbor's education (no schooling, an eighth-grade education, or a college B.A.).

93. The average marginal component effect (AMCE) for co-*jati* neighbors was 9.66 pp, while for clients it was only 0.8 pp (a difference significant at the 92% confidence level). Similarly, AMCEs for shared religion and shared state are stronger for neighbors than clients, and these are respectively significant at the 99% and 95% confidence levels.

94. The difference between effects was significant at the 99% confidence level.

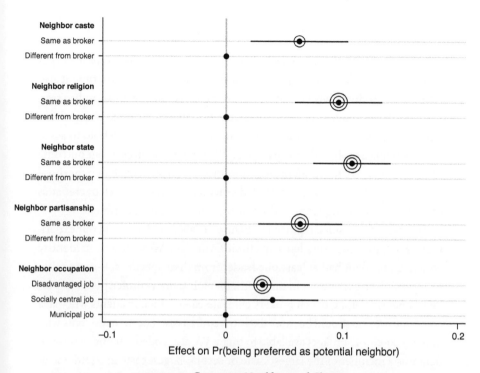

FIGURE 3.5. Comparing Neighbors and Clients

Notes: The figure shows estimates for the effects of the randomly assigned attribute values on the probability of a resident being preferred by a broker as a neighbor. Estimates based on OLS models with standard errors clustered by respondent; bars represent 95% confidence intervals. The points without horizontal bars denote the reference category for each attribute. Rings indicate significant differences between the AMCEs in the client (Figure 3.3) and neighbor models (1 ring = $p < 0.1$; 2 rings = $p < 0.05$).

from the baseline municipal job to disadvantaged occupations in the neighbor experiment is significantly smaller than the corresponding impact on our client experiment. This difference aligns with our theoretical expectation of a specifically political value to cultivating disadvantaged clients, which does not extend to evaluations of neighbors.

Overall, Figure 3.5 confirms that the characteristics of residents have distinct impacts on broker preferences for clients and for neighbors, which improves our confidence that our initial experiment was inducing brokers to make specifically political evaluations.

Who Actually Receives Help?

Another way we assess social desirability concerns is to see whether the types of resident traits that most impacted broker evaluations in our experiment also reflect the residents who reported receiving assistance from slum brokers. Here, we draw on our 2015 survey of slum residents, which asked respondents whether a slum leader had met with someone from their household to assist with resolving a problem in the past year.[95] This response gives us our outcome of interest, coded 1 for residents who reported receiving help, and 0 for those who did not. Our survey also provided us with data on various characteristics of residents, including many of the traits included in our experiment.

Several of the results, reported in Figure 3.6, align with those of our experiment. First, we find no evidence of ethnic favoritism. We were able to identify whether a resident had at least one leader from their specific sub-caste, faith, or region-of-origin present in their settlement. If shared ethnicity is an important dimension along which brokers cultivate clients, then residents who have co-ethnic brokers should be more likely to report assistance than residents who have no co-ethnic brokers available to them. We also coded whether a respondent was a member of the largest caste or second-largest caste in a settlement. Here we wanted to assess a slightly different potential use of ethnicity in "vote-bank" politics. Perhaps brokers use ethnic markers not to identify co-ethnics, but rather to identify the largest pools of available clients. If brokers construct client bases through these ethnic lenses, we should expect residents in the largest castes within a slum to be prioritized. Yet *none* of these ethnic variables registered significant effects, broadly aligning with our experimental findings.

Second, residents who have spent more time in the settlement are more likely to report receiving recent attention. Since time in the settlement (measured in years) was the one continuous variable in our model, we re-scaled this measure by two standard deviations to ease the comparability of its impact with binary predictors.[96] The re-scaled coefficient shows that a change in two standard deviations (roughly from the low to high end of observed values)

95. We preferred this to asking residents if slum brokers had successfully helped them. This measure better matches our experiment, which follows most experimental studies of political responsiveness in conceptualizing responsiveness in terms of *willingness* to assist, not *efficacy* in request fulfillment. We also avoided asking respondents to identify which leader they had approached, as this line of questioning appeared too sensitive to us, especially if local leaders were to hear we were asking residents to evaluate their performance.

96. See Gelman 2007.

corresponds to an eight-to-nine percentage point increase in the likelihood of reporting assistance ($p < 0.05$).

Our results regarding residents with disadvantaged occupations are more nuanced. We coded residents who worked in relatively disadvantaged occupations matching those in our experimental category (see Online Supplement Table S3.3). Overall, we find such residents are more likely to report receiving help. However, this result is not statistically significant. Upon further inspection, this result appears to be heavily inflected by gender. Residents employed in the thirty-two male-dominated disadvantaged professions (667 respondents, roughly thirty percent of our sample) are seven (7.1) percentage points more likely to report receiving help than other residents.[97] This category is composed of professions like laborer, autorickshaw driver, and house painter. However, those employed in the five female-dominated disadvantaged professions (268 residents) are just over nine (9.1) percentage points less likely to report receiving help than other residents.[98] This second category includes jobs like housemaids, cleaners, and cooks.

Given our experiment presented brokers only with male residents, and our examples of disadvantaged jobs conformed more to male-dominated professions, our experimental findings partially align with this observational data. However, this result also suggests future work should examine how broker responsiveness is shaped by a potential client's gender. We do find an overall gender gap in who gets help from political brokers. Among the 1,518 surveyed residents who acknowledged the presence of local brokers in their settlement, only fifty-four percent of female residents reported receiving recent assistance, compared to sixty-three percent of men. Second, in sixty-six settlements with no female brokers, fifty-three percent of female residents reported receiving assistance, whereas in twenty-one settlements with two or more female leaders, sixty-two percent of women reported the same. Our limited sample size, and lack of knowledge of which individual broker helped which client prevents us from drawing firm conclusions from these patterns. Overall, these simple descriptive findings underscore the potential importance of closer attention to gendered dimensions of brokerage.[99]

Overall, these tests show that the broker evaluations in our experiment align in some key respects with their actual patterns of responsiveness,

---

97. This difference was statistically significant at the 95% level.

98. This difference just misses statistical significance at the 95% level ($p = .053$)

99. e.g., Daby 2021; Goyal 2022.

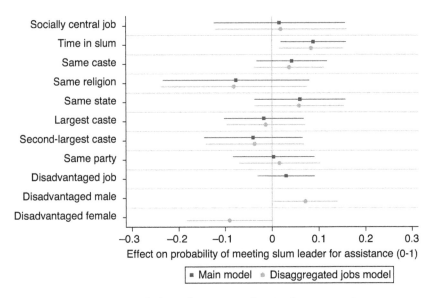

FIGURE 3.6. Which Residents Receive Slum Leader Assistance?

Notes: N = 1,514. The figure reports results from OLS regressions in which the outcome variable identifies respondents who reported receiving assistance from a local slum leader. All models also included slum-fixed effects and standard errors clustered at the slum level. Explanatory variables not shown in the figure included household income, age, and whether the respondent was literate. All explanatory variables displayed in the figure are binary indicators except time in the settlement, which has been divided by two standard deviations for comparability. See, Gelman 2007. Dots indicate coefficients recovered from the regression analysis; bars indicate 95% confidence intervals. "Disadvantaged Job Female" refers to the five disadvantaged jobs with female majorities (Housemaid, Cleaners, Domestic Cooks, Washers, and Sweepers). "Disadvantaged Job Male" refers to the 32 other disadvantaged jobs. See, Supplement Tables S3.3 and S3.4 for coding breakdown.

reducing concerns that our experimental results reflect cheap talk. That said, two observational results were not anticipated by our experiment. We do not find significant positive correlations for residents who work in "socially central" jobs (see Online Supplement Table S3.4 for the coding of these jobs). We also do not find residents who have at least one co-partisan leader in their settlement to be more likely to report receiving assistance than residents who do not. This muted importance of partisanship may in part reflect the shifting nature of partisan loyalties within slums, which makes it hard for brokers to target along partisan lines. Thirty percent of respondents who identified as BJP partisans, and just under twenty-eight percent (27.75%) of respondents who identified as Congress partisans, reported that they frequently shifted their vote choice from election to election. In this respect, our fixing of hypothetical residents as partisans of one party or another on the experiment may reflect a certainty that is not always assured in reality.

Overall, the results reported in Figure 3.6 largely reinforce the notion that brokers prioritize clients whose attributes are beneficial for reputation-building, including veterans of the settlement, and those in (male-centered) disadvantaged professions. By contrast, brokers do not appear to favor residents with traits thought to facilitate monitoring their voting behavior (such as shared ethnicity and partisanship).

Do Slum Brokers Really Have Multi-ethnic Support Bases?

We argue that slum brokers display ethnic indifference to help attract multi-ethnic clienteles. This argument implies that brokers should possess ethnically diverse followings. To assess this, we asked our 629 slum brokers to recall the last five residents who approached them for help. We then asked them to list the surnames of these five residents. This information allowed us to code the *jati* and faith of those residents.

A striking seventy-seven percent of slum brokers named at least one client from a different *jati* than their own. By contrast, a mere five percent listed only clients from their *jati* (18% provided no answer).[100] These patterns extend to broader religious identities. Here we examine those slums in which our resident survey indicated the presence of multiple faiths (79 of 110 settlements). In such settlements, forty-six percent of brokers reported serving recent clients from multiple faiths, typically Hindus and Muslims, compared to forty percent who only provided names of a single faith.[101] Recall this figure refers only to recent clients, and the number of brokers serving residents of multiple faiths might have been even higher if we had asked for a more expansive list.

100. 15 slum brokers helped clients of other faiths in settlements where we did not randomly draw a religiously diverse resident sample. We took advantage of this additional information and coded them as having helped non-coreligionists.

101. This data reduces ecological validity concerns regarding presenting brokers with potential clients who were not religious co-ethnics in our experiment. In addition to a high proportion of brokers with religiously-mixed clienteles, we find rates of helping clients from other faiths are stable for Hindu and Muslim brokers across slums with Hindu and Muslim majorities, varying levels of religious fractionalization, and levels of trust between residents. Fuller results reported in Auerbach and Thachil 2020.

Our in-depth interviews with residents corroborated the ethnic inclusivity of brokers. We interviewed thirty-six randomly sampled residents in two Jaipur slums in which we have conducted extensive fieldwork.[102] Interviewed residents were diverse, representing twenty-two *jati* and three faiths. Our interviews established the importance of political brokers, with thirty of thirty-six residents reporting having sought help from a slum leader. Second, the interviews revealed that many residents do not even have the option of going to a leader from their own caste. Only seven respondents had a leader from their own *jati* in their settlement. Yet this did not prevent them from seeking help, as twenty-five of the twenty-nine respondents without co-*jati* brokers still approached a broker for help. Furthermore, even when residents do have brokers from their caste available, they often seek help from non-co-ethnic brokers. Of the seven respondents with co-*jati* brokers, four sought help at least once from a leader from a different *jati*. Overall, these patterns confirmed that caste divisions do not firmly demarcate the scope of potential broker-resident relations.

Considering results across our various analyses, our findings demonstrate consistent support for two resident qualities linked to reputational concerns: ethnic indifference and favoring veteran residents. We find less consistent support for our other indicator of social centrality based on occupation. Our results for co-partisanship are mixed. Changing a resident's partisan affiliation to match the broker has a sizeable positive impact in our original experiment. The lack of a corresponding influence in our neighbor experiment suggests this preference is explicitly political. Yet our observational evidence suggests that responsiveness does not always occur along partisan lines. These disparate findings may reflect the difficulties of partisan-driven responsiveness in places where the partisan attachments of many residents are fluid over time.

Alternatives Interpretations of Results

Finally, let us consider alternative interpretations of our main findings. Our central argument suggests that reputational concerns drive the prioritization of disadvantaged and socially central clients. But perhaps brokers value such residents for other reasons. For example, brokers may target residents in low-status jobs not due to reputational concerns, but rather because they are the cheapest votes to buy. Our survey data does not align with these expectations

102. We selected these settlements because they were ethnically diverse, average in terms of population, and exhibited multi-focal slum leadership.

of a minimalist, transactional model. In contrast to the minimalist model expectations, our surveyed brokers viewed cheap strategies of election-day gift-giving as relatively unimportant and ineffective with the vast majority of residents.[103] Instead, brokers noted the importance of everyday, relational activities that appeal to all residents.

Second, if brokers target cheap, low-status residents, the latter should display higher electoral turnout—*the* crucial act of client reciprocation within such transactional models.[104] Yet self-reported turnout among "disadvantaged" job-holders (934 respondents) was just under ninety percent (89.60%), essentially equal to the nearly ninety-two percent (91.86%) rate for residents in government and other "high-status" jobs (86 respondents). Far greater is the difference between reported slum turnout (nearly 90% across our sample) and general turnout in urban local elections (50%–65% in our study cities in recent elections). Practically all slum residents turn out to vote, irrespective of their occupation.

Finally, if brokers focus only on attracting the most marginal residents, they should prefer relatively new clients, who are more likely to require the cheapest and most basic services. For example, obtaining ration cards is cheaper than fulfilling requests to obtain piped water or streetlights. Sixty-three percent of residents who had arrived in the slum within the past five years still required a ration card, compared to just ten percent of those who had lived in the settlement for ten years or more. Yet our experiment reveals broker responsiveness actually increases in going from a newcomer to veteran resident, and our observational evidence finds veteran residents are more likely to report receiving help in the past year.

A different possibility is that brokers target residents who are firmly embedded within slum social networks because these networks can be used for monitoring their electoral behavior.[105] We view this possibility as unlikely for several reasons. First, this logic is precisely what should lead to ethnic favoritism, especially along narrow *jati* lines, given that these dense kinship ties are seen as especially helpful to monitoring. Second, while the vast majority (89%) of brokers expressed confidence in their abilities to assess the general direction in which the settlement voted, less than half that many (43.6%)

103. A majority of surveyed leaders (55.29%) said less than ten percent of residents would have their vote affected by such gifts.

104. Nichter 2008.

105. Cruz 2019.

believed that they could assess how individual residents voted. Furthermore, even among such "monitors," only about thirteen percent (13.5% or roughly 5.9% of the full sample) of brokers said they used a voter's social networks to find out how they actually voted. Instead, most brokers (61.1%) said their verification relied on a voter self-reporting. However, reliance on self-reports is hardly convincing evidence of monitoring prowess. The voters we interviewed often spoke openly of telling brokers they had indeed supported them, even if they had not actually done so.

Another possibility is that the positive impact in shifting a potential client's occupation from a privileged to disadvantaged job does not reflect a desire for building inclusive reputations, but rather the fact that a slum leader's services are only valuable to a slum's poorest residents (wealthier residents may have more direct avenues of claim-making). In contrast to this explanation, our data show that slum brokers are almost uniformly in demand across income groups: surveyed residents in the bottom and top per capita household income quintiles turned to slum brokers for assistance at similar rates (35% and 41%, respectively). This is likely the product of widespread pessimism among slum residents regarding their ability to command the attention of officials alone, without the help of an intermediary. In an earlier 2012 survey we conducted in 80 of the 110 settlements, only twelve percent of 1,925 resident respondents believed that they would get attention from public officials if they went to them alone.[106] Such pessimism holds across income groups: residents in the bottom and top asset index quintiles reported broadly similar expectations of responsiveness (11% and 15%, respectively).[107] Such broad pessimism may reflect the fact that even the top quintile of households in slums are far from well-off. Slum brokers, therefore, have an expansive pool of potential clients that cuts across income groups within slums.

Conclusion

This chapter builds on Chapter 2 to further unpack the processes through which political networks form to connect poor migrants to the wider world of city politics. We began by showing that many of the qualities poor migrants value in their local leaders do in fact reflect actual leaders in their settlements. The kinds of brokers migrants want are the kind they get. Such alignment

106. See Auerbach 2016 and Auerbach 2020.
107. Auerbach and Kruks-Wisner 2020.

powerfully suggests an important and often overlooked dimension of representation within urban politics, albeit one that is outside of formal elections. Furthermore, actual slum leaders are especially distinguished by qualities residents view as indicating their problem-solving effectiveness. These findings illustrate how paying attention to the formation of political machines can reveal neglected channels of bottom-up accountability within these networks.

Next, we build on Chapter 2's analysis as to how poor migrants select whom among them rises to local leadership. Here, we invert our gaze to study which residents these leaders choose to cultivate as supporters through acts of everyday problem-solving. These quotidian decisions not only cement the ties between leaders and residents, but also shape larger patterns of inclusion and exclusion within the city.

Our analysis once again calls for greater recognition of the agency of poor migrants, in this instance the migrants who rise to leadership positions. Brokers are often dismissed as perpetual intermediaries deployed to check up on voters during elections on behalf of party elites. In these descriptions, brokers seek little more than to dispense with their duties most cheaply, so as to maximize the resources that remain within their own pockets. This portrayal has fueled assumptions regarding the types of residents brokers are expected to favor: residents from their own partisan or ethnic communities whose behavior brokers can most confidently verify.

Our time spent with brokers in Jaipur and Bhopal revealed the inadequacies of such simplified portrayals. The slum leaders we worked with are not content to remain the henchmen of their superiors. Rather, they are ambitious entrepreneurs seeking upwardly mobile political careers. These ambitions motivate them to craft large personal followings, to mobilize broadly rather than monitor narrowly. A wide array of evidence shows such desires compel brokers to build reputations as inclusive problem-solvers, eschewing narrow forms of parochial favoritism, and favoring residents best poised to spread word of their assistance.

However, our findings should not be read as providing a triumphal view of slum politics. After all, we uncover not only dimensions of inclusion, but also of exclusion, in the patterns of representation and responsiveness that we study. This chapter speaks to the need to move beyond a narrow focus on ethnicity and partisanship as solely structuring patterns of exclusion within the politics of the Global South. For example, the fact that brokers disproportionately reflect indicators of efficacy that residents value also results in residents who lack those traits being underrepresented within such positions of authority. For example, less educated residents, or those who work as manual laborers or homemakers are especially unlikely to become influential within migrant communities. Less socially influential or embedded residents are also less likely to have their demands responded to by brokers, including women and recent arrivals in the settlement.

So far, our analysis has been contained to political processes within the world of the informal settlement. In Chapter 4, we move to how these processes connect to political forces outside of slums. In particular, the nodes of informal leadership that migrants create within slums have direct implications for higher levels of politics and party organization in the city. Urban political elites looking to recruit support within informal settlements must decide which local leaders to incorporate into their party organizations. Such decisions will again have crucial implications on who is represented and responded to within urban politics. It is to these crucial decisions that we next turn our attention.

4

How Patrons Select Brokers

HARISH CHANDRA, AN ELECTED WARD councilor in the city of Bhopal, begins his work the moment he steps outside his front door.[1] During one cool January morning, we joined Chandra on a routine drive to visit constituents in his ward. Our destination is a large, sprawling slum settlement known as Gagan Nagar. Chandra stops just short of the settlement and tells us he prefers to approach on foot: "If people from the slum see me coming in my car, it gives the impression that I am trying to show off. It hurts my *chavvi* [image]."[2]

As soon as we enter the slum, we are joined by a slim man with a trimmed mustache and neatly combed hair. Chandra introduces him as Ashok *sahib*, Chandra's most senior party worker in the slum.[3] Ashok *sahib* proceeds to guide us through the settlement. As we walk, residents stream towards Ashok *sahib* and Chandra for help with issues ranging from a broken streetlight to a recent theft of petrol from an area where motorcycles park in the settlement. (See Table 4.1 for a list of issues.) Ashok *sahib* stands by Chandra throughout the walk, jotting down instructions and making calls whenever he is instructed.

We ask Chandra if these "slum walks" are a frequent part of his routine. He responded that he usually relies on Ashok *sahib* to bring him people and problems—to be his eyes and ears in the settlement. "But sometimes it is good to have him walk me through the settlement. That way people see that I am not just a *gadiwala neta* [which roughly translates to "an elitist leader who doesn't get out of the car"], that I can walk amongst them and understand their problems.

1. Name anonymized.
2. Author field notes, February 5, 2017.
3. An honorific equivalent to "sir." Name anonymized.

TABLE 4.1. Slum Resident Complaints to Chandra (Councilor) and Ashok (Broker)

Location	Issue	Action Taken
Home		
1	Electricity loss	Phone to supplier
2	Sewer line extension	Work order
3	Housing scheme form	Form from office
Slum		
1	Broken garbage-collection cart	Repair request by phone
2	Cooking gas connection	Form from office
3	Cleaning gutter	Request by phone
4	Exposed water pipe	Work order promised in April
5	Pension fund access	Form from office
6	Clearing garbage dump	Work order promised in April
7	Invitation to school function	Accepted; went next day
8	Broken streetlight	Instructed fortnightly repair truck
9	Pension fund access	Form from office
10	Sewer line extension	Work order already submitted
11	Dispute; trespassing cow	Warning to owner
12	Complaint—boys drinking	Requests 1 am police rounds for 1 week
13	Housing scheme funds	Refused—ineligible
14	Complaint; petrol theft	Subsidizes fence around motorcycles
15	Dispute resolution—unpaid loan	Arranges installment plan for lower interest
16	Repaving road	Refuses—too expensive
17	Replace drain cover	Repair request by phone

Source: Author Field Notes, February 5, 2017.

But it also it helps Ashok *sahib* to show people that he can get them an audience with me, either here or in my office."

In advance of his campaign to run for councilor, Chandra recruited Ashok *sahib* to be his main party worker in Rajiv Nagar. "I needed to build up our organization within the slum or I stood no chance of winning. This slum has become bigger and bigger, and by now it is clear—to win the ward, you have to win Gagan Nagar." In Gagan Nagar, Chandra was drawn to Ashok *sahib*, who residents identified as a capable problem-solver.

Ashok *sahib* has several of the qualities we have identified as attractive to slum residents. First, he is educated, which draws many within the community to him for help with government forms and applications. Second, he has great "mouth-publicity," an English phrase which Chandra loosely translates as the ability to mobilize a large number of slum residents quickly. "If he needs to, he can have fifty people lined up for a rally or protest within a few hours." Ashok *sahib*'s prodigious mouth-publicity stems from his long tenure in the settlement

FIGURE 4.1. Ward Councilor Making His Local Rounds
Front right: Councilor Chandra. Center back (striped shirt): Ashok *Sahib*. Front left: residents.
Photograph by author, January 2017.

(over thirty years). He was also one of the few residents in the slum with his own mill for grinding flour, and would let residents come to grind wheat for a nominal fee. This service brought him into regular contact with residents from across the slum and placed him at the center of local social networks. Mouth-publicity matters—and not just at election time. Chandra often has to bring supporters to party rallies and protests against the rival BJP government. The more people he brings, the more likely he is to receive "bites"—media coverage in the local newspapers and on social media that captures the attention of party superiors. "Without crowds, you can't get bites; without bites, you can't get party candidate tickets," Ashok *sahib* tells us.[4]

For his part, Ashok *sahib* agreed to work for Chandra. In return, he requested a formal position (*pad*) within the local Congress party. More than receiving handouts or election-time payments, Ashok *sahib* prioritized such formal organizational inclusion. Chandra arranged for him to receive the position of ward

4. Interview with Ashok *sahib*, Bhopal, February 6, 2017.

president in the Congress Party's youth wing. While there were other local leaders Chandra could have picked in Gagan Nagar, he credits his decision to pick Ashok *sahib* as central to his own success. "Every councilor has an Ashok *sahib*," Chandra says, "they wouldn't be a councilor otherwise." Ashok *sahib*, however, has quiet aspirations beyond his settlement. He hopes to graduate to a position in the main Congress party. "Who knows," he speculates to us privately, "perhaps one day I will even get a councilor ticket from the party?"

How do party leaders like Chandra select which brokers to formally include within their local organizations? Chapters 2 and 3 explored how political networks form between slum residents and local leaders within their communities. This chapter moves outward, examining how such networks connect to the wider world of city politics beyond the slum. It does so by focusing on how political patrons choose which local brokers from slums to formally provide with organizational positions. For reasons we detail in this chapter, this important choice has been largely ignored within studies of machine politics, again due to insufficient recognition of the significant competition between brokers that affords patrons the opportunity to choose between multiple aspirants.

The importance of organizational inclusion was repeatedly noted to us by the brokers in our study. In this chapter's first sections, we draw on data from ethnographic fieldwork, and our survey of 629 slum leaders in order to examine why brokers prize such inclusion. We find brokers value the upward connectivity such positions confer, which aids in their efforts to solve resident problems and thereby maintain standing in the settlement. Furthermore, we find that this desire for party positions reflects brokers' careerist ambitions to rise within party ranks. In this chapter we present novel data from the careers of slum leaders to show that many can and do experience some upward mobility within party organizations.

The fact that brokers almost universally desire party positions creates a surfeit of choice for political party leaders in the intensely competitive environments we work within. To study how patrons decide which brokers to grant positions to, we draw on interviews and an experiment embedded within a survey of 343 local party patrons across Jaipur and Bhopal. Briefly, we find that patrons strongly value indicators of partisan loyalty as well as personal loyalty to the patron. The importance of loyalty reflects the uncertainties wrought by the high degrees of inter-party competition and intra-party factionalism found in India, which grant brokers exit options within and between parties. Moreover, traits suggestive of a broker's everyday efficacy in helping residents, notably high levels of education, prove to be more significant than indicators of the brokers' episodic election-time efficacy. We finish the chapter by examining whether the findings from our experiment align with the political careers of actual slum leaders.

How patrons decide which brokers to bestow positions to is of obvious importance for understanding the ways in which newly urban poor communities are politically integrated. First, the organizational inclusion of slum leaders, who we have shown are also themselves predominantly poor migrants, is an important channel through which these communities obtain representation within city politics. Such representation has been unacknowledged by scholarship that views these communities as either uniformly excluded from city politics, or as solely incorporated through shadowy and informal mechanisms of "political society."[5] Instead, we show slum leaders actively inserting themselves into the organizational structures of mainstream political parties, and often ascend to occupy important positions within these structures.

Studying how patrons incorporate local brokers also furthers our understanding of channels of bottom-up accountability within machine organizations. Importantly, both our qualitative and quantitative evidence suggest that patrons actively consider the views of ordinary slum residents in choosing which brokers to incorporate. For example, we find that patrons value educated brokers in our experiment, mirroring the preferences of slum residents in Chapter 2. Furthermore, education is associated with promotion patterns among actual slum leaders. Our interviews with politicians support interpreting such alignment of findings as consistent with patrons seeking brokers who are popular among ordinary residents, affording the latter a modicum of influence in shaping the structures that govern them.

Finally, this chapter also helps build our sense of the very clear limits of this form of machine politics. While the efforts of slum leaders in elbowing their way into partisan organizations are remarkable, slum leaders also face considerable hurdles. Not every leader is organizationally included, and not every leader who is included actually experiences upward mobility. Moreover, even those brokers who rise to positions of prominence hit glass ceilings, especially with respect to obtaining political candidacies which often require deep financial resources.

5. On "political society," see Chatterjee 2004.

Why Do Brokers Join Parties?

In Chapter 2, we saw how neighborhood leaders emerge in slums through the support of local residents and not due to the prior backing of party elites. Parties then seek to integrate these locally influential leaders in order to gain political footholds in vote-rich settlements. This begs the question, what do slum leaders want from parties in return?

The most obvious answer is that slum leaders seek immediate payoffs from parties to deliver votes. Conventional models of clientelist vote-buying often portray intermediaries as having such transactional motivations, just as such studies view client electoral reciprocity as primarily motivated by campaign handouts.[6] Brokers are said to receive direct payments for good performance, and to pocket some party resources meant for vote-buying in their localities.[7] The slum leaders we interviewed secure both kinds of immediate benefits. They also receive some payments from clients, usually in the form of small fees for assistance in certain kinds of problem solving.

Yet, if slum leaders were solely motivated by election-time payments, it is hard to explain why so many of them (88%) consistently sought more permanent inclusion within a party organization. A chief objective for most slum leaders we interviewed was to be granted a formal position or *pad* within a party.[8] In the words of one interviewee, "my getting a position in the party was crucial—like a naked man putting on clothes."[9] Of our 629 sampled slum leaders, 415 (66%) held such positions at least once. Importantly, almost none of these positions came with fixed benefits, such as a salary or office space; nor are such positions prerequisites for receiving campaign payments from parties in our study cities.

---

6. Larreguy et al. 2016, p. 161, write, "Brokers hired by political parties play the essential intermediary role in this process, mobilizing voters on election day in return for cash and bonuses."

7. Regarding Latin American machines, Stokes et al. 2013, p. 81, write that a broker "receives two types of benefits. If the party wins, then she receives an exogenous post-election payoff R. In addition, the broker may extract pecuniary 'rents' r by failing to pass on some measure of resources to voters." Regarding machines in Africa, Koter 2013, p. 197, similarly notes, "There are two types of rewards that politicians can offer [intermediaries]: direct payments or gifts in kind during electoral campaigns and promises of future rewards contingent on electoral results."

8. Chapter 1 details the organizational pyramid of the Congress and BJP in Indian cities. Parties and their affiliated wings (youth wings, women's wings, etc.) are organized into tiers, ranging from the local level polling station to the ward, block, city, and district levels.

9. Interview with Shiv, Gulab Colony, July 4, 2016.

Why then do slum leaders so keenly seek to formally join parties? First, this desire is better explained by understanding broker support from clients as rooted in their abilities to spearhead bottom-up claim-making, rather than in directing top-down vote-buying. As we argued in Chapter 2, leaders emerge first and foremost through selection by clients. Yet under competitive conditions, leaders must deliver for residents or risk losing their influence to other aspirants. As we have argued, slum residents we spoke to appeared quite unmoved by campaign gifts. Instead, they seek out leaders who can help advance their everyday demands for essential public goods and services.

Viewing brokers as selected by clients to help advance their claims, and not simply as rented funnels for election payments, helps make sense of why brokers seek party positions. Organizational inclusion bestows brokers with privileged connections to the political and bureaucratic elites who are in a position to address everyday resident concerns. A formal position or *pad* is a useful signal to bureaucrats and politicians, including those a broker may not know personally, that they have connections to leverage and enough political clout to cause trouble if their demand is not heard. Numerous brokers spoke of such benefits of organizational inclusion:

> I saw that the people in the slum were beset by problems. I wondered about how to get our concerns heard. I met a couple of political leaders, and they told me to join a party and only then I'd be able to get work done. I thought it over, and started going for [*sic*] party meetings. Once I got a position, I found when I filed applications, they were resolved much faster.[10]

> When I met 2–3 party leaders they asked me to join Congress and become a member. They promised that they will solve the issues. So, I joined. I met politicians, many other people. When I got associated with the party, then I got the post of [ward] president. They also looked after the problems of people in the slum. I solved many issues of water, roads, electricity, etc.[11]

Political elites offered similar views on the value of formal inclusion in aiding a slum leader's ability to serve their followers. A Congress ward president in Jaipur told us:

> See, the thing about slum leaders is that they give us their presence, their reach, within the slum. They do not have personal friends in the JDA

---

10. Interview with Broker 21, Settlement 22, June 23, 2016.
11. Interview with Broker 22, Settlement 23, June 11, 2016.

[Jaipur Development Authority], in the municipality, but they are living in
the areas with the most problems, in need of the most help. That is why they
approach us for inclusion within the party, for a position. If they don't,
they will not get their problems solved fast enough, and then they will lose
their leadership position within the slum.[12]

The city president of the Congress made a similar observation:

You need to build that *juraav* [attachment] with local leaders, and the way to
do that is by giving them a position. See, they need to feel like they have the
weight of big leaders like me behind them. They want it so that if they have a
problem—when they need to get their neighbor's son admission to a local
school, when they want a water tanker to come to their neighborhood—that
they have the weight of a leader like Pratap Singh [the speaker] and the
"*haath*" [hand, the symbol of the Congress party] with them. Giving them a
position is the way to do this.[13]

Formal inclusion thus helps brokers meet bottom-up resident demands,
thereby helping them consolidate their own followings. This logic is hardly
unrelated to rent-seeking, as brokers need followings to receive payments from
parties.

However, our fieldwork also made clear that brokers seek organizational
inclusion for reasons beyond immediate rent-seeking. As we argued in Chapter 3, slum leaders are ambitious entrepreneurs whose aspirations extend beyond the settlements from which they emerge. They seek political careers of
their own, not to forever remain rentable intermediaries for politicians. Such
long-term ambitions are an acknowledged motivation of brokers. Yet prior
studies have not assessed whether broker trajectories in parties reflect the mobility of ambitious careerists, or the plateaus of permanent brokerage.[14]

Such ambitions further clarify the premium leaders put on formal inclusion
within party networks. Slum leaders told us they covet *pads* precisely because
these positions serve as toeholds from which to climb up the party ranks:

The thing with *pads* is they depend on who can do good work for the party.
So, if today I have a low *pad*, but I do work then tomorrow I will get a better

12. Interview with Patron 1, Congress Party Ward President, Jaipur, February 9, 2017.

13. Interview with Pratak Singh Khaachariwas, Congress City President, Jaipur, February 9, 2017.

14. Stokes et al. 2013; Camp 2017. Szwarcberg 2015 is an important exception.

one. The party leaders will promote you. They will not stop you if you are doing good work; they will support your rise within the party.[15]

It is tempting to dismiss such statements as wishful thinking. The absence of systematic data on the trajectories of brokers within parties contributes to a vision of these actors as perpetual intermediaries. Yet the quotation above comes from Vimla, a female slum leader who has enjoyed precisely the ascent she described. She began as a ward-level (Level 2) president for the BJP's women's wing. Her next position was as general secretary of the *mandal*-level (Level 3) women's wing, followed by becoming *mandal* president of the women's wing (Level 3). Finally, she was appointed general secretary of the city-wide women's wing (Level 4).

To provide another example: Satish, a popular informal leader in Jaipur's Ganpati slum, was, at the time of our fieldwork in 2015, the ward president of BJP. His appointment to this prominent position followed a gradual climb up lower rungs of the party hierarchy—president of the BJP's student wing in his college, local general secretary of the party's youth wing, a committee member at the *mandal* level, general secretary of the main BJP party at the ward level, and then party president at the ward level. Prospects for further advancement were bright for Satish when we last spoke, including possibly securing the opportunity to run for municipal office. Indeed, Satish's senior BJP worker in Jawahar Nagar was able to reach that lofty perch. With a college degree, a highly frequented general store, and more than two decades worth of problem-solving activities in Jawahar Nagar, Satish may very well become a BJP ward councilor in the future.[16]

These individual trajectories counter the idea that leaders like Satish can never rise beyond their slums. But are such trajectories exceptional? Our survey data provides an unprecedented glimpse into the careers of Indian brokers. We collected information on all current and prior positions held by surveyed brokers who had held at least one position. The trajectories of these 415 leaders are mapped out in Figure 4.2. The horizontal axis groups leaders by the total

15. Interview with Vimla, Settlement 24, June 9, 2016.

16. Author field notes, February 4, 2011. A number of slum leaders we interviewed went on to either contest or even become councilors. These include Broker 25 (Settlement 25, Bhopal, July 10, 2016); Broker 23 (Settlement 23, Jaipur, June 14, 2016) who fought and won as an independent after being denied a Congress ticket; Broker 26 (Settlement 26, Jaipur, June 15, 2016); and Broker 15 (Settlement 18, Jaipur, June 22, 2016).

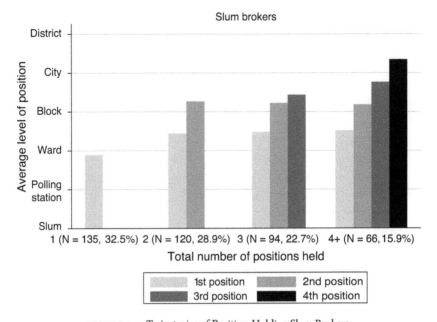

FIGURE 4.2. Trajectories of Position-Holding Slum Brokers
Notes: Percentages in parentheses indicate proportion of position-holding brokers (N = 415) within each category.

number of positions they have held (1, 2, 3, or 4+). The height of the columns indicates the average level of each position occupied.[17]

Figure 4.2 makes clear that slum leaders are not engaging in purely wishful thinking when aspiring to rise within a party. Leaders who were able to secure multiple *pads* did tend to follow an upward political trajectory. Take, for example, the ninety-four slum leaders who held a total of three *pads*. Their careers are depicted in the third cluster of columns in Figure 4.2. These leaders jumped a full level of positional rank between their first positions (which were held at an average level of 2.47, between a ward- and block-level post) and third positions (at an average of 3.51, between a block- and city-level post). Similarly, slum leaders who held a total of four *pads* went from a starting level of 2.29 to a finishing level of 4.36, equivalent to a jump from a ward-level post to a city-wide

17. For the "4+"column, the far right black bar depicts the average rank of the fourth position, even for those brokers with 5 or more positions.

post. Indeed, 176 leaders (28% of the entire sample) held a city-wide post at least once in their career.

Given such broad recognition of the value slum leaders place on inclusion, one might ask why political leaders do not simply give *all* slum leaders formal positions, and even regular promotions? After all, slum leaders openly admitted that they exert a higher level of effort on behalf of the party after receiving a position:

> It is important to have a *pad*. Because a post gives you dignity, and this dignity gives me the passion to serve the party to the fullest. And through this I can also serve the people. It's considered very good to have the post. Even the senior leaders think that the person who gets it will work actively.[18]

Yet Figure 4.2 shows inclusion and regular promotion is far from a universal experience. Over a third of surveyed slum leaders (214) had never received a single *pad*. Even among those that do, many often are not promoted. One-third of our 415 position-holders did not manage to secure more than a single *pad*, and over half had not secured more than two by the time of our interviews.

Our research revealed both strategic and logistic reasons for this slippery slope. Strategically, the motivational value of a position in inspiring hard work diminishes if the benefit is universally dispensed to all leaders irrespective of their achievements. Indeed, the value of positions is rooted in scarcity, in the promise of relatively privileged connections to elites and ascension up a party hierarchy. Second, endlessly proliferating positions to ensure broad personnel inclusion would necessitate the sacrifice of other purposes of party organizations. In particular, constructing bloated organizations would compromise the ability of local chapters to hold meetings, chart cohesive action plans during campaigns, and even manage expenses. If a ward committee was to include six treasurers and twelve secretaries, for example, even basic tasks like managing expenses and organizing meeting agendas would face hurdles of coordination. As a prominent city politician in Jaipur told us, local party committees cannot be "jumbo jets," taking in all of those local brokers seeking positions.[19]

---

18. Interview with Broker 16, Settlement 19, Bhopal, July 3, 2016.

19. Interview with former city president of the Congress Party, Jaipur, May 28, 2016.

Slum leaders themselves recognize that parties cannot grant every aspirant within a slum a position.

Positions are not distributed like *prasad* [food distributed as religious offerings]. Not everyone gets this.[20]

There is a limit to how high many of us leaders [from the slum] can rise . . . After all, if there are 100 people like us working hard in the slums, but only 10 posts at the ward level, most will not get it.[21]

In short, slum leaders desire formal inclusion, both to service client demands, and to enable their chance at upward ascension. Parties recognize the value of granting their wishes, but cannot bestow such largesse on every aspiring broker.[22]

How, then, do parties decide which leaders to prioritize in building their urban machines? Before answering this analytical question, we must address two prior descriptive ones. First, how do slum leaders garner the attention of party elites? Second, who in the party typically makes these selection decisions?

How do Brokers and Politicians Meet?

For slum leaders to be integrated into parties, they must first come into the latter's field of vision. To understand this process, we asked each surveyed slum leader to describe how they were brought into a party organization. We recorded, transcribed, and coded their open-ended answers.[23] In this section, we draw on some of the responses we found to be both representative and informatively articulated.

20. Interview with Broker 50, Settlement 43, Bhopal, February 20, 2017.

21. Interview with Rajesh, Tulsi Nagar, January 17, 2017.

22. Similar observations have been made about US and European machines. McCaffery 1992, p. 447, discusses how the Republican machine in Philadelphia during the early twentieth century "distributed nominations (as they did political appointments and opportunities to participate in 'honest graft') strictly on a performance-related basis . . . and not on the basis of personal resources . . . Such a strategy . . . did more than simply maintain discipline among party workers. It also instilled over time a terrific sense of loyalty among the party's rank and file." Chubb 1982 similarly describes position-holders in the Christian Democratic Party in southern Italy. While regular membership of the *tesserati* was allowed to proliferate among ordinary supporters, actual positions in the organization were more defined and limited, much like in the BJP and Congress in our study sites.

23. We had seven non-responses to this question.

Take, for example, Shekhawat, a slum leader in Jaipur's Bhojpura settlement. Shekhawat is one of the slum's more educated residents, and because he is the owner of a small general store where residents pass time, he is entrenched in the social networks of the settlement. Shekhawat led a sustained fight with the state government for sewer lines, which attracted the attention of the local MLA from the Bharatiya Janata Party (BJP). Local party workers then approached Shekhawat and took him into the party organization. At the time of our fieldwork, he occupied the position of vice-president of the *mandal* (Level 3), a senior post.[24]

Slum brokers could come to the attention of party elites through quieter, everyday work, or through visible acts of responsiveness in times of crisis.

> I am a seamstress in the settlement, and a lot of women who approach me for my services also share with me their joys and sorrows. I try to help them as much as I can, and that's how I got to know most of them ... if someone needs a loan, I would go with them, or advise them on forms to fill, or how to re-pay the loan. I have also helped folks get ration cards, BPL cards, or ID cards. I got involved in the women's wing of the Congress since the party saw that I helped a lot of women and led them.[25]

> I organized protests to secure water taps. As this matter unfolded, gradually the Congress felt that this man has some weight, he is the one who talks, and the public is with him ... every single man and child knows Fauji *sahib*, and says his name with a lot of love. That is why they gave me the post.[26]

> The slum used to get flooded quite often. Together with my friends I used to collect money and distribute food packets ... In times of crisis the leaders come on their own ... So the leaders came and saw that I did good work.[27]

While everyday problem-solving dominated leader accounts, one in five leaders (21%) identified a "big event" as crucial in enabling initial contact with party elites.

In other cases, slum leaders recalled taking the initiative in directly approaching political parties for inclusion. When making such overtures, leaders

---

24. Author field notes, November 1, 2010.
25. Interview with Broker 18, Settlement 20, Jaipur June 16. 2016.
26. Interview with Broker 28, Settlement 27, Jaipur, June 10, 2016.
27. Interview with Akram, Gulab Colony, Bhopal, July 4, 2016.

must signal their local standing and influence. One way of doing so is to bring supporters to party rallies.

> I first began by offering free tuition to people's children. Then people began to know me; that this is someone who can get work done. One-by-one, people began attaching themselves to me . . . Congress has a lot of support- ers in the area, but I approached the BJP, and told them that . . . I wanted to be a party worker, and was happy being a party worker. I went for a meeting, and brought 10 to 20 people. When party leaders saw that, they were im- pressed, and made me the ward vice-president.[28]

> If there was a rally then there would be buses and I was asked to send two busloads of people to the rally. I would fulfill the task and that's why I got the position.[29]

Another is to organize an event to demonstrate the size of one's own following, and invite party leaders to it.

> I used to organize various religious programs in the temple here, which people really liked. I would collect money from the residents, and organize feasts and other religious events, where I would also invite party leaders. Residents soon felt like I was someone who could get things done, which is why they started approaching me with their problems. Party leaders also realized that I knew people in the settlement who could work with them. So, this worked both ways.[30]

> I also organized cricket tournaments for kids in the neighborhood, and invited government ministers to it. That's how people got to know me, and my popularity in the neighborhood increased.[31]

Perhaps the most extreme tactics for gaining attention we saw were slum leaders contesting elections against a potential patron as an independent can- didate, if only to show the depth of their own support. As Mumtaz, from Gulab Colony in Bhopal said:

> I contested the election as an independent candidate for the post of coun- cilor. I contested against Asha Jain [the current councilor]. The councilor, she got scared that she might lose. I told her that for me it was a gamble and

28. Interview with Broker 30, Settlement 28, Jaipur, June 10, 2016.
29. Interview with Broker 31, Settlement 29, Bhopal, June 28, 2016.
30. Interview with Broker 32, Settlement 30, Jaipur, June 15, 2016.
31. Interview with Broker 33, Settlement 31, Jaipur, June 21, 2016.

win or loss was in the hands of the Almighty. It wouldn't bother me if I lose [*sic*]. That I'd make a name for myself even if I lose and it was essential that I fought. When counting started and the boxes opened, I got 200 votes. That made her break into sweat; her margin of victory was not much more. When she won, she came to me and treated me with respect. She took me to a rally and directly made me the president of the party at the ward level. She told the leaders that she'd keep me with her.[32]

In sum, slum leaders can become visible to political operatives outside the settlement through a variety of channels: organizing protests, attending party meetings, doing their everyday work within the settlement, and even fighting elections. Elites must then decide which of these leaders to allocate valuable positions. Who within party organizations makes these critical selections?

Who Decides? "Low" Patrons in Indian Cities

Often the focus of machine politics is on charismatic leaders at the very apex of party hierarchies. Yet these "high patrons"—the Tweeds and Plunkitts of the city—do little of the day-to-day work of party-building in India, including decisions over which local broker to bring into their fold. Instead, these decisions are made by "low patrons:" political leaders whose influence is also locally contained. In their study of machine politics in Chicago, Bradley and Zald note that local ward committees "constituted the core of the party machinery. They controlled the selection of candidates for public office as well as the operation of the election machinery that elects the candidates."[33]

In Indian cities, these low patrons frequently operate at the level of the municipal ward. Most prominent are elected councilors like Chandra, who featured in this chapter's opening vignette. Others include the runners-up in ward-level elections; such figures are often the most prominent figures for the losing party. And beyond political candidates are individuals such as the ward- and block-level presidents of party organizations.

These low patrons are often tasked with listing and recommending people for formal *pads* within local party organizations. When asked how local positions were granted, state-level senior party leaders told us:

We consult with our ward level leaders. We say ok, we have to make *padad-hikaris* [officers/position-holders], so give us your feedback about who is

32. Interview with Mumtaz, Gulab Colony, Bhopal, July 4, 2016.
33. Bradley and Zald 1965, pp. 165–6.

deserving for these positions. We have extensive discussions before any selections—ultimately it is their decision. They know what is happening in the ward.[34]

Ward-level patrons repeatedly told us of their recruitment activities:

First, we look for active party workers. We hold meetings, and we see who comes, but also who comes and asks questions, or [who] provides suggestions to questions we ask. Then we ask our workers to hold events—blood donation camps, food donations, and we see who does that? We then look at who is bringing us the concerns of their alley, their area, saying, "brother, help us with this." Finally, we live in this ward, so we go and ask people in their neighborhoods to see who has a good *chhavi* [image].[35]

To select a leader from a *basti*, we go there and see how the person is, how his overall behavior and nature is, which means determining not only whether this person is doing work but also whether people listen to him or not. If we find out that people listen to him, obey him, then we give him give him a small position in the ward.[36]

Many of the areas in which these efforts are made are within slum settlements. Indeed, slum leaders' own statements affirm that ward-level patrons are at the forefront of their integration into a party:

The ward president was the owner of the building where I worked. He asked me to join him in the BJP as a party worker. I joined on the condition that if people came to me for help, he would take the matter further in the party, to people who have political clout, and can get things done. He said yes, and I joined him.[37]

Our interviews confirm the centrality of ward-level operatives in integrating slum leaders into their parties. When asked how they ended up formally joining a party, the most common answer slum leaders gave was through a personal tie to a leader (40% of responses). Further, these interviews reveal their most common initial contact within a party to be a councilor or other

---

34. Interview (part 1) with Patron 2, BJP party worker and Patron 3, BJP ward councilor, Jaipur, February 5, 2017.

35. Interview with Patron 1, Congress Party Ward President, Jaipur, February 9, 2017.

36. Interview with Patron 4, BJP Councilor, Bhopal, February 15, 2017.

37. Interview with Broker 8, Settlement 13, Jaipur, June 4, 2016.

ward-level actor (60%), compared to only twenty-four percent who identified high-level leaders such as a state-level representative (MLA) for their initial contact within a party.

To understand how low patrons make these selection decisions, we conducted a systematic survey of these actors across Jaipur and Bhopal in January–March 2017. Our sampling frame consisted of all municipal councilors as well as the second-place candidates in the past two elections in each city. Given that both cities were dominated by two parties (the BJP and Congress), the inclusion of winners and runners-up usually ensured we were contacting the leading political figure of each party in each ward. Overall, we were able to interview 343 out of a total of 611 such low patrons (a 56% response rate).[38]

It is helpful to combine this 2017 data on patrons with our surveys of 2,199 slum residents (described in Chapter 2) and 629 slum brokers (Chapter 3). This reveals how ward-level patrons, on average, stand above slum leaders within party and social hierarchies, yet are also as embedded within the same localities as slum leaders. This combination of relative privilege and social proximity makes low patrons ideal interfaces between party and slum.

Figure 4.3 compares the career trajectories of low patrons (top panel) and slum brokers (bottom panel). Low patrons enter the party with substantially higher average starting positions (the average level of their first position was 3.28 to 2.24 for slum brokers). Low patrons were also more likely to hold multiple positions, with fifty-six percent of position-holders securing more than two positions, compared to only thirty-nine percent of slum leaders. Those securing multiple positions also rose faster than their slum leader counterparts. On average, among low patrons holding multiple positions, the average rank of their second position was already at a city-level. By comparison, slum leaders only achieved the equivalent average rank by their fourth position.

Demographic comparisons may help account for these differing fortunes. Figures 4.4 and 4.5 illustrate that low patrons are more privileged than both slum leaders and residents. Patrons are less likely to come from minority religions than are slum leaders and residents. Our data reveals that slum leaders enjoy higher monthly household incomes ($341) than the average resident ($190). Yet this difference is dwarfed in magnitude by the gap between both

---

38. 182 of our interviews took place in Jaipur, and 161 in Bhopal.

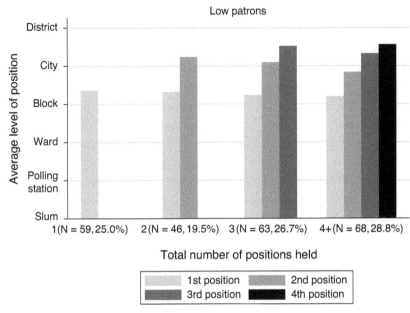

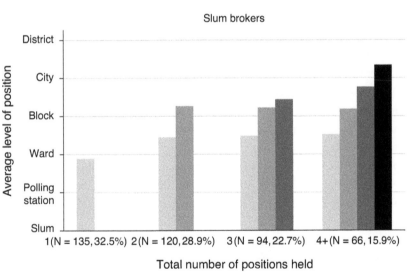

FIGURE 4.3. Comparing Trajectories of Low Patrons and Brokers

Notes: Percentages in parentheses indicate proportion of position-holding low patrons (N = 236) and position-holding brokers (N = 415) within each category.

groups and patrons ($1,620/month).[39] Patrons are also significantly more educated (12 years of schooling on average) than both slum leaders (8 years) and residents (5 years). Notably, our slum leader sample has a much higher proportion of men (88%) than our low patron sample (58%). However, this difference primarily reflects the fact that a third of councilor seats are reserved for female candidates via seat quotas. Patrons are also more likely to have been locally born than slum leaders and ordinary residents. Sixty-nine percent of sampled patrons were born in Bhopal or Jaipur districts, compared to fifty-eight percent of sampled slum leaders and fifty-one percent of sampled slum residents.

Within local party hierarchies, wealthier, predominantly Hindu patrons thus sit firmly above poorer, ethnically diverse slum leaders who are more likely to be migrants.[40] This relative privilege makes sense, given the nontrivial expenses incurred by ward-level electoral candidates. Low patrons self-reported spending an average of Rs. 4.89 *lakhs* (about $7,000, equivalent to roughly four months of the average household income for low patrons in our sample) for their last election campaign. Low patrons reported seventy-one percent of these funds came from their own pockets. Such an amount far exceeds what most slum leaders can afford; it is the equivalent to a slum leader's average income for eighteen months.[41]

Despite their relative privilege, low patrons are also socially proximate to slum leaders, frequently interacting with them to mobilize voters, put on rallies, and discuss resident complaints. The vast majority of the low patrons (79%) live within their local ward, and reported being regularly approached by slum residents and their leaders for assistance. This combination of authority and proximity vaults low patrons to the forefront of deciding which slum

39. Using Rs. 65/$1 conversion (July 12, 2017). Three extreme outliers excluded in slum resident sample ($5 *lakhs* per month and above).

40. We do find low patrons and slum leaders display some important similarities. In terms of caste, the low patron sample is impressively diverse, with 133 distinct Hindu *jati* and Muslim *zat*. 17.2% of respondents were Scheduled Caste and Scheduled Tribe, while 33.53% were intermediate caste (Other Backward Classes); 47.81% were upper caste. The vast majority of sampled low patrons were from the two study states, Rajasthan and Madhya Pradesh (188 respondents, or 93.88%), with the small remainder hailing from Chhattisgarh, Haryana, and Uttar Pradesh.

41. As one leader grumbled, "they saw I was a good activist and connected with me and slowly started to give me posts. But despite being so senior the party didn't give me the councilor's ticket . . . getting a ticket is all about the money today." Interview with Broker 35, Settlement 33, Bhopal, July 1, 2016. Financial concerns may inform the slippery slope slum leaders face in becoming low patrons themselves.

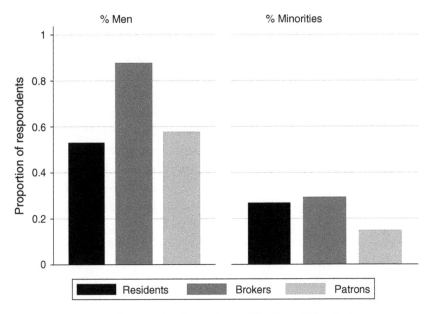

FIGURE 4.4. Demographic Comparisons of Gender and Minority Status
Notes: N (Patrons): 343; N (Slum Leaders): 629; N (Resident): 2194. Source: Author Surveys (2015, 2016, 2017)

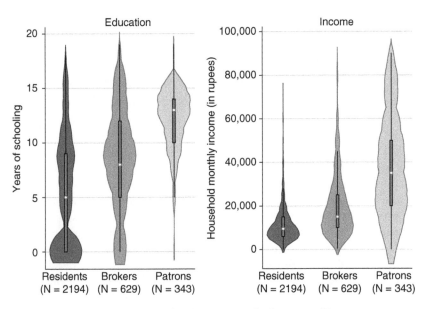

FIGURE 4.5. Demographic Comparisons of Education and Income
Notes: White dots indicate median values. Thick grey bars indicate interquartile range. Outer shape provides kernel density curves. Source: Author Surveys (2015, 2016, 2017).

leaders receive the formal positions the latter crave. And low patrons face strong incentives to get these selections right because effective recruitment enhances their own prospects for rising up the party's hierarchy.[42]

Loyalty and Efficacy: The Twin Concerns of Patrons

How do patrons select the brokers responsible for the daily operations of their local organizations? Processes of broker selection by parties are often obscured by the presumption that such intermediaries exist, and are employed by parties. Studies consequently focus on how parties confront problems with brokers already in their employ, most of which stem from conflicts or misalignments between the various groups' priorities. Studies of how party patrons select brokers have also been limited by an assumed lack of competition between brokers within many formal models of clientelism. An absence of competition renders questions of local selection redundant.

Yet, as we have shown, patrons in competitive environments must carefully choose which brokers to incorporate into their local party networks. Two broad concerns that animate such evaluations emerge from our fieldwork. The first concern is one of loyalty, rooted in the *patron-broker* relationship. In competitive situations, where brokers have options to switch parties, and even to switch bosses within parties, patrons prefer brokers of whose loyalty they can be more assured. We define two types of loyalty: *partisan* loyalty to the party organization, and *personal* loyalty to the patron. The second concern is one of efficacy, and centers on the *broker-resident* relationship. Low patrons looking to advance within party hierarchies must recruit brokers who enjoy popularity among residents, and who can translate that popularity into support during elections. Patrons thus evaluate two dimensions of broker efficacy: a broker's everyday ability to problem-solve for residents, and the broker's election-time ability to mobilize residents to vote and attend rallies.

Personal and Partisan Loyalty

Earlier studies of clientelism assumed brokers were loyal partisans whose interests aligned with those of their party superiors.[43] Recent studies have usefully theorized brokers as autonomous actors with agency and independent

---

42. A majority of low patrons identified slums as the most important constituencies for winning elections (58%), far more than those who identified middle-class (38%) or wealthy (4%) neighborhoods.

43. Stokes 2005; Nichter 2008.

political motivations.[44] However, these accounts typically focus on interactions between a dominant party and a single, locally dominant broker.[45] In these models, both sides have limited options. Parties decide whether to employ a given broker or not, rather than select between brokers. Brokers have no alternative to employment with the dominant machine. Under such conditions, commitment issues are primarily rooted in either different preferences between patrons and brokers over which voters to target, or broker susceptibility to shirk and pocket party resources intended for voters.[46]

The competitive conditions we examine highlight a different concern. Parties must choose *between* multiple brokers within a given locality, rather than decide whether to employ a locally dominant broker or not. Furthermore, brokers can leave their party to join a rival organization, taking supporters with them.[47] Some brokers in our study cities openly discussed their willingness to retaliate against patrons who did not help them meet resident demands, or to support their rise within the party. These brokers noted that they were willing switch parties if their patron was especially neglectful:

> I was in Congress party and I was there for 40–50 years, yet they didn't give me the promotions I deserved. Instead, my [party] seniors started admonishing me, saying without them I am nothing. When they started passing these comments I didn't like them. When Ashok Parnami [from the rival BJP], the chairman of the municipal corporation, who was very courteous in nature asked for my help in the election, I welcomed it and gave him my support and got associated with him.[48]

> I was in the BJP . . . but if the person above you wants to curb your talent, you cannot let your talent be curbed. I am not married to the BJP. I can then move to the Congress party, which salutes me and says, "come join with us, *Sahib*, we will respect you, we will give you posts."[49]

---

44. Stokes et al. 2013; Camp 2017; Larreguy et al. 2016.

45. For single broker models see Gingerich and Medina 2013; Rueda 2015. For multiple brokers with local monopolies, see Gans-Morse et al. 2014; Camp 2017.

46. On differences in the voters each prefers to target, see Stokes et al. 2013; Camp 2017. On incentives for brokers to shirk in their duties, see Larreguy et al. 2016. On efforts by brokers to pocket resources given to them by their superiors to pass on to voters, see Aspinall 2014.

47. Novaes 2017.

48. Interview with Broker 41, Settlement 39, Jaipur, June 7, 2016.

49. Interview with Broker 28, Settlement 27, Jaipur, June 10, 2016.

Over one in four surveyed slum leaders (26.83%) openly stated that they had switched parties at least once. Further, this substantial figure is likely to be an underestimate given that desirability concerns may prompt some brokers to be reticent about directly admitting such acts of disloyalty.

This reality colors the selection decisions of patrons when evaluating brokers. It especially prompts patrons to place a high premium on a broker's *partisan* loyalty, as several ward patrons confirmed.[50] A key way to demonstrate such loyalty is to demonstrate small acts of loyalty to the patron's party *before* seeking a position. For example, brokers may choose to register as formal members with the party, or to show up to party meetings and events.

> I began small—with doing small things for the local meetings the party held—spreading the blankets for people to sit on, providing them tea.

When the interviewer asked, "Why did you do these things?" this broker explained:

> In order to get a little ahead. I thought that if I provide tea and things like that, if I can just put myself in their line of sight, I have a chance of getting ahead. I volunteered to go and hang posters and banners for them, and I began attaching myself to them. Doing little things like this, I managed to sneak myself into the party like a monkey. Over time, as they saw my activities, they saw my value and loyalty to the party, and agreed to make me ward president. Like this, I climbed the ladder.[51]

In other cases, pre-existing affiliations with a party serve as indicators of genuine ideological attachments. While such attachments are less common than instrumental careerism, twenty percent of surveyed brokers mentioned ideological alignment as their primary motivation for joining a specific party.

> The reason behind [my] joining the Congress Party was that it puts weight on Hindu-Muslim unity, puts weight on poor sections of society, SC [Scheduled Castes], ST [Scheduled Tribes], or those of working classes, and the farmer class. I was from a farmer family myself, and my views matched their ideology, so I got connected, that was the main reason. In terms of my post, I am a member, and have been a post-holder. The people

50. As one leader (Patron 14, Bhopal BJP, February 15, 2017) told us, "Loyalty to the party; he must be loyal to the party. This comes first."
51. Interview with Broker 40, Settlement 38, Bhopal, June 28, 2016.

on the top of the party, they decide based on our work who to give the post to. I took the responsibility, fulfilled it on time, and after fulfilling was asked to give it up. That is fine. Whatever responsibility I am given, I fulfill.[52]

I joined the BJP because of the party's ideology. The ideology of *Hindutva* [Hindu nationalist ideology], which is about the nation . . . So many people lured me into leaving the party. They asked me to join their party. They said they'll give me the ticket and a car. But I didn't go.[53]

Slum leaders with pre-existing partisan affiliations might also be seen as more loyal because shared partisan networks enable patrons to collect information about their behavior and commitments before extending a position.[54] Sixty-four percent of surveyed patrons said they used party meetings to obtain information about their cadres, and slum leaders cited regular attendance and assistance at party meetings and events as strengthening their own abilities to get a position.[55]

Concerns over partisan loyalty are complemented by concerns of a broker's *personal* loyalty to the patron. The latter are fueled by the divisive pressures of intra-party factionalism that is widespread across India.[56] Factionalism compels patrons to create personalized networks of power within their own parties in efforts to minimize the risk of losing personnel to rival factions.

Party workers work hard only for those who are close to them. For example, in our area there are ten workers of Congress. Two are very close to me. So, these two workers work very hard for me as compared to the rest of the eight workers who work more for the party or other leaders. It works according to factions. Sometimes workers of the other faction also engage in scheming against workers of my faction. They create roadblocks. It is true that, ultimately, we must fight a different party, but sometimes we have to fight people within your own party. Either you compromise with them or you fight them.[57]

52. Interview with Broker 29, Settlement 27, Jaipur, June 4, 2016.
53. Interview with Ramu, Tulsi Nagar, Bhopal, December 16, 2016.
54. Larreguy et al. 2016.
55. Interviews with Ranvir, Jamun Nagar, Jaipur, June 19, 2016; and Broker 20, Settlement 21, Jaipur, June 4, 2016.
56. Brass 1965; Nellis 2015.
57. Group interview with Congress Party Workers, Bhopal (gas station), January 23, 2017.

Patrons with deep personal networks can also help their own loyalists replace them as they move up the party ladder. As one slum leader told us, "You get promoted within the party when you associate yourself with a local party leader, and work hard for them. When they get promoted, they want to you to take their place since they know you will work hard for them."[58]

It is this imperative for personal loyalty that often compels patrons to choose brokers with whom they share familial or ethnic social ties. Two different brokers explained how they connected with local patrons in this manner:

We connected there and the three of us started working. Because we were *Yadavs* [an intermediate caste][59] and we were close friends, it was my duty to support them. One of them said that he wanted to become the district chairman if he had our support. So we started to reach out to more people in our *Yadav* community. Then we made a team.[60]

One reason for me to join the party was that Surendranath Singh was the district chairman and my older brother was given a post with him. Slowly, slowly he [Surendranath] brought me into the party to work with him.[61]

Conversely, other slum leaders complained that they believed their local patron would not include or promote them, as they came from a different caste:

For instance, both our ward president and vice-president are upper caste. They do not give posts to any SC [Scheduled Caste] and ST [Scheduled Tribe] people. It's not only about me. This is a very bad thing. The general category [upper caste] people don't want SCs and STs to rise in life. It was like a play of kings where a king can only be replaced by his son.[62]

Such tensions were especially apparent as slum leaders in many wards are more likely to come from different ethnic backgrounds than higher-ranking patrons.

There are thus strong reasons to anticipate parties will prefer brokers with shared partisan or ethnic backgrounds. However, especially in competitive

58. Interview with Broker 35, Settlement 32, Jaipur, June 12, 2016.

59. In both of our study states, Yadavs are members of the Other Backward Classes (OBC) administrative caste category.

60. Interview with Broker 39, Settlement 37, Bhopal, July 4, 2016.

61. Interview with Harish, Tulsi Nagar, Bhopal, July 1, 2016.

62. Interview with Broker 38, Settlement 36, Jaipur, June 9, 2016. "General category" refers to members of upper caste communities.

settings, loyalty cannot be the sole consideration. Patrons must consider brokers who are poised to enlarge their own support base. As one patron put it:

> We consider how much support the person gives to the party, how much public following he has, and how much capability he has to connect new people with the party. Whatever support is there already for the party, that won't go anywhere; what matters is how much new support the person can generate. It is based on these criteria that we select people for positions.[63]

Consequently, patrons may weigh the security of loyal brokers against the vote-maximizing benefits of picking off swayable brokers from rival partisan or ethnic networks. While the fealty of poached brokers is highly suspect, the electoral bonus they provide might be considerable. The example of Arun, a slum leader who changed affiliation from the Congress to the BJP is instructive. After several years with the Congress, Arun approached the BJP and told them how he and many of his clients were dissatisfied with how little the Congress had done for their settlement.

> We had a lot of issues with water. So, I went to BJP leaders, and told them that if they arranged water on a regular basis, they would get my supporters' votes. When I first approached the party, they said that since we had supported Congress before, we were going to vote for them again. I assured them that the Congress had not helped us at all. So, we did not want to be associated with them anymore.[64]

Such an offer was risky, but attractive to the local BJP councilor, as successful poaching could deliver a double bonus, enlarging the party's support while also cutting into their rival's base.

Similarly, another leader in Bhopal told us that his upper caste patron specifically looked for a lower caste broker like him to help break into that support base. As one broker explained, he got his post because:

> The BJP didn't have the support of the Scheduled Caste [SC] people. The upper caste leaders wanted people like me to gain access among the SCs. They created a mood of social ease and came to our houses for tea and conversation. They had water at our houses.[65]

63. Interview with Patron 5, Bhopal BJP, February 5, 2017.
64. Interview with Arun, Settlement 35, Jaipur, June 11, 2016.
65. Interview with Ramu, Tulsi Nagar, Bhopal, July 2, 2016.

Thus, patrons must evaluate this trade-off between loyalty and growing their support base when considering privileging shared ethnic and partisan ties with brokers.

Electoral and Everyday Efficacy

Conventional models of clientelism emphasize the role of brokers in monitoring support. Yet, as we have argued, brokers do not simply verify votes, they help win them. Most often, scholars have conceptualized this ability in *electoral* terms, with reference to a broker's capacity to mobilize voters at the polls.

Such electoral efficacy can be gleaned by visible measures such as the size of campaign rallies brokers organize.[66] Some interviewed slum leaders suggested similar measures can prove important:

> A couple of party workers from Congress approached me once in order to get people to attend one of their meetings. They sent around 8 buses, and I got all of them filled with people from the neighborhood; each bus had around 50–60 people . . . That's how party leaders got to know me.[67]

Yet brokers also admitted that slum residents would frequently attend the campaign rallies of multiple brokers, and even multiple parties. As one BJP broker told us:

> Look, just because someone comes to my rally doesn't mean he will vote as I say; he can turn around the next day and go to the Congress rally. He has to *want* to vote for us.[68]

Residents concurred, saying they that would often go to rival party rallies for the food or entertainment, with no compulsion that attendance would obligate them to vote for a particular candidate or party.[69]

More broadly, our interviews suggested the need to look beyond a broker's electoral efficacy, and towards their *everyday* efficacy in claim-making. So how do patrons assess such efficacy? They might cue on the same observable indicators that Chapter 2 demonstrated that clients use to assess broker efficacy.

---

66. Szwarcberg 2015.

67. Interview with Broker 34, Settlement 32, Jaipur, June 4, 2016.

68. Interview with Rajesh, Tulsi Nagar, January 17, 2017.

69. Jamun Nagar Respondent 12, Jaipur, August 18, 2017; Amaltas Colony Respondent 9, Jaipur, August 17, 2017.

In particular, patrons mentioned a broker's education, a trait we argue residents prize in assessing broker capabilities for effective claim-making.

> When looking at *karyakartas* [*party workers*], we do look at education. It is not just about their popularity. Because their skill [*kshamata*] and attitude [*charitra*] is also very important. And if these are not good, then they may do something wrong or stupid, and today's popularity will go in an instant.[70]

> Education is very important for any party worker or party politician. Whether for getting a position in the party or working for the party, education is an important medium for filing applications, getting scheme benefits, so it is important to be educated.[71]

Slum leaders concurred:

> I come from an educated family. So, whenever someone in the slum needed a form filled or help of this sort, I would fill it out. In this way once or twice people came to my place for help. I also went with them to get their official work done. People got to know about me, and then I developed a connection with the people.[72]

> I helped inform people about various government welfare schemes. I also helped the MLA send forms to folks in the settlement . . . to assist them in filling up the forms and submitting them at the right place, which I did.[73]

Of course, everyday efficacy and electoral efficacy can be tightly linked. A broker who is capable in everyday problem-solving also may be able to mobilize more attendees for electoral rallies. Still, the two are analytically distinct, as one patron we interviewed articulated:

> As a *mandal adhyakash* [Level 3 president] in the BJP, I am responsible for identifying who are the most efficient local workers. When judging workers, *we look at some level of education*, the person's behavior, his character, and of course how much *janadhaar* [mass base] he has. It can happen that you select someone who is famous and has a mass base but is uneducated. Their lack of schooling may cause them to make mistakes, and lose their existing support and potential followers.[74]

70. Interview with Patron 6, BJP *mandal* president, Bhopal, February 6, 2017.
71. Interview with Patron 7, BJP ward councilor, Bhopal, February 9, 2017.
72. Interview with Broker 27, Settlement 26, Jaipur, June 15, 2016.
73. Interview with Broker 36, Settlement 34, Jaipur, June 16, 2016.
74. Interview with Patron 6, Bhopal BJP *mandal* president, February 6, 2017. Emphasis added.

The skills required for effectively organizing eye-catching campaign events, bussing supporters to rallies, and other election-time responsibilities are far from identical to those required for mundane but essential tasks such as filling out applications, finding information regarding potential schemes, and contacting government officials. Yet the latter, more mundane skills may prove more crucial in indicating a broker's genuine popularity within the settlement.

Broker Localities

The framework we have outlined thus far largely focuses on individual characteristics indicating a broker's loyalty to patrons or reputation among clients. Yet attributes of a broker's locality may also shape their worth to patrons. For example, parties might consider the size of the neighborhood in which a broker is active.[75] In our setting, brokers embedded in large slums might be considered more valuable than those in small slums.[76]

Party leaders might also weigh the partisan profile of a leader's locality in assessing their worth. Party leaders may prefer to integrate leaders who emerge from strongly co-partisan or co-ethnic settlements. Alternatively, party leaders may regard adding such brokers as redundant, as support from such settlements is more highly assured even without them. Patrons may prefer to incorporate brokers within swing or rival settlements who may enlarge the party's support base. Some slum leaders we interviewed claimed to have leveraged this potential in securing a position:

> Congress has a lot of supporters in the area, but I approached BJP, and told them that people are opportunistic these days, and change party affiliation when provided an attractive enough incentive . . . Once I went for a meeting, and brought 10 to 20 people with me. When [BJP] party leaders saw that, they said that I was helping make the party popular among potential members. They were impressed with that, and made me the *upaadhyaksh* [vice-president].[77]

Thus, patrons in Indian cities must juggle multiple concerns in selecting brokers to include in their parties. The question, then, is how do they balance evaluations of personal and partisan loyalty, and of everyday and electoral efficacy?

---

75. Auerbach 2020.

76. Given that slum leader authority is circumscribed by settlement boundaries, the former has a higher ceiling on a potential following than the latter.

77. Interview with Broker 30, Settlement 28, Jaipur, June 10, 2016.

How Do Patrons Select Brokers? An Experiment

To help understand how political leaders in the city evaluate slum leaders, we embedded a forced-choice conjoint experiment within our survey of low patrons. The experiment was designed to mirror those presented to slum residents and brokers in Chapters 2 and 3. Respondents were asked to evaluate two slum leaders aspiring to be the next ward-level president of their political party. The full question read as follows:

> *Recently, I was speaking to a leader like you in this city. This leader had to advise his party on whom to select as the next party president for his ward. Two local leaders, each from a different slum settlement within the ward, wanted the position. Since there can be only one ward president, the politician could only support one of the two slum leaders for the position. I would like to tell you about these two slum leaders.*

Following this prompt, we provided residents with six pieces of randomized information about each of the two hypothetical slum leaders. This information was presented on a tablet, and was read out loud first, after which respondents were given an opportunity to re-read the information.[78] Respondents were then asked:

> In your opinion, which of these two candidates would you choose to appoint as ward president?
> • First candidate
> • Second candidate
> • Don't know[79]

We presented respondents with four randomized individual leader characteristics—two were conceptualized as indicators of broker loyalty to party and patron (ethnicity and partisanship), and two as indicators of local efficacy with clients (rally size and education). We also varied two traits specific to the settlement the leader resided in (size and partisan composition).

---

78. We preferred this approach to asking the respondents if they wanted to read the question themselves first. This latter approach risked respondents with low levels of education agreeing to read the question rather than risk embarrassment at admitting they may face trouble in reading the text. While most of our respondents were literate, we did not want to bias the experiment against the few who had relatively little schooling (11% had an eighth-grade or lower education).

79. This option was not read out by survey enumerators, but could be marked if the respondent volunteered a "don't know" answer.

The manner in which we conceptualized and randomized each of these six attributes is listed as follows.

Trait 1: Ethnic Identity

To randomize each hypothetical slum leader's ethnicity, we varied their sub-caste or *jati*. To do this we utilized a similar name manipulation as in the prior experiments conducted with slum residents and leaders (Chapters 2 and 3). This manipulation created a *jati* match or mismatch between the patron and the slum broker.[80] These names also identified a respondent as Hindu or Muslim, allowing us to code religious matches and mismatches.[81] Finally, we varied each broker's region-of-origin in the same fashion as in Chapters 2 and 3.

Trait 2: Partisan Identity

With equal probability, we randomly assigned brokers either to be longtime members of the respondent's party, a new arrival into the respondent's party, or a member of the rival party who is considering defecting to the respondent's party. This treatment allows us to examine how shifts in a broker's partisan status influence their probability of being selected by the patron for a party position. We can thereby assess how patrons weigh rewarding members of their own party compared to poaching from rival partisan networks, as well as the significance of differing lengths of shared partisan affiliation.

Trait 3: Electoral Efficacy (Rally Size)

To measure the election-time mobilizing power of a broker, we manipulated the size of a rally the broker was said to have organized during the previous state elections held in the city. Brokers were assigned with equal probability to have organized a 50 (small), 250 (medium), or 400 (large) person rally.

Trait 4: Everyday Efficacy (Education)

We presented qualitative evidence earlier in this chapter suggesting that patrons view education to be an important indicator of an aspiring broker's everyday efficacy among clients. To assess the importance of this trait, we manipulated

---

80. Respondents who were from one of the three pre-fixed upper caste, lower caste, or Muslim *jatis* utilized in the experimental treatments were also coded as co-ethnics of the aspirant.

81. Recall that over 95% of the residents in our sample were Hindu or Muslim.

the broker's level of education. Brokers were randomly assigned to have no schooling, an eighth-grade education, or a college B.A, mirroring the manipulations in Chapter 2.

Slum Trait 1: Population Size

We also manipulated two attributes of the settlement from which the slum broker hailed. In order to vary the electoral heft of the settlement, we manipulated its size. With equal probability, we assigned brokers to reside in slums with a population of 1,000 (small), 3,000 (medium), or 5,000 (large) people. We chose these thresholds because they roughly corresponded to the mean slum population in our sample (2,395), and one standard deviation above and below this mean value.

Slum Trait 2: Partisan Composition

Finally, we manipulated the partisan profile of the slum from which a leader came. Overall, these categories allow us to directly assess how shifts in the partisan status of a slum impacted the likelihood of a broker from that slum being preferred for a party position. Our manipulations were grounded in two different theoretical arguments. The first is a longstanding debate on whether parties will prefer to favor areas of consistent "core" support, or swayable "swing" voters.[82] The second is a more recent argument that politicians will favor slums that vote cohesively over those that have fractured preferences.[83] The latter are seen as providing more efficient electoral yields than slums where individual households have to be wooed one by one.

To explore the role of overall slum partisanship, we made four manipulations with equal probability (25% each). In the first two, a slum was either said to typically come together to vote cohesively and consistently for the BJP, or come together to vote cohesively and consistently for the Congress. In the third manipulation, the slum was said to vote cohesively, but sometimes for the BJP and sometimes for the Congress. In the fourth and final manipulation, households in the slum were said to be fractured, and to vote independently for different parties. In both of the last two treatments, slum residents have exhibited a willingness to vote for either Congress or BJP, but only in the former do residents do so as a cohesive "vote-bank."

---

82. Cox and McCubbins 1986; Stokes 2005.
83. Spater and Wibbels 2020.

These manipulations allow us to code a broker as residing in a slum that was either a "core slum" for the respondent (a BJP-voting slum for BJP patrons, or Congress-voting slum for Congress patrons), a "rival slum" (a BJP-voting slum for a Congress patron or vice versa), a "swing slum" (the third treatment), or a "fractured slum" (the fourth treatment).[84]

How Do Patrons Evaluate Brokers? Some Answers

What traits do party patrons most value in the brokers they seek to incorporate into their local organizations? As with the choice experiments used in Chapters 2 and 3, the experiment here allows us to assess how much each of the traits discussed increases (or decreases) the likelihood of a slum leader being preferred by a patron over another. Our primary interest is in estimating the average marginal component effect (AMCE). The unit of analysis is the rated slum leader profile. Our dependent variable was coded 1 for profiles that were selected from within a pair, while those not selected were coded 0. Each councilor rated three pairs of slum leaders, or six profiles total. With 343 respondents, and no non-responses on this question, we ended up with a total of 2,058 rated profiles.[85]

Figure 4.6 reports the overall results for this experiment. The figure displays both the AMCEs (points) and the ninety-five percent confidence intervals (bars). Recall each AMCE is measured against the baseline values for a given attribute, which are depicted by points without bars.

Let us first consider the results regarding partisanship. According to our results, changing a broker's partisan status from a potential defector from the rival party to a member of the patron's party significantly increases a broker's average probability of selection.[86] This holds true both for longtime members

84. 95% of our patron sample was affiliated to either the BJP or Congress. For independent patrons, we coded both BJP and Congress voting slums as "rival slums." Our results for this attribute do not change if we exclude independent leaders.

85. Recall we attempted to reach each and every eligible candidate for our survey, so our sampled respondents represent an upper bound for the number of subjects who could have been interviewed for this study. Using the cjpowR package in R (Schuessler and Freitag 2020), we calculate the minimal detectable effect (MDE) with this sample size is 6.2 pp for the three 2-level variables, 7.5pp for the four 3-level variables, and 8.7pp for the one 4-level variable.

86. A small number of low patrons (N = 25, 7.3% of all respondents) in our sample professed no partisan affiliation. While these non-partisan respondents have no "party," we include them in our analysis. Given the highly factionalized nature of politics, we believe the partisan loyalty

of the patron's party (9.7 percentage points), as well as new arrivals (7.7 percentage points).[87] This finding suggests that indicators of loyalty are more likely to boost the likelihood of a broker being included within a party network than the vote-maximizing potential of a rival defector.[88]

Second, Figure 4.6 suggests that the role of co-partisanship versus rival defectors is broadly comparable for longtime loyalists and for new arrivals.[89] Thus, the impact of partisan loyalty does not appear to markedly intensify with longevity in the party. We cannot empirically ascertain reasons for this result in our experiment. However, when observing patrons taking our survey we noticed several verbally commenting on the costs and benefits of longtime loyalists relative to new recruits. On the one hand, the fealty of loyalists is more certain, yet, on the other, loyalists also tend to be more assertive and demanding in terms of seeking continued promotions.

Changing a broker's caste from one that differs from the patron to one that matches the patron's caste increases the broker's probability of selection by five and a half percentage points.[90] However, there was no evidence of comparable ethnic favoritism on the broader identity dimensions of religion or region-of-origin. We interpret this as consistent with patrons viewing shared ethnicity as a mechanism for ensuring *personal* loyalty, rather than as a tool for voter mobilization. Using ethnicity as a tool for mobilizing votes would incentivize patrons to privilege relatively broad dimensions for ethnic coalition-building or to abandon ethnic favoritism altogether.[91] Using ethnicity to ensure personal loyalty to the patron conversely privileges the narrowest possible dimension of ethnicity, for which social networks are most likely to be the most tightly knit.

This logic also helps explain the divergent results concerning ethnicity between slum leaders and patrons. Recall that when brokers were asked to

treatment can still be intelligible to non-partisan patrons in factional terms, who can encounter longtime loyalists, new arrivals, and even rival defectors with respect to their personal factional followings. Excluding these 25 respondents does not change any of our substantive results.

87. Both effects are significant at the 99% level.

88. A descriptive preference for partisan loyalists over rival defectors is also apparent if we examine marginal means for all three categories.

89. This conclusion is supported by examining our results using longtime loyalists as the baseline. The AMCE for new arrivals relative to longtime loyalists is only -2pp and not significant (p = 0.436), while for rival defectors it is negative (-9.6pp and significant). An analysis of marginal means also shows preferences for longtime loyalists and new arrivals are similar.

90. This result is significant at the 95% level.

91. Posner 2005.

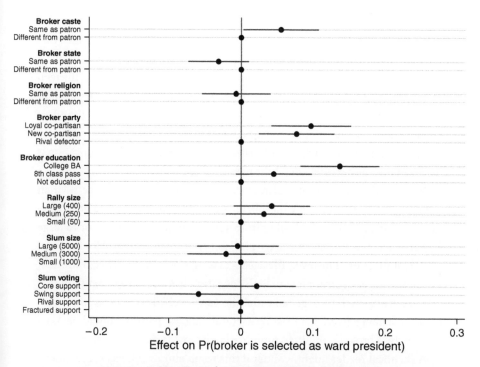

FIGURE 4.6. How Do Broker Traits Impact Patron Preferences?
Notes: N = 2,058 rates profiles. The plot shows estimates for the effects of randomly assigned slum leader attribute values on the probability of being selected for ward president of a local party organization. Estimates are based on an OLS model with standard errors clustered by respondent. Bars represent 95% confidence intervals. The points without horizontal bars denote the reference category for a given attribute.

evaluate potential clients to help (Chapter 3), we did not find a comparable positive effect of shared *jati*. However, we did find that changing a resident's region-of-origin to match a broker's increased the former's likelihood of receiving help. We reasoned this result makes sense given that brokers face incentives to build the most inclusive and broadest possible set of followers in the settlement. By contrast, patrons undertaking the specific task of machine-building arguably face different incentives. Selecting a single ward president is less a game of numbers, and more one of quality control. The penalty of having a disloyal broker to organization-building is likely to be more severe than the penalty of a disloyal voter. Such differences may inform the ways in which ethnicity shapes, and doesn't shape, selection decisions at distinct levels of machine anatomy.

Our overall results reveal the importance of loyalty concerns in shaping patron preferences for brokers. We also find evidence of the importance of a broker's client-facing efficacy. Changing a broker's level of education from no schooling to a college BA increases their probability of selection by over thirteen percentage points (13.6), while the corresponding impact of secondary schooling is four and a half percentage points.[92] As with clients in Chapter 2, the effect of going from no education to college education is the largest registered by any manipulated attribute. In direct comparisons, the impact of college education is higher than that of shared *jati* (at the 96% level) on patron decisions.

Interestingly, this indicator of everyday efficacy is also more impactful than our measure of election-time mobilizing power. Changing the size of an election rally organized by the broker from small to medium (3.2 pp) or to large (4.3 pp) increases a broker's average probability of being preferred for the ward president position. However, these effects were not statistically significant.[93] Furthermore, going from low to high education has a larger impact than that of going from small to large rallies (at the 98% level). This latter result is particularly striking given that existing accounts suggest patrons should be most affected by a broker's ability to mobilize large crowds during elections.

A skeptical reader might wonder if this result simply reflects canny politicians giving us a socially desirable answer: that they simply want to reward well-educated leaders without any thought to narrow electoral concerns. Yet we read this result as entirely consistent with political motivations. We have argued previously that residents are most likely to be swayed by slum leaders who have helped them in everyday claim-making, not those who give them handouts at election time rallies. Moreover, we presented qualitative and quantitative evidence that residents view education as a preeminent indicator

92. The effect for college education is significant at the 99.9% level and for secondary education at the 90% level. AMCEs for both partisan attributes are larger than the MDE for a 3-level variable for our sample size (see footnote 85). However, the AMCEs for our three ethnicity variables are smaller than the MDE for a 2-level variable (6.2 pp). For shared state-of-origin, we note the possibility that the lack of significance for the AMCE (-3.2 pp) may reflect insufficient power (for religion the AMCE is extremely small, at 0.7 pp). For *jati*, we note that our significant result, given power constraints, might be susceptible to Type M and Type S errors. Gelman and Carlin 2014. We find a negligible—less than a 0.0006%—chance of a wrong sign (Type S), and an exaggeration ratio of 1.367 (Type M) indicating slight overestimation (for reference, the exaggeration ratios in the two studies examined by Gelman and Carlin 2014 were 8 to 9.7).

93. For the large rally coefficient, we note that the lack of a statistically significant AMCE (p = 0.114) again may reflect a lack of statistical power.

of a broker's everyday efficacy in Indian slums (Chapter 2). Our experimental results, therefore, are consistent with a view of patrons as valuing educated slum leaders because they believe such leaders are valued by ordinary residents, a squarely strategic calculation. Also, as we show later in this chapter, education positively correlates with actual observed promotion patterns of brokers within party organizations.

Finally, we find that slum-level characteristics play a minimal role in shaping patron preferences in broker selection. We do not find any effects of a broker going from representing a small settlement to a medium or large one. With respect to the partisan status of a broker's slum, we find no impact in shifts from a settlement with fragmented voting to one that cohesively votes for either the patron's own party or rival party.[94] The only slum-level attribute that appears to matter is when we shift the broker's slum to a "swing" status, which decreases their chance of selection by nearly six percentage points.[95]

As in prior chapters, our online supplement includes analyses of our main results partitioned by key respondent characteristics, notably gender, median education (12 years), migrant status, and whether the patron has ever held the ward councilor post.[96] These analyses are for descriptive interest, and should be viewed with caution, given the limitations of our sample size in meeting the

94. As previously noted, a small number of respondents (25 out of 343, 7.3% of our sample) were "non-partisan." In instances where these respondents received petitions from "BJP" or "Congress" slums (79 out of 2,058 rated petitions, 3.8% of our sample), their perception of the settlement could therefore not be coded as "core" or "rival." Instead, we coded such settlements as "fragmented" rather than "swing." We chose to do so because a non-partisan low patron, when considering such a slum electorally, is unlikely to assume they can capture the entire settlement as a cohesive vote-bank (unlike a partisan actor for whom "swing" slums at least sometimes do collectively vote). Non-partisan patrons are more likely to view the settlement as one in which they will need to engage with individual households, some of which can be won over. We also find our results are substantively unchanged if we drop the 25 "non-partisan" respondents from our sample.

95. Note that this AMCE, while statistically significant, is below our MDE for a 4-level attribute (8.7 pp). Therefore, we are again mindful of the chance of Type S or M errors. We find less than a 0.01% chance of a wrong sign (Type S), and an exaggeration ratio of 1.44 (Type M) indicating slight overestimation.

96. The choice of reference category can complicate the use of AMCEs for comparing preferences across different subsets of voters. Leeper et al. 2020. We therefore show conditional marginal means, which allow us to assess differences in preferences in a manner robust to reference category choice. We also provide conditional AMCEs, which show the causal impact of slum leader features relative to the baseline for each subgroup.

substantial power requirements for systematically assessing significant differences across subgroups.[97]

Overall, our results suggest that in making machine-building decisions, patrons are not simply obsessing over the election-time performance of brokers. Instead, patrons primarily evaluate brokers based on indicators of the loyalties and everyday problem-solving capabilities of the individual they are looking to integrate into their partisan and personal team.

Which Brokers Get Promoted?

As in prior chapters, we examine whether our experimental findings align with data on actual outcomes in our study setting. We have already presented considerable qualitative evidence outlining the importance of efficacy and loyalty in patron decision-making. In this section, we seek to validate our experimental findings against observational data collected in the field.[98] Specifically, we examine which kinds of slum leaders experience upward mobility within local party organizations.

To examine broker promotion patterns, we draw on data we collected on the personal career histories of the 629 slum leaders we surveyed. We examine the correlates of the current rank level leaders hold at the time of the broker survey, the highest rank they have ever achieved, and the change in positional rank from their first position to their most-recently held one. Our survey also captured a number of leader traits that are plausible indicators of broker loyalty and efficacy, the twin concerns highlighted in our experiment. Figure 4.7 reports coefficients indicating the impact of a given trait on a broker's current and highest-ever positional rank.

The career histories of the 629 slum leaders lend strong support to our experimental findings. First, several measures associated with everyday efficacy are highly important. Broker education has a strong positive correlation with positional rank. Brokers with some high school (Eighth Class Pass) and college education (College) have a positional rank that is on average 0.8 to 1.4 levels higher than brokers with middle school or less education.[99] Furthermore, engaging

97. Schuessler and Freitag 2020.

98. A recent review essay cites our validation analyses as one of only two such efforts within conjoint experiments in political science reviewed by the authors. Bansak et al. 2020.

99. As we have noted in Chapter 2, education does not serve as an indicator of wealth or privilege in our study settings. Further, in additional models not reported here, we find no

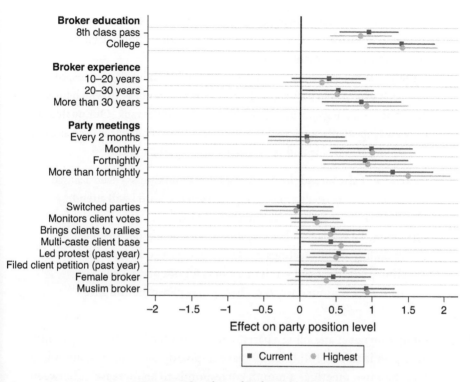

FIGURE 4.7. Correlates of Broker Achievement

Notes: The figure reports results from OLS regressions in which the outcome variable identifies the level of a broker's then-current position (Current), and highest position ever achieved (Highest). Variable ranges from 0 (no position held) to 7 (state-level position). Explanatory variables include three ordinal variables: broker education (omitted baseline is less than eight years), experience as broker (omitted baseline is less than ten years), and broker attendance at party meetings (omitted baseline is no attendance). All other variables are binary indicators.

in both quiet (filing petitions) and disruptive (leading protest) claim-making within the previous year for clients also corresponds to a higher rank, and three of the four coefficients reported in Figure 4.7 are statistically significant. In contrast, we find no strong evidence that parties reward brokers for measures of their election-time efficacy. We do observe positive correlations between positional rank and brokers reporting that they tried to monitor a resident's vote, and reporting they took clients to campaign rallies. However, neither correlation is statistically significant for either outcome variable.

––––––––––

positive result for broker household income, or for brokers who come from politically active or connected families.

Overall, there is stronger evidence as to the importance of everyday efficacy in shaping of broker trajectories, relative to election-time activities, which aligns with our experimental findings.

There is some evidence that traits associated with loyalty correspond to broker achievement in party rank. Notably, the frequency with which brokers attend party meetings positively correlates with broker rank. Our qualitative interviews repeatedly suggested that such meeting attendance is used as a key channel for establishing and verifying loyalty to party and patron.

> BROKER: I also attend the meetings. I don't bunk [miss] even a single meeting. Any small meeting anywhere in the ward I will attend.
> INTERVIEWER: So how did you get this post?
> BROKER: I got this post because they saw my work too. That I am attending all the meetings. So, I keep going to every meeting. This is why they said—this one works for our party; he is a trustworthy ground worker—hence they chose me and gave me this post.[100]

Going from never attending a party meeting to attending one every month corresponds to one full level increase in positional rank, and attending more than two meetings a month corresponds to an increase of between 1.3–1.5 levels. However, perhaps surprisingly, party-switching—a clear sign of disloyalty—is not negatively correlated with achieved rank.[101]

With respect to demographic indicators, broker achievement within party organizations positively corresponds to the self-reported length of their tenure as slum leader. This result makes sense given that such tenure indicates the robustness of a leader's standing within his or her support base. Interestingly,

---

100. Interview with Broker 51, Settlement 41, Bhopal, June 20, 2016.

101. We do not have a firm explanation for this result. Party-switchers are not systematically different from brokers who do not report switching across several observable traits; we find no positive correlation between switching and age, gender, education, or leadership experience. We do have some further information on defections from a follow-up question posed to defecting brokers on their reasons for switching parties (N = 169). Only 10% said they defected because of their previous party losing their majority in an election. More important were concerns about lack of promotion or internal competition within their party (36%) and overtures from rival party workers (16%). These responses further underscore the careerist ambitions motivating broker decisions. These results may also hint at the fact that defecting brokers may switch parties with some informal arrangement to receive a promotion or position as a reward, which might mitigate penalties for defection in overall promotion patterns.

we find no evidence of female and/or minority Muslim brokers holding systematically lower-ranked positions. Seventy-two percent of the female leaders we surveyed held party positions, compared to sixty-five percent of male leaders. Moreover, the average rank of positions women held (2.45) was comparable to that of men (2.50). The chief difference was that women's positions were less likely to be located within the main party organization (27%) than men (43%), and more likely to be in specialized wings, especially within the women's wing (59% of female positions).

Coming from a Muslim background actually corresponds to an increase in expected positional rank. While we cannot definitively explain this result, it may reflect that parties face scarcities in finding minorities to staff key organizational positions. While a similar proportion of Muslim leaders were given positions within the main party as Hindu leaders (38% to 42%), the need to staff the "minority wing" of parties provides an additional place for Muslim leaders to obtain positions.

Figure 4.8 illustrates the results of a similar analysis in which the outcome variable indicates the *change* in a broker's positional rank from their first position to their current position. Most of the key results from Figure 4.7 are replicated in Figure 4.8: broker education is significantly correlated with an increased positional rank, as is attendance at party meetings, and leading protests. Switching parties, monitoring voters, and bringing clients to rallies register no impact. The main differences with the results in Figure 4.8 and those in Figure 4.7 are that broker experience does not systematically correlate with upward trajectories.

Finally, and perhaps surprisingly for many observers of Indian politics, these results are remarkably consistent across the partisan divide. Scholars and observers frequently describe the Congress and BJP as having disparate organizational ethos, stemming principally from the latter's role as the political arm of a wider Hindu nationalist movement. Due to its embeddedness within this wider movement, the BJP is often seen as more organizationally dense than the Congress, staffed by a more ideologically committed cadre drawn to its Hindutva ideology, and with access to a range of grassroots affiliates within the Hindu nationalist "family of organizations," the Sangh Parivar.[102] Yet, among slum leaders, a minority of both Congress and BJP brokers said that they joined their parties for ideological reasons, with the rates highly comparable across both parties. We also see few differences in promotion

102. Anderson and Damle 1987; Jaffrelot 1998; Thachil 2014.

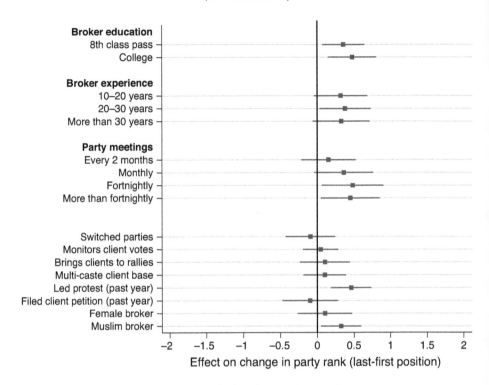

FIGURE 4.8. Which Brokers Get Promoted?

Notes: The figure reports results from OLS regressions in which the outcome variable identifies the difference between the level of a broker's current position and their first position ever held. Variable ranges from -5 to 5. Explanatory variables include three ordinal variables: broker education (omitted baseline is less than eight years), experience as broker (omitted baseline is less than ten years), and broker attendance at party meetings (omitted baseline is no attendance). All other variables are binary indicators.

patterns. We coded a binary variable identifying BJP-affiliated leaders (N = 321, almost exactly half the sample). We then interacted this indicator variable with each of the explanatory variables in our models. For each of our three outcome variables (current position, highest position, and positional rank change), we fail to reject that these interaction effects are jointly indistinguishable from zero at conventional levels.[103]

103. All three F-tests failed to reject the null at 95% levels, and two failed at the 90% level. The one exception (for Current Rank, p = 0.088) is largely driven by female BJP leaders having higher positional ranks than female non-BJP leaders.

Overall, our analysis of broker promotion patterns underscores the importance of partisan loyalty and everyday efficacy, which are also the two dimensions most strongly emphasized in our experiment. Further corroboration of the importance of these traits comes from a phone survey we conducted with 321 slum brokers in 2020, at the onset of the Covid-19 pandemic and subsequent national lockdown. The full results of this analysis are reported elsewhere, but two findings bear mentioning.[104] First, we asked brokers to enumerate (without prompting) any emergency relief schemes they were aware of that were launched during this period, and from which slum residents might derive benefit. We also assessed whether the brokers were contacted by a senior politician in the city offering to provide assistance during the lockdown.

A broker's education (as measured on our 2016 survey) positively correlates with both the number of new welfare schemes they could correctly identify, and whether they had been contacted by a politician during the lockdown.[105] Substantively, a single standard deviation increase in broker education (4.5 years) corresponds to a just over seven percentage point (7.2) increase in the broker's likelihood of being contacted during the 2020 lockdown.[106] Similarly, party meeting attendance in 2016 positively correlates with the broker's likelihood of being called by politicians in 2020. Going from reporting "never attending meetings" to "attending monthly meetings" in 2016 corresponds to a nearly ten percentage point (9.6) increase in the likelihood of being called by a politician during the lockdown in 2020.[107]

The 2020 survey results thus provide compelling evidence that the markers of efficacy and loyalty we highlight throughout this chapter correspond strongly to variations in the performance of slum leaders during a sudden, unexpected, and uniformly imposed test of their problem-solving abilities.

104. Auerbach and Thachil 2021.

105. Our scheme information outcome was measured as a five-point index, where a respondent earned one point for each scheme they were able to identify without prompting.

106. This association was significant at the 95% level. The full results of this analyses are reported in Auerbach and Thachil 2021. Other variables included were leadership experience, partisanship, gender, religious minority status, household income, age, city of residence, alignment with local and state governing party, and whether the leader currently held a party position.

107. This association was significant at the 99% level.

Loyalty *or* Efficacy?

We can combine our experimental data from patrons and our observational data from brokers to assess how the former weigh potential trade-offs in the loyalty and efficacy of different brokers. First, our survey of brokers helps establish that patrons face these tradeoffs in real life. Ideally, patrons would have a surfeit of brokers who are both intensely loyal and highly effective. Figure 4.9 plots the distribution of surveyed brokers along a key dimension of loyalty (frequency of party meetings) and efficacy (years of education). As the sparsely populated top right quadrant of Figure 4.9 shows, ideal brokers—those who are both highly effective and loyal—are relatively rare. Only thirty-six brokers, or roughly six percent of our sample, had *both* at least some college education and also attended party meetings or gatherings on a weekly basis. Overall, broker achievement along these two dimensions is also weakly correlated ($r = 0.14$). Consequently, patrons will frequently choose between brokers who rate highly on only one of the two characteristics.

Our experiment provides some insight into how patrons might make such hard choices. Figure 4.10 compares four candidate profiles, indicating different permutations of education and partisan loyalty from our experiments. Candidate A represents a college-educated co-partisan. Candidates with this mixture of traits in our experiment were selected just over fifty-eight percent of the time in our sample. At the other extreme is Candidate D who has no college education and is a rival defector; this type of candidate was preferred just over thirty-nine percent of the time. Candidates B and C are mirror images, scoring high on education and partisanship respectively, and low on the other dimension. Interestingly, Figure 4.10 illustrates that, on average, highly educated, non-partisan brokers (B) were preferred at a higher rate (56%) than low-educated co-partisans (C, 50%).[108]

We also investigate whether such patterns align with those we observed concerning actual broker achievement. Once again there is evidence of alignment between our observational (Figure 4.11) and experimental data (Figure 4.10). Figure 4.11 charts how brokers with differing blends of efficacy and loyalty fare in terms of their upward mobility within partisan organizations (as measured by the difference in rank between their first- and last-held positions). Consistent with our experimental evidence, brokers who are both highly loyal (attend weekly party meetings and gatherings) *and* highly effective

---

108. This difference is significant at the 90% but not the 95% confidence level (two-tailed).

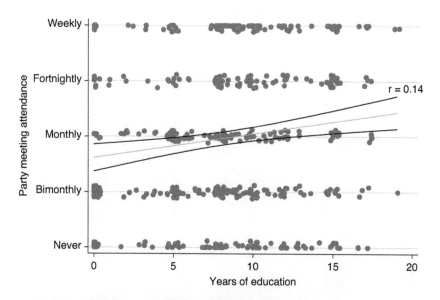

FIGURE 4.9. Loyalty versus Efficacy in Broker Achievement
Notes: The figure is a jittered scatterplot of broker education (x-axis) and party meeting frequency (y-axis). The solid gray line indicates the line of best fit, and the black lines indicate 95% confidence intervals.

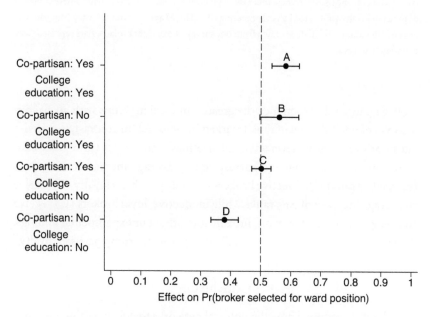

FIGURE 4.10. Loyalty versus Efficacy in Patron Choices (Experimental)
Notes: The plot shows the average probability of being preferred for selection as a president of the slum development council. The estimates are shown for profiles with traits specified on the vertical axis. Bars represent 95% confidence intervals.

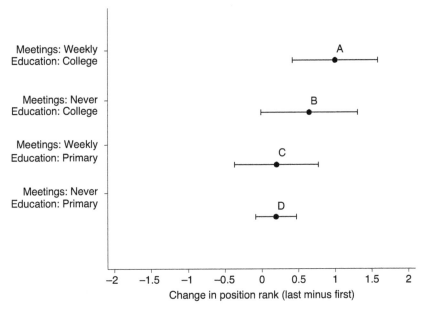

FIGURE 4.11. Loyalty versus Efficacy in Broker Achievement (Observational)
Notes: The plot shows the average increase in positional rank for brokers with different blends
of partisan loyalty (indicated by party meeting attendance) and everyday efficacy (indicated by
level of education). The data is drawn from our survey of 629 slum brokers. Bars represent 95%
confidence intervals.

(college educated) experience the greatest upward mobility, with an average
increase of one full level of rank (marked by point A). In contrast, those who
rate poorly on loyalty (never attended meetings) and efficacy (fifth-grade education or less) experience a corresponding average increase of only 0.19
(marked by point D). Effective brokers who rate poorly on loyalty (B) receive
an average increase of 0.65 ranks while ineffective, loyal brokers (C) receive
an average increase of only 0.2, broadly mirroring our experimental findings.
When forced to choose, everyday efficacy appears to trump partisan loyalty.

Conclusion

This chapter examined how the political networks that form within poor migrant slums, as explored in Chapters 2 and 3, connect to the larger world of
machine politics beyond the settlement. We focused on an important and
neglected channel through which such connections are forged: the selection

of local brokers by party patrons for formal inclusion within party organizations. Focusing on this arena of selection once again highlights underacknowledged aspects of competition, accountability, and representation within the political machines we study.

Competition is essential to the very premise of our inquiry. Prior studies have often ignored the question of how patrons select brokers, because of a deeper neglect of the competition that affords such choice. We show how competition shapes the ways in which such choices are made, underwriting the importance of loyalty in patron evaluations.

Other aspects of our findings illustrate important forms of bottom-up accountability within the hardscrabble world of urban politics in India. Under competitive machine politics, incorporating effective brokers is crucial not only for the patron's own fortunes, but also to keep popular intermediaries away from rival parties. Yet, contrary to common assumptions, patrons do not appear to primarily cue on election-time mobilizing as a signal of broker popularity. Instead, evidence from our interviews, experiments, and data on the career trajectories of actual slum leaders all suggest that patrons place greater emphasis on a broker's ability to help residents, signaled by high levels of education. Indeed, read together, Chapters 2 and 4 reveal that brokers are "twice selected" for their education. First, education positively distinguishes which residents become brokers (Chapter 2). Second, education positively distinguishes which of these brokers will be selected by patrons for inclusion or promotion within their partisan organizations (Chapter 4). This repeated emphasis on education speaks to the importance of problem-solving abilities in machine-building. The fact that patrons are concerned with the efficacy of brokers in helping clients further reveals bottom-up channels of accountability within these organizations.

This chapter further reinforces our call to move away from viewing brokers primarily as shadowy operatives snooping on voters on behalf of their political superiors. Instead, brokers should be viewed as conduits for local representation. Chapters 2, 3, and 4 collectively show that brokers are actively selected by their local communities, and then a subset of these figures are selected for formal inclusion by political leaders. In other words, many of the chosen representatives of slum residents go on to populate mainstream political parties, and some of these chosen leaders even ascend within party hierarchies.

Finally, as noted previously, any analysis of political inclusion also reveals forms of political exclusion. The fact that high levels of education and experience correlate with broker success in party organizations suggests that settlements lacking such leaders are less likely to see their representatives fare well within city politics. For example, roughly a third of the settlements we surveyed did not have a single leader with a college education, while a fifth had three or more such leaders. Newer settlements by definition will have a ceiling on how experienced their local brokers can be. The heightened importance of caste in patron evaluations of brokers, especially relative to broker evaluations of residents detailed in Chapter 3, also hints at dynamics of exclusion. Chapter 5 explores further dimensions of inclusion and exclusion by focusing more squarely on how patrons evaluate requests for assistance put forward by brokers on behalf of their settlements.

5

How Patrons Respond to
Brokered Requests

MUKHTAR'S HOUSE IS PERCHED AT the entrance of Lal Puliya slum, at an intersection where the local road abruptly narrows into a dusty, crooked alleyway that serves as the main thoroughfare of the settlement. If those directions are not specific enough, residents point visitors to the massive green water tank that hovers over Mukhtar's house, which is plastered with a banner bearing his image and a photograph of Ashok Gehlot, the Chief Minister of Rajasthan. A two-time ward councilor between 2004 and 2014, Mukhtar is the most prominent politician in Lal Puliya and the slums surrounding it. He climbed the organizational ladder of the Congress Party in the late 1990s and early 2000s, and, through daily acts of problem-solving, grew such a sizable following in Ward 80 that he could not be denied a party ticket.[1] Mukhtar would have likely still been councilor during the course of our research if his ward had not been reserved for female candidates in 2014.

Ward 80, like many other wards in Jaipur, is almost exclusively composed of slums. The barrage of problems that face local residents is relentless. Most homes are settled on sand dunes, exposing them to the constant risk of soil erosion.[2] Few residents have access to bathrooms. As a result, a four-kilometer-long strip of desert serves as an open-air bathroom for tens of thousands of people. A storm drain running through the center of the ward remains uncovered, creating a breeding ground for mosquitos. Jaipur's sanitation workers rarely come to remove trash. As a result, vacant plots have become impromptu trash dumps. Accessing water is a daily struggle for residents, who

---

1. Author field notes, October 30, 2010; author field notes, July 2016.
2. See Figure 5.1 for a photograph of slum settlements in this part of northern Jaipur.

rely on truck-fed tanks and sparsely placed community water taps. Resident efforts to address these problems are largely targeted at the councilor. Indeed, during his time as councilor, Mukhtar's home was frequently buzzing with constituents seeking assistance.

Most residents in Ward 80 did not have unfettered access to Mukhtar, and, by extension, to his political influence and the public resources under his control. In a context of widespread need and meager public funding, residents must jostle with one another to have their problems addressed, often with the assistance of a local political broker. Indeed, the resources necessary to address even a small fraction of Ward 80's problems far outstrip the modest personal constituency funds allocated to Jaipur's councilors—in the early 2010s, the annual allocation was Rs. 30–40 *lakh* ($60,000–$80,000). Mukhtar, like his counterparts elsewhere in India's cities, was forced to decide how and where to allocate his scarce time and resources. Projects completed during his time as councilor include building a primary school, paving alleyways, and installing two public water tanks.[3] Selecting these projects, and placing them in certain areas of Ward 80 and not others, meant that many other resident requests were neglected. Some petitions must take a backseat to others.

Why are patrons like Mukhtar responsive to some resident claims and not others? Recent scholarship on politician responsiveness has primarily approached this question by examining *unmediated* claims of *individual* voters for *private goods*. Yet the most pressing needs of poor citizens are often for goods and services for their entire community, not simply their own households. Requests for such larger forms of assistance are seldom made directly to politicians by low-income voters. Instead, as in the slums we worked in, requests for *local public goods* were typically made by *brokers* on behalf of *groups* of voters.

Such forms of claim-making play important roles across much of the Global South. For example, the 2016 Afrobarometer survey, conducted across thirty-six countries, finds that the majority (67%) of citizens who contact local officials do so for community problems, and that most (61%) do so in groups.[4] The dearth of studies on brokered group claims is surprising given the rich literature on the role of brokers in mediating citizen access to public services.[5] We view this neglect as rooted in two factors. First, studies of accountability

---

3. Author field notes, October 30, 2010.
4. Afrobarometer (Round 6) 2016.
5. Gay 1994; Burgwal 1996; Auyero 2001; Krishna 2002.

and elite responsiveness emerged from scholarship of elite behavior in the United States, and developed separately from scholarship on machine politics.[6] Second, scholarship on machines has focused on how brokers facilitate top-down vote-buying, rather than bottom-up claim-making.

This chapter addresses this gap by knitting together a focus on elite responsiveness with an attentiveness to the organizational dynamics of machine networks. In particular, we focus on examining distributive preferences of politicians when evaluating claims for local public goods made by brokers. We consider elite responsiveness to brokered requests as important not only for their distributive consequences in shaping citizen access to public goods, but also because these interactions are formative of the machine networks we study.

In assessing mediated claims for local public goods, we argue that politicians like Mukhtar prioritize foremost those petitions that lend themselves to personal credit-claiming. Politician responsiveness is not simply driven by factors emphasized in many studies of distributive politics, namely whether a given locality is a bastion of "core" partisan or ethnic support, or dominated by persuadable "swing" or fixed rival voters. Instead, our data suggest that elites prioritize actions that cut through the complexity of the many state actors and institutions involved in public service delivery to ensure that voters see the politician as the primary benefactor. As we noted in Chapter 4, low patrons in India's cities are themselves ambitious political entrepreneurs who are jostling for promotions and party candidacies. We argue that their responsiveness to constituents is shaped by an understanding that the provision of local public goods ideally should provide opportunities to cement their own personal reputations within electorally influential slums. Consequently, politicians evaluate petitions from slums with an eye towards requests that best afford such credit-claiming opportunities.

Our qualitative fieldwork highlighted three features of petitions that facilitate credit-claiming. The first and perhaps most novel feature was the nature of the good itself. Local public goods vary in the ease with which politicians can take credit for their provision, a fact that has been largely untheorized within studies of distributive politics. Those goods that can be durably and clearly claimed by a politician will be prioritized over those goods that are fleeting in their provision or opaque in their source. The second feature is the population of voters who make up the target audience behind the petition.

6. Butler and Broockman 2011; White et al. 2015; McClendon 2016.

Slums vary widely in their sizes. Word of a politician's assistance can reverberate across a more expansive number of voters in larger slums—even beyond those residents who immediately benefit from the delivered good—giving politicians bigger reputational spillovers for the same unit of resources.

The third feature highlighted by our framework concerns the nature of the broker spearheading local demands. Existing scholarship on unmediated exchange has often focused on whether a politician is directly aligned along partisan or ethnic lines with his or her constituency. By contrast, our focus on credit-claiming and mediated exchange makes a novel theoretical intervention by considering the ethnic and partisan nature not only of the constituency, but also of the petitioning broker. Our qualitative work especially highlights the importance of a broker's partisan identity to patron evaluations. Co-partisan or persuadable, unaligned brokers facilitate credit-claiming efforts in a variety of ways, from spreading word of the politician's patronage to mobilizing crowds for ribbon-cutting ceremonies. Rival party brokers are less likely to assist in these efforts, reducing incentives for politicians to respond to their petitions.

To investigate the factors that shape the responsiveness of city politicians to mediated claims for local public goods, we conducted a petition experiment with the 343 low patrons across Bhopal and Jaipur we first introduced in Chapter 4. Low patrons in urban India are routinely bombarded with petitions for public services, forcing them to decide where to allocate scarce resources. Our experiment provided three broad types of information to politicians: the social and political characteristics of the broker (a slum leader) making the claim; the larger demographic and political characteristics of the slum settlement for which the claim was being made; and the nature of the local public good requested—which varied in the degree to which the good enabled credit-claiming activities.

Our first set of findings align closely with a credit-claiming logic. We find that politicians are more likely to respond when the local public good in question will be durable in its presence and can be easily physically tagged by the politician—qualities that facilitate credit-claiming. Indeed, shifts in the nature of the good requested produced the strongest impact on a petition's likelihood of eliciting a response across all the attributes manipulated in our experiment. More modest evidence indicates that a slum's population—the number of voters through which word of a politician's patronage can spread—can influence political responsiveness.

FIGURE 5.1. A Squatter Settlement in Northern Jaipur

Our second set of results concern partisanship. Consistent with our theoretical framework, patrons are sensitive to shifts in the partisan profile of brokers, evidenced by a penalty against rival party brokers. We interpret this result as reflecting that opposition party brokers are less likely to help broadcast word of a politician's patronage, diminishing the latter's opportunity to cleanly claim credit. However, contra conventional expectations, we do not find that changing the partisan profile of the settlement has an effect on patron evaluations of petitions.

Our third set of findings concern ethnicity. Again, our results cut against prior assumptions in scholarship on distributive politics. We find no evidence of ethnicity playing a significant role in structuring politician responsiveness to brokered, group-based claims. Changing the ethnicity of the petitioning broker, or the broad ethnic composition of the settlement, to match the patron's does not increase the likelihood of the petition being prioritized. These results are consistent with evidence presented throughout this book on the need for politicians to construct multi-ethnic coalitions in diverse Indian cities. As documented in Chapter 3, slum brokers also construct multi-ethnic followings, creating linkages among residents, brokers, and patrons that are not constrained by co-ethnicity. We also have demonstrated that slums are not rigid ethnic "vote-banks," most strikingly evident in patterns of Muslim involvement with the Hindu nationalist BJP. Fluid patterns of electoral support and inter-ethnic networks muddle expectations of how a slum's ethnic composition will predict electoral behavior, encouraging politicians to look elsewhere for reasons to respond to or to ignore a petition.

This chapter begins with more in-depth descriptions of India's ward councilors—the "low patrons" of urban machines—based on our interviews and survey data. We first introduced these individuals in Chapter 4, where we emphasized their roles in incorporating brokers into party organizations. In this chapter, we focus on describing these patrons' problem-solving activities, and the public resources they have at their disposal to meet resident demands. Erecting this descriptive scaffolding is important, as there are few studies on local representation in India's cities. Indeed, our survey of ward-level politicians is, to our knowledge, the first detailed, face-to-face survey of these actors in India. Our data establish these actors as key players in distributive politics, motivating our study of their distributive preferences.

India's Municipal Councilors at Work

Following India's decentralization reforms in the early 1990s, municipal governments became a constitutionally enshrined third tier of government, with regular elections every five years and responsibilities over public service provision.[7] Municipalities are divided into wards, with each ward having an elected councilor (*parshad*) who represents that ward in the municipal body. At the time of our councilor survey in January 2018, there were ninety-one and eighty-five wards in Jaipur and Bhopal, respectively. Municipal elections in both study states are partisan, with candidates running on party labels. The elections also feature reservations for women, Scheduled Castes, Scheduled Tribes, and, in some states (including Rajasthan and Madhya Pradesh), Other Backward Classes.[8]

Ward councilors are the most accessible points of elected representation in India's cities. In a nationally representative survey of over 40,000 citizens, respondents were asked whom they would approach if they had difficulty in getting important work done. Among the nearly 13,000 urban respondents, nearly twenty-seven percent (26.7%) mentioned the ward councilor, compared to just under twelve percent (11.7%) who mentioned state-level MLAs and just over two percent (2.1%) who mentioned national MPs.[9]

In Jaipur and Bhopal, the average ward populations during the 2009–2014 period were 39,557 and 25,689 people, respectively.[10] State assembly constituencies

7. See Bardhan and Mookerjee 2006; Baud and de Wit 2008.
8. On municipal reservations in India, see Bhavnani 2009 and Auerbach and Ziegfeld 2020.
9. Only one selection was permitted. Data from: Azim Premji University and Lokniti 2019.
10. Census of India 2011.

in Rajasthan and Madhya Pradesh have roughly 350,000 constituents—an order of magnitude larger than city wards. Parliamentary constituencies across India have on average 2.5 million constituents.[11] Most of the then-current or former ward councilors we surveyed (161 of 201) live within the wards they represent, further underscoring their status as grassroots representatives. Describing the proximity of the ward councilor vis-à-vis their constituents, one councilor said:

> I call being a *parshad* "*rajniti ki* nursery" [the nursery of politics]. Because this is where we have the most direct contact with our voters—the very bottom level of elected office. This means we are involved in every aspect of a voter's life—we will even be involved in familial disputes where we have to help. Now compare that to an MLA or MP who lives in a bungalow with armed guards. Very few people have the *himmat* [courage] to approach them. But we are in close contact; just like a *sarpanch* [village council president] is in a village, so a *parshad* is in town.[12]

Councilors attract a dizzying variety of claims for public goods and services, even for goods and services over which they have no direct authority. Councilor positions can serve as springboards to higher offices and government departments under the control of the state government, or provide enough political leverage to get a recalcitrant official to move forward with a project for constituents. One councilor in Jaipur described the variety of problems that make their way to him and his counterparts in the city:

> If you have a water problem, call your *parshad*; if you have a light problem, call your *parshad*; if you have an overflowing gutter, call your *parshad*; if a cow is blocking your garage, call your *parshad*; if your son got into a fight with the police, call your *parshad*; if the mother-in-law is fighting with the daughter-in-law, call your *parshad*![13]

In most wards in Jaipur and Bhopal, councilors have their own offices where day-to-day constituency service is conducted.[14] Nearly half (49.75%) of our

---

11. Vaishnav and Hintson 2019.

12. Interview with Patron 8, Congress Party ward councilor, Bhopal, January 19, 2017.

13. Interview with Patron 9, Congress Party ward councilor, Jaipur, February 7, 2017.

14. The descriptive statistics in this section are based on the 201 (of 343) politician respondents who won a municipal election (either in 2009 or 2014) and served as councilors. The remaining 142 respondents ran for municipal office but came in second place, and so they lacked

surveyed councilors reported that they meet with constituents at these ward offices. The second most common location is a public place (22.39%) like a community center or park. To provide an example, there is a public square in New Market, Bhopal, where you can often find the local councilor passing time and meeting with constituents. Nearly eighteen percent (17.91%) of surveyed councilors noted that their public business is primarily carried out in their home. In Rudra Nagar in Bhopal, for instance, the councilor turned his living room into a place for meetings with constituents. Salty snacks and tea are always available. Other councilors reported meeting constituents in party offices or the municipal building. There is some evidence of gendered differences in these frequencies, with surveyed female councilors more likely than surveyed male councilors to meet constituents in their ward office (55.56% vs. 45.05%) or a public place (25.56% vs. 19.82%), and less likely (13.33% vs. 21.62%) to hold meetings in their own homes.[15]

The average councilor in our sample visited the *nagar nigam* (municipal building) nearly seventeen (16.47) times a month. Male councilors tend to visit the *nagar nigam* more often than their female counterparts (17.31 times vs. 15.44 times).[16] These visits are not usually to perform legislative activities, but more often to push city bureaucrats into releasing funds for local development projects. When such efforts fail, councilors sometimes resort to protests as means of intensifying pressure on officials. On average, nearly sixty percent (59.20%) of our surveyed councilors (63.06% among male councilors and 54.44% among female councilors) reported having organized a protest to demand attention to ward-level problems.[17]

Councilors are allocated discretionary funds that they can use toward local public works. While modest, especially in comparison with the discretionary resources at the disposal of MLAs and MPs, councilor funds are nevertheless actively sought out by constituents. We find slum leaders to be well-versed in how to request these funds. For example, Jagdish, the slum leader of Saraswati

---

the councilor experience required to answer these specific survey questions. 90 of our 201 respondents (44.78%) who were current or former ward councilors were women.

15. These differences are not statistically significant at conventional levels. This lack of statistical significance may reflect insufficient power to detect within-sample differences between men and women.

16. This difference is statistically significant (Welch two-tailed t-test, $p < 0.05$).

17. This difference between male and female councilors is not statistically significant at conventional levels.

that we met in Chapter 2, knew to petition his councilor for paying for piped water and drains, and even knew how much funding his councilor receives and used that information to persuade him. With the permission of the city commissioner (an unelected bureaucratic official), councilor budgets can cover local public goods such as storm drains, water tanks, paved roads, community centers, spot cleaning, sewers, and streetlights. To provide a few examples from Jaipur: in 2010, Rs. 1.67 *lakh* (U.S. $2,570) was spent in Ward 35 for sewer, road, and drainage work. In 2008, Rs. 0.78 *lakh* ($1,200) was spent in Ward 66 to install a water tank.[18] These types of public works are multiplied thousands of times over across the city in any given year.

We asked the 201 current or recent councilors in our sample to list the last several types of public services that they had provided constituents through their annual discretionary budget.[19] The most common type of project was roadwork (148 respondents)—specifically, paving and repairing streets. The second most common project involved water provision (111 respondents)—for example, laying water pipes, installing hand pumps, digging bore wells, and placing water tanks. Other common projects included sewer work (63 respondents), constructing parks (44 respondents), installing or fixing streetlights (48 respondents), and dispatching sweepers to remove solid waste from drains and streets (42 respondents). Less common were building community centers (9 respondents), health facilities (6 respondents), and public schools (14 respondents), as well as dealing with electrical maintenance (10 respondents).

Councilor efforts to solve constituent problems are not conducted with a quiet modesty. Instead, councilors exert considerable energy to make sure that constituents are aware of their efforts. Councilors will often "tag" infrastructure they provide to neighborhoods—for example, community centers and water tanks—with painted signs. Some neighborhoods even have massive gates that display the name of their political patrons. Other acts of credit-claiming take place in public gatherings, where councilors give speeches and remind residents of their acts of patronage. These events often coincide with the construction of a local project. Local party workers are tasked with organizing these events and bringing out crowds of residents.

18. These examples come from ward-level councilor expenditure reports that we collected from the Jaipur Municipal Corporation in 2011.

19. 197 of 201 respondents provided at least three examples.

FIGURE 5.2. Credit-Claiming on Social Media

Notes: Photos from the Facebook page of Chandra, Congress Ward Councilor, Bhopal. Photo on the left is from a *bhoomi-pujan* [equivalent to a ribbon-cutting] ceremony for a new gutter in a slum. Photo on the right is from a protest with Congress leader P.C. Sharma, a then-current state-level legislator [photos from public Facebook page, used with permission, granted 2/7/2017].

Reputation-building strategies take on more technologically savvy forms as well. Many of the politicians we encountered in Jaipur and Bhopal have carefully curated Facebook pages that document their acts of constituency service. Take Chandra, the Bhopal councilor we met in Chapter 4. An eager party worker maintains a Facebook page for Chandra that is devoted to broadcasting Chandra's *samaj seva*, or social work. This page regularly features pictures of Chandra at public events (see Figure 5.2). Some photographs show off his connectivity, with him standing next to state and national-level politicians. In other photographs, Chandra is surrounded by party workers, distributing food to poor constituents.

These efforts are not simply self-aggrandizing behavior. The need for patrons to craft individualized reputations is understandable given the considerable personal risks and expenses they are expected to bear in order to contest municipal elections. Even relatively powerful parties like the BJP and Congress rarely provide the majority of campaign funds needed by candidates for low-level councilor positions. While exact figures on campaign finance in India are notoriously difficult to collect, we did ask patrons to estimate the proportion of funds they received from different sources.[20] Respondents estimated that on average only about five percent of their campaign expenses

20. Kapur and Vaishnav 2018.

were funded by the party, compared to seventy-one percent that they self-financed (the remaining 24% came from private donations from supporters).

In summary, India's municipal councilors are important nodes of problem-solving and public spending. They possess discretionary budgets, and are able to exert influence over municipal government as well as other departments engaged in public service delivery. The resources and time for these activities are limited in the face of widespread claims, forcing councilors to prioritize the needs of some constituents over others, and to seek to maximize credit for their acts of responsiveness.

How do Slum Residents Make Claims for Public Services?

Before considering the factors that guide political responsiveness to resident claims, it is important to first establish, in context, how citizens make those claims. This is because the shape of how claims are made—the actors involved and the strategies those actors employ—inform what political elites must consider in deciding which claims to respond to and which claims to ignore. In this section, we draw on our survey data and fieldwork to establish that slum residents' demands of urban patrons are often marked by three traits: they tend to be group-based, mediated, and related to assistance for local public goods.

A first important element of claim-making in India's slums is that it is often conducted in groups on behalf of the neighborhood. This is especially note-worthy given that much of the literature on politician responsiveness within local distributive politics focuses on how ordinary citizens directly engage with the state as individuals.[21] While this premise captures an important form of citizen engagement with the state, it overlooks the frequent group-based nature of claims for local public goods.

Slum residents often present themselves to officials in numbers to signal *lok shakti*, or people power. For example, they gather in groups to travel to government offices to raise demands and submit petitions. In an earlier author survey conducted within eighty slum settlements in Bhopal and Jaipur, an impressive eighty percent of resident respondents (1,544 of 1,925) reported that people in

---

21. Such studies of responsiveness in India include Gaikwad and Nellis 2017; Kruks-Wisner 2018; Bussell 2019; Vaishnav et al. 2019.

their settlement engage in this activity.[22] Fifty-two percent of respondents said that they had engaged in forms of group claim-making in the previous twelve months.[23] Group claim-making is not a male dominant activity—nearly fifty percent of female resident respondents (48% or 433 of 897) reported personally engaging in group claim-making within the previous twelve months.[24] In some instances, a slum leader acts on behalf of the group and visits the official alone to submit a petition. These petitions frequently include appended pages of resident signatures and fingerprints, making it clear that a group of voters stands behind the request, and that failure to act may force residents to protest.

A municipal councilor in Bhopal provided an example of a group claim:

> Two months ago, about fifty people came to me. Forty were women and [the] rest were men. One person said, "We don't have a gutter in our area." The women said, "We don't have [a] road;" and someone said, "We don't have water." I asked them, "What is it that you would want to be resolved first?" I said, "Is it water?" They said, "No, we will arrange for filling water." Then I asked, "Do you want a gutter?" They said, "No, we want a road first." Now, there are four streets, which one should be paved first? All four will cost a lot of money. There is only one main road and that should be paved first; everyone agreed to work on the main road first; alleyways can wait . . . So, we have initiated the process for the main road. It will cost Rs 4.5 *lakh* [US$6,500]; its tender has been passed and work will begin by 5 March.[25]

Group claims highlight the importance of the neighborhood and not simply the individual citizen within distributive exchanges. Residents and slum leaders submit petitions for public services for their settlements. Politicians, moreover, do not look out across their constituencies and see a mass of spatially undifferentiated voters. Instead, our interviews with politicians revealed that they have a detailed sense of the neighborhoods in their respective constituencies. The

22. Survey respondents were asked, "Do people in this slum ever gather together in groups to meet political leaders (the ward councilor, MLA, or MP) or government officials to ask for development or solve a problem in the slum?" Auerbach, 2020, p. 95.

23. Auerbach 2016.

24. Auerbach 2020, p. 95.

25. Interview with Patron 10, Congress Party ward councilor, Bhopal, February 14, 2017.

hundreds of petitions we gathered from slum leaders—most of which are composed on letterheads that state the settlement's name—demonstrate that the *settlement* is firmly situated within the framing of claims:

> **Petition 1:** In the last 15 years, the residents of *Rudra Slum* have not received any government services meant for them. Efforts at poverty relief, especially those meant for the empowerment of the settlement's women as well as those meant for family welfare, have been absent.[26]

> **Petition 2:** In *Pahari Slum* there are three dangerous pits. When it rains they completely fill with water. Because of this, life is very difficult for the people living here. Moreover, children go into the pits to bathe. This water is dirty and as a result children suffer from skin problems. Moreover, children sometimes die when jumping into the pits. We request the minister solve the problems of the poor residents of *Pahari*.[27]

> **Petition 3:** We live in *Durga Slum*. Sewage water from the officials' houses is seeping out of the drains and coming into our shanties . . . because of this, most small children are sick with fevers. Water and trash are accumulating. We request you, sir, to stop this sewage water from coming into our shanties. Properly drain the water so we can be rid of this filth.[28]

A second important element of claim-making in India's slums is that slum leaders are frequently at the helm of resident efforts to petition officials for public services. Our data from residents, ward councilors, and slum leaders themselves attest to the centrality of these actors in spearheading resident claims. Sixty-five percent of resident respondents who acknowledged group claim-making noted that slum leaders are involved at least sometimes.[29] Seventy-two percent of surveyed councilors reported that slum leaders sometimes make in-person demands on behalf of residents.[30] Of this subset of

26. Petition sent to area MLA and mayor, December 24, 2000. Italics used to indicate slum name.

27. Petition written by Bhaiya to state minister, July 24, 1998. Italics used to indicate slum name.

28. Durga development committee documents, October 8, 1994. Italics used to indicate slum name.

29. Auerbach 2020, pp. 95–96.

30. Only 31 of 201 councilors said there were not any slums in their ward. The average councilor said that 28.24% of their ward's population is in slums, with a standard deviation of 25.74%.

councilors, forty-one percent mentioned that slum leaders mostly visit them alone to make claims. A similar percentage (40%) reported that slum leaders are usually accompanied by a group of residents; the remainder stated that slum leaders visit both alone and alongside residents.

Surveyed slum leaders corroborated this pattern of intermediation. Ninety-three percent of our surveyed slum leaders (587 of 629 slum leaders) reported heading resident efforts to demand public services. Eighty-six percent (542 of 629 slum leaders) also claimed to have filed a petition for public services in the past year, and sixty-six percent (418 of 629 slum leaders) reported having organized protests, also within the past year. These efforts align with the careerist ambitions of slum leaders in competitive settings. As our analysis in Chapter 4 showed, organizing protests and filing petitions both positively correlate with a slum leader's achieved rank within party organizations.

Political Responsiveness to Slum Resident Claims

City politicians must prioritize among the many daily requests they receive from slum residents; there just isn't enough time or financing to do them all. How, then, are such decisions made? Our framework emphasizes the importance of credit-claiming in structuring politician responsiveness. Second, we center our analysis on mediated, group claims for local public goods. These contributions jointly focus attention on several relatively under-emphasized features of claim-making: the nature of the good requested, the characteristics of the broker spearheading the claim, and the size of the settlement making the request. In the following sections, we outline the specifics of how these concerns manifest within patron evaluations of petitions, alongside a more typical focus on the ethnic and partisan profile of the constituency from which a demand emanates.

The Type of Good

A small yet burgeoning literature on the political economy of development describes divergent forms of political responsiveness based on the extent to which a politician can claim credit for providing a public good or service. Harding and Stasavage, for example, find that governments in Africa's democracies are more likely to emphasize policies within the public education sector that can be clearly traced back to their actions (for example, the abolishment of school fees) rather than policies over various educational inputs that are muddied in their attribution because of the involvement of local governments and various service providers.[31]

We encountered many examples of India's city politicians going to great lengths to claim credit for having provided local public goods. When government medical camps or ration card drives were held in slums, the MLA or ward councilor often attended the event to be seen as the benefactor. Water tanks were tagged with the names and party symbols of those elected representatives who placed them in the locality (see Figure 5.3). When infrastructure was placed in settlements, elected representatives would frequently organize ribbon-cutting ceremonies. Party workers gathered crowds of residents and distributed sweets. These credit-claiming efforts are central to political reputation building.

Public goods and services are not equal in the clarity of their attribution. Consider the following three types of goods or services, which sequentially diminish in the ease with which politicians can claim credit for them—water tanks, health camps or "ration card" drives, and paved roads.[32] Water tanks are permanent fixtures in slums that are located in areas where crowds of residents gather to wait for water trucks and trade gossip. A tagged water tank can double as a billboard that permanently advertises the patronage of the politician. A government health camp or ration card drive provides very public opportunities to engage a crowd of residents. Residents must attend the event to avail themselves of these services, ensuring politicians a large crowd. These events, however, are more fleeting in their presence than a water tank, diminishing their usefulness as a visual source of the politician's patronage. Paved local alleys can neither be easily tagged, nor are they amenable to the broadly attended credit-claiming events associated with health camps or ration card drives. We expect petitions for public goods and services that lend themselves to durable credit-claiming, such as water tanks, to be prioritized over those that are more challenging to claim credit for, such as paved roads.

Neighborhood Size

Our qualitative work revealed that a settlement's *population* is another important factor from a credit-claiming perspective. The population sizes of the slums in India's cities vary widely. The average slum in our sample has 2,395

---

31. Harding and Stasavage 2014. See also Harding 2015.

32. "Ration cards" in India grant the holder's family access to subsidized food purchases through a public delivery system.

FIGURE 5.3. Water Tank Tagged by Area Ward Councilor

residents with a one standard deviation of 2,957 residents. Our smallest settlement has just 307 residents; the largest, 23,811. A slum's population is an obvious
indicator of the number of votes that can be attracted from that settlement.[33]
A unit of resources spent in a larger settlement can have greater reputational
reverberations than a unit of resources in a smaller settlement.

This simple logic of numbers emerged as a key theme in our interviews
with city politicians. To provide just one example, in response to a question
as to which kinds of *bastis* [slums] usually attract the parties, one politician
responded:

Bastis where the number of people is large.[34]

Against the backdrop of the literature on distributive politics, it is not
obvious that patrons will be more responsive to requests from larger slums.
First, much of the valuable literature on politician responsiveness centers analytically on individual voters, not the demographics of the neighborhoods in
which they reside.[35] Second, some studies of clientelism in fact anticipate that
machines will target *smaller* settlements because those are precisely the types
of places that are easier to monitor.[36] Along these lines, Veenendaal writes,
"in small societies there is a direct, unfettered, and reciprocal relationship between patron and client, resulting in a stronger position of clients vis-à-vis
patrons."[37] In contrast, our framework anticipates that larger settlements
should receive disproportionally more attention because of their more expansive numbers of voters.

Partisanship in Brokered Exchanges

How might the political characteristics of localities shape political responsiveness? Scholars have long asserted that the allocation of public resources
flows along partisan lines in settings marked by non-programmatic distribution. Politicians have been argued to favor *core* settlements—those that

33. Our qualitative and historical research demonstrates that inter-settlement political organization—thereby increasing numbers—is exceedingly rare. See Auerbach 2020.

34. Interview with Brajesh Singh Rajput, Fall 2017.

35. Examples include McClendon 2016; Bussell 2019; Gaikwad and Nellis 2021.

36. See Stokes 2005, pp. 322–23; Nichter 2008, p. 28; Nichter and Peress 2017, p. 17. This expectation is again often formulated with a focus on individual-level benefits.

37. Veenendaal 2019, p. 1035.

overwhelmingly support their own party, and do so in a stable, predicable manner. This preference might reflect risk-averse actors favoring areas most likely to repay the favor, or the fact that the loyalty of these areas is endogenous to benefit receipt: politicians must favor core supporters to keep them as core supporters.[38]

In our study cities, municipal politicians illustrated how this preference for core settlements might manifest. One noted that, "The first priority is given to the slums where you are "damn sure" [said in English] you have support from the slum."[39] Another municipal politician echoed this sentiment, "We will first help those who are aligned with us, those who have always helped us, and stayed with us."[40]

A contrasting expectation is that politicians will target swing neighborhoods, that is, those that oscillate in their partisan support.[41] The logic here is that, assuming core neighborhoods are likely to support the politician anyway, it is more expedient to allocate scarce resources to neighborhoods that are on the fence. One councilor, for example, noted, "See, there are many slums that frequently switch between parties; we would like those slums . . . where our vote bank can be converted into a permanent one."[42]

However, irrespective of whether politicians favor core or swing areas, an underlying assumption of both models is that patrons can easily classify localities into either category. However, in reality, India's urban politicians are often stymied in such efforts by slums that exhibit substantial volatility in their patterns of electoral support. Rarely can they be "damn sure" of the extent to which a slum is a "core" or "opposition" settlement. A substantial proportion of our resident respondents across the 110 sampled slums are swing voters (34%), changing the party they support from election to election. Furthermore, these

---

38. Numerous studies of machines demonstrate core targeting. Democratic party ward bosses in cities like New York and Chicago famously doled out jobs, money, and public services to party supporters in low-income neighborhoods. Gosnell 1937; Erie 1988. Chubb 1982 documented how the Christian Democratic Party in southern Italy targeted party supporters for particularistic benefits. More recent literature finds similar targeting across the Global South, including Argentina (Calvo and Murillo 2013; Camp 2017), Mexico (Diaz-Cayeros et al. 2016), and rural India (Dunning and Nilekani 2013).

39. Interview with Patron 8, Congress Party ward councilor, Bhopal, January 19, 2017.

40. Interview with Patron 12, ward councilor, Bhopal, February 20, 2017.

41. Dixit and Londregan 1996; Stokes 2005.

42. Interview with Patron 13, Congress Party ward councilor, Bhopal, February 6, 2017.

voters are well distributed across settlements: in 100 settlements at least twenty percent of sampled respondents identified as swing voters.

Many settlements, moreover, are not only fluid in their electoral behavior but are also internally fractured in the partisan preferences of residents. Across our 110 sampled settlements, forty-seven percent of respondents supported the BJP (with a standard deviation of 21 percentage points) and forty-one percent of respondents supported the Congress (with the same standard deviation). In an impressive fifty-eight settlements, at least thirty percent of sampled respondents identified as supporters of the BJP while another thirty percent identified as supporters of the Congress.[43] In this political context, politicians cannot be too confident about the current partisan leanings of a settlement. Such fluidity may lead politicians to be more open to considering requests from nominally "rival" settlements.

Our focus on brokered claim-making highlights the importance of the petitioning broker's partisan profile in addition to that of the settlement. A broker's partisan status is especially important from the perspective of politicians who are driven by credit-claiming concerns. After all, brokers are embedded in the community for which the claim is made, and thus have influence over the extent to which local residents will come to know that the provided good or service is due to the politician's actions.

In such a context, patrons might favor co-partisan brokers, who are expected to gather crowds of residents for ribbon-cutting ceremonies and spread word of the politician's patronage, facilitating the politician's credit-claiming efforts. Opposition party brokers, conversely, may be more hesitant to lend their support in these efforts. They may even actively sabotage the credit-claiming efforts of the politician to prevent the latter's electoral support from rising in the community. The compulsions of credit-claiming thus make petitions made by opposition party brokers especially unattractive.

In addition to co-partisan brokers and opposition-party brokers, there are independent brokers who are considered (or consider themselves to be) non-partisan but might ally with a given party for a particular event or election. In our survey of 629 slum leaders, we found that eighty-five slum leaders (13.51%) were not affiliated with any particular party. Among those with explicit party affiliations (544 slum leaders), eighty-three slum leaders (15.26%) had switched their parties of affiliation at some point. These non-aligned and

---

43. Twenty-five settlements had at least 40% of residents supporting the BJP and at least 40% of residents supporting the Congress.

"swing" brokers (168 of our 629 sampled slum leaders) nevertheless have incentives to assist a politician in their local credit-claiming efforts in order to secure the requested good or service. These incentives flow from the fact that non-aligned brokers have to indicate their connections to political elites, especially since they lack formal ties. As such, these brokers will look to participate in joint activities with the providing patron to show off their own connectivity, and thus expand their own reputations for efficacy in problem-solving—the source of their local popularity. Patrons, for their part, might be attracted to the potential for such brokers to have clienteles beyond the patron's core base. Credit-claiming events organized by independent brokers therefore might be especially attractive, and even offer lower-cost opportunities for collaboration than formal inclusion, in which loyalty will be more prized.

Ethnicity in Brokered Exchanges

Finally, our attention turns to how ethnic considerations shape patron evaluations of demands for local public goods. The most obvious concern for scholars has been the broad ethnic composition of a given locality. In much of South Asia and Sub-Saharan Africa, for example, shared ethnicity has been seen to facilitate the mutual trust needed for distributive exchange. Co-ethnic neighborhoods are therefore expected to be favored over neighborhoods that are not co-ethnic.[44] In his seminal study on ethnicity and politics in Sub-Saharan Africa, Bayart described how ethnic groups expect disproportionate shares of public resources when their co-ethnics are in power.[45] Yet other studies have revealed how politicians in these contexts look to craft multi-ethnic coalitions, and sometimes can even disfavor co-ethnics, while citizens can cross ethnic lines in voting.[46]

For urban politicians in India considering demands from slums, co-ethnic targeting is complicated by the rich ethnic heterogeneity within these settlements, particularly along the lines of sub-caste (*jati*). While such identities are important for rural politicians presiding over ethnically segregated and less diverse villages, *jatis* are hard identities for city politicians to use as a basis for decisions. Politicians are unlikely to know the exact mix of *jati* in a slum with any precision, especially given that such data is not officially collected.

44. On South Asia, see Chandra 2004; Anderson et al. 2015. On Africa, see Posner 2005.
45. Bayart 1993.
46. Kasara 2007; Arriola 2012; Ichino and Nathan 2013; Koter 2013.

Politicians, though, may deploy more encompassing ethnic identities.[47] These broader categories [*varnas*] in India are composite groupings of *jatis*: the Scheduled Castes (SCs), Scheduled Tribes (STs), Other Backward Classes (OBCs), General Castes, and Muslims. Scheduled Castes are a collection of castes that were historically treated as "untouchables" and experience the worst forms of social discrimination and exclusion within the Hindu social order. Scheduled Tribes are a collection of "indigenous" communities that historically populated isolated forest areas, but are now present in some urban slums. Other Backward Classes are a collection of castes that traditionally have faced disadvantage within the caste system as well, although they can sometimes occupy dominant positions in specific localities. The General Castes consist of those in the upper tiers of the caste hierarchy.

Yet, the significant volatility in patterns of party support in India's slums suggests that these broad ethnic categories may not be a reliable basis upon which to condition political responsiveness either. Even among our Muslim resident respondents, twenty-one percent stated they support the Hindu Nationalist BJP. Among General Castes, OBCs, and SCs, the support patterns were remarkably fluid, even across the two parties within our surveyed slums. Furthermore, as seen in Chapter 3, India's slum leaders stitch together client bases that cut across ethnic lines. In such electorally fluid contexts that lack rigid and dependable ethnic "vote-banks," urban patrons have incentives to build reputations for ethnic inclusivity in an effort to expand their base of support among voters.

A second characteristic is the ethnicity of the broker making the claim. The literature on ethnic politics anticipates that ward councilors would prefer to respond to the petitions of co-ethnic brokers over those who are not co-ethnic due to greater expectations of trust and reciprocity with the former.[48] Yet, to a politician bent on credit-claiming, ethnicity is likely less important than co-partisanship in assessments over petitions because there are few sharply defined "ethnic rivals" within diverse cities. It cannot be assumed that a broker will necessarily sabotage credit-claiming efforts because of their ethnicity. Underscoring this last point, over twenty-seven percent (27.22%) of the Muslim slum brokers (46 of 169 Muslim slum brokers overall) in our sample are

47. A rich literature in India has explored how *jatis* have been politically mobilized into larger aggregate categories, and even multi-ethnic coalitions. Srinivas 1955; Rudolph and Rudolph 1960; Bailey 1970; Kothari and Maru 1970; Jaffrelot 2000.

48. Habyarimana et al. 2007; Corstange 2016.

affiliated with the BJP, and that percentage rises to just under one-third (31.29%) if we only consider Muslim slum leaders (147) who are explicitly affiliated with a political party.

Consistent with our findings on the responsiveness of brokers to resident requests for assistance, we expect India's city politicians to exhibit an ethnic indifference in assessing petitions from brokers. As we demonstrated in Chapter 3, political brokers in India's cities most often have multi-ethnic client followings. The crowd of voters standing behind a petition cannot be easily read off the ethnicity of the broker submitting that petition. The usefulness of co-ethnicity in coordinating distributive exchanges between voters and politicians is diminished in settings where political brokers articulate claims for public goods on behalf of diverse groups of voters.

Interestingly, this expectation differs from the logic of party organization-building explored in Chapter 4. When seeking the brokers who will serve as their most trusted daily lieutenants, especially in settings rife with partisan and factional competition and fears of defection, considerations of personal loyalty are paramount. Such concerns drive politicians to privilege brokers from their own *jati* to a modest degree in making the less frequent, and more valuable, decisions about whom to award a party position. In prioritizing among the daily petitions they receive from citizens and brokers, politicians are more concerned with how an act of responsiveness will reverberate across a group of voters, specifically, how it can help them to expand their personal reputation for being an effective patron.

How Do Patrons Evaluate Group-based Demands? A Petition Experiment

To assess the broker- and neighborhood-level attributes that command the responsiveness of India's city politicians, we conducted a petition experiment with the same sample of party patrons in Bhopal and Jaipur discussed in Chapter 4. Recall our sampling frame consisted of all winners and runners-up in the 2009 and 2014 municipal elections in the two cities. These winners and runners-up collectively represent the "low patrons" of India's cities, individuals who have amassed enough local support to be given a party ticket and secure enough votes to either win or come in second place. Such low patrons are crucial targets in India's cities for slum dwellers' claims. In total, we were able to conduct the petition experiment with 341 of these low patrons.

Each patron was presented with two petitions. Respondents were told these petitions were sent by slum brokers, on behalf of slum residents, to a politician like them in their city. Seven key attributes of each petition were experimentally manipulated using language similar to what we observed in the hundreds of actual petitions we gathered from slum leaders in Bhopal and Jaipur. Following the presentation of the two petitions, respondents were asked which of the two petitions he or she would address first. Below we detail each of the seven attribute manipulations.

Trait 1: Broker Ethnicity

Our treatments randomly varied whether the petitioning broker belonged to one of five broad ethnic categories in India: Scheduled Castes (SCs), Scheduled Tribes (STs), Other Backward Classes (OBCs), Muslims, and General Castes. Each larger ethnic category had an equal probability of being randomly selected for a petition. These treatments produced a caste match or mismatch between the respondent politician and the broker making the claim. The treatments additionally created a religious match or mismatch—either Hindu or Muslim—between the respondent politician and that broker. The salience of shared caste or faith is provided by examining how going from a co-ethnic to non-co-ethnic broker on a given dimension affects the probability of a petition being prioritized.

Trait 2: Broker Partisan Profile

For partisanship, our treatments randomly varied (with equal probability) whether the slum leader was a BJP worker, an INC worker, or a broker who was not attached to any one party. This allowed us to code a leader as a co-partisan of the respondent politician, a partisan rival, or an independent non-partisan. This enables us to assess the impact of shifts in partisan status on the probability of a petition being prioritized.

Trait 3: Request Type

Petitions then stated the local public good or service being requested. This treatment had four options (assigned with equal probability), each representing a good or service that slum residents commonly demand from politicians.

These four requests were paving the slum's alleyways, installing a public water tank, organizing a public health camp (*sarkari chikitsa* camp), and organizing a ration card drive.[49]

Our interest in these four goods and services lies in the extent to which they lend themselves to credit-claiming. Paving streets, we have argued, is the least amenable public good to credit-claiming because it cannot be easily "tagged." A politician can hold a public event to declare that they have paved the road, but since the good has already been provided, residents have fewer reasons to attend. Second, these local alleys are usually only used by households in that section of the settlement.

At the other end of the spectrum, water tanks are highly amenable to credit-claiming. These goods can be tagged (see Figure 5.3) and claimed during a public event, making it an attractive good to provide. It can also be accessed via tap to a wide swathe of slum residents. Moreover, water tanks require ongoing, daily water delivery, ensuring a degree of dependency on the politician to keep the pipes flowing. Between these two poles lie public health camps and ration card drives, which afford a middling opportunity for credit-claiming. Because residents need to attend to avail themselves of the services, these events typically attract large crowds, giving the politician an immediate audience. Yet such events do not become a part of the built space that can be tagged.

Trait 4: Settlement Size

The final three attributes center on settlement-level characteristics: the population of the settlement, the general partisan leanings of the settlement, and the broad ethnic makeup of the settlement. With respect to population, our politician respondents were assigned, with equal probability, to assess petitions that state the settlement as having either 2,000 or 5,000 residents—the first representing an average sized settlement in our study cities and the second representing a settlement that is one standard deviation above average in population. These figures signal to politicians the size of the settlement's "vote-bank"—the total number of voters through which gossip of the politician's patronage will diffuse.

---

49. We specify alleyways (*galis*) because these are the local roads within squatter settlements for which residents request paving work. Squatter settlements typically lack main thoroughfares as a consequence of their unplanned, haphazard establishment.

Trait 5: Settlement Partisan Profile

For partisanship, each petition presented its settlement as being a BJP strong-hold, a Congress stronghold, a swing settlement in which residents vote together but oscillate between Congress and BJP, or a fractured settlement in which every house votes its own way (each with equal probability). As in Chapter 4, these manipulations allow us to code a petition as coming from a slum that was either a "core slum" for the patron, a "rival slum," a cohesive "swing slum" (the third treatment), or a "fractured slum" (the fourth treatment).[50] These final two sce-narios represent distinct ways that a slum can be seen as an electorally un-committed settlement, with a "swing slum" signaling greater local electoral coordination than a "fractured slum."

Trait 6: Settlement Ethnic Profile

Each petition described the ethnic makeup of its settlement in one of the fol-lowing six ways: as majority SC, ST, OBC, Muslim, General Caste, or, finally, a settlement that housed a mix of these larger ethnic categories. This generated three categories of settlements: those with a majority from the same ethnic group as the patron, those with a majority from a different ethnic group, and those with mixed ethnic groups. We observe the salience of ethnicity in driv-ing political responsiveness by examining how shifting the ethnic status of the settlement affects the probability of a petition being prioritized.

Trait 7: Settlement Name

Three sets of fictitious settlement names differentiated the petitions: Peepal (a type of fig tree) Nagar Slum and Uttar ("North") Nagar Slum; Hawa ("Wind") Nagar Slum and Chand ("Moon") Nagar Slum; Suraj ("Sun") Nagar Slum and Neem (a type of mahogany tree) Nagar Slum. We selected these names because of their neutrality—none signal a settlement's ethnic or religious com-position (such as Bismillah Nagar or Durga Nagar, the former potentially suggest-ing a Muslim-majority settlement and the latter a Hindu-majority settlement) or a settlement's partisan leanings (such as Digvijaya Singh Nagar or Vajpayee

50. 95% of our patron sample was affiliated to either the BJP or Congress. For independent patrons, we coded both BJP- and Congress-leaning slums as "rival slums." Our results for this attribute do not change if we exclude independent patrons.

Box 5.1. Text of Petition

[**Preamble**]: Politicians face many demands from residents but have limited resources to satisfy all of those demands. I recently visited a politician just like you in [Jaipur/ Bhopal], who receives many requests for help from slum dwellers. Two slum leaders, each from a different slum, approached the politician for help in making a request for a service from the city government. The politician would like to help both people, but only has the resources to help one slum. I would like to show you the two petitions.

[**Petition Text (two petitions presented)**]

Header: Name of Settlement

Subject: Request for help from *basti* residents.

I am a *basti* leader, from the [LEADER ETHNIC] community, and a party worker for [LEADER PARTY].

I write on behalf of the residents of our *basti*, who request your help without which we will face a big difficulty. We are requesting you to provide our settlement with a [GOOD].

Our *basti* is made up of [*BASTI* SIZE] people, who come from [*BASTI* ETHNIC] communities. In the past, in our *basti* supported [*BASTI* PARTY].

We hope you are able to help us with our problem. Thank you.

Nagar, the former named after an influential Congress state leader and the latter a former BJP Prime Minister).[51]

Box 5.1 presents the verbal preamble and written text included within the petition experiment. Respondents were presented with two such petitions, and then asked the following question:

> Which of these two settlements would you choose to help first with your ward development funds?

The petitions containing these randomized pieces of information were printed on paper to emulate how they appear in reality and then handed to each politician respondent for their consideration. We present these pieces of information through the medium of a petition because that format best matches how claims are presented to political elites in our study setting. Figure 5.4 reproduces one of the many petitions we obtained during fieldwork, while

---

51. In practice, we find that very little can be gleaned from a settlement's name in terms of the ethnicity or partisan leanings of its residents. For example, a settlement called "*Koli basti*" does not indicate a majority or even a plurality of residents from the Koli caste. Nevertheless, within the context of our experiment, it was important to use neutral settlement names.

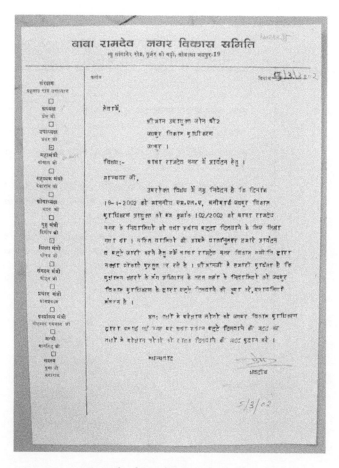

FIGURE 5.4. Example of Actual Petition Crafted by Slum Broker

Figure 5.5 shows a sample petition generated for the experiment, with the settlement name provided as the header.

Our work builds on prior studies examining government responsiveness in India that focus on requests from individual citizens.[52] Some of these prior studies have also used text messages or emails sent from fictitious citizens. Responsiveness is then measured by whether the politician responded to the text message or email. We did not deploy this approach, as we did not observe text messaging to be a common way for slum residents to contact elected representatives, especially for more local public goods and services.

52. Gaikwad and Nellis 2017; Bussell 2019.

नं-49

पीपल नगर कच्ची बस्ती

विषय:- बस्ती में रहने वालों की मदद के लिए प्रार्थनापत्र.

महोदय,

मैं पीपल नगर बस्ती का नेता हूँ और सामान्य बिरादरी का हूँ. और मैं भाजपा का कार्यकर्ता हूँ.

मैं अपनी बस्ती में रहने वाले लोगों की तरफ से आपसे मदद मांगने आया हूँ, जिसके बिना हमको बहुत समस्या है. इसलिए हम आपसे अपनी बस्ती में सामुदायिक वाटर टैंक के लिए पानी का टैंकर भिजवाने के लिए निवेदन करते हैं.

हमारी बस्ती में लगभग 5000 लोग रहते हैं, जो कि ज्यादातर मुस्लिम बिरादरी के हैं. और हमारी बस्ती में लोग एक साथ मिलकर कभी कांग्रेस और कभी भाजपा का समर्थन करते हैं.

हम आपसे आशा करते हैं कि आप हमारी मदद करेंगे.

धन्यवाद

FIGURE 5.5. Sample Petition Provided in Experiment

In our study cities, we witnessed claims usually being made either in person or through written petitions—often both, as noted previously. Ward councilors, and a much larger cast of bureaucrats in the city government, are routinely bombarded with petitions for public services. The circulation of paper is central to everyday governance in South Asia, and written claim-making has been documented among the poor, who must cobble together paper "proofs" to access state services.[53] We thus crafted our experiment to mirror the types of claims that emerge from India's slums—claims voiced by slum leaders through written petitions, on behalf of residents (see Figure 5.6 for a councilor assessing

53. On the centrality of paper circulation in governance see, Gupta 2012; Hull 2012. On written claim-making among the poor see, Tarlo 2003; Das and Walton 2015; Auerbach 2018.

FIGURE 5.6. Petition Experiment with Patrons

two of the petitions). However, we deliberately chose not to send in written petitions from "fictitious" brokers and settlements, another approach in studies of responsiveness.[54]

54. In addition to ethical considerations raised by having public officials consider and respond to such fictitious requests (McClendon 2012; Teele 2021), our setting was not conducive

Results and Discussion

Our main results present average marginal component effects (AMCEs) estimated through a simple OLS model. Once again, these results show how the probability of a petition being prioritized changes with a shift in the value of a given attribute (e.g., slum size) from its baseline value (e.g., a small slum) to a given value (e.g., a large slum). The unit of analysis is the rated petition, which is coded 1 if the respondent politician selected the petition within the pair and coded 0 if they did not. Our respondent politicians rated three sets of petitions, generating a total of 2,058 observations. We cluster our standard errors at the respondent level.[55]

Figure 5.7 presents our results. The first major finding concerns the type of request raised in the petition. Changing the good requested from the baseline category to one that lends itself to credit-claiming increases the probability of the petition's selection. The baseline category here is paving an alleyway—the requested good least amendable to being credibly claimed or durably tagged by politicians. The biggest jump in probability of selection corresponds with going from alleyway paving to water tanks (23.3 percentage points, $p < 0.00$). We hypothesized water tanks to be the most attractive of the four treatments given their ability to be tagged and publicly claimed, as well as to ensure a degree of ongoing dependency. Moving from paving alleyways to the two goods with middling credit-claiming opportunities—health camps (10.5 percentage points, $p < 0.01$) and ration card camps

---

to the anonymity presumed by such designs. It was highly unlikely that patrons would not know all brokers (especially from their own party), and settlements in their wards, and so fictitious brokers and settlements would quickly be recognized as such.

55. Recall we attempted to reach each and every eligible candidate for our survey, so our sampled respondents represent an upper bound for the number of subjects who could have been interviewed for this study. Using the cjpowR package in R, we calculate the minimal detectable effect with this sample size is 6.2 pp for the two 2-level variables, 7.5 pp for the four 3-level variables, and 8.7 pp for the two 4-level variables. To account for the non-independence of ratings from the same respondent, we cluster standard errors by slum leader, as suggested by Hainmueller et al. 2014. Our results are unchanged if using a logit specification, or if estimating our models without clustered errors, as recent work has suggested for certain experimental designs (Abadie et al. 2017), including conjoint experiments (Schuessler and Frietag 2020).

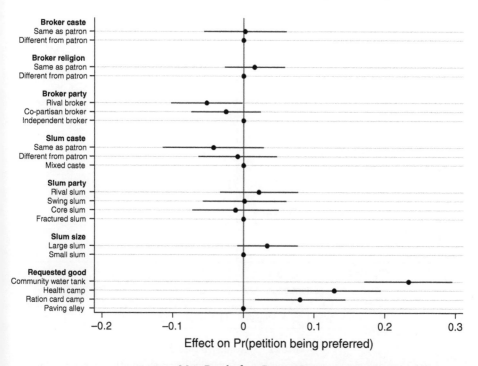

FIGURE 5.7. Main Results from Petition Experiment

Notes: This plot shows estimates for the effects of the randomly assigned petition attribute values on the probability of having a petition prioritized by a municipal politician. Estimates are based on an OLS model with standard errors clustered by respondent; bars represent 95% confidence intervals. The points without horizontal bars denote the reference category for each attribute.

(8.0 percentage points, p < 0.01) also increases a petition's likelihood of being prioritized.[56]

The results depicted in Figure 5.7 are all relative to paved roads. Figure 5.8 represents the average probability that a petition will be preferred for each of the four requested goods in turn. Overall, petitions for a community water tank were selected just over sixty-two percent (62.1%) of the time within a pair.

56. Our AMCEs for water tanks and health camps are both greater than the MDE for a 4-level variable, and the AMCE for ration card camps is slightly underpowered (at the 73.3% level). We find a negligible (0.0004%) chance of a wrong sign (Type S error) and an exaggeration ration of 1.17 (Type M error) indicating very slight overestimation.

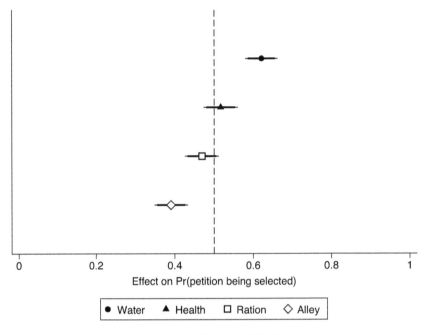

FIGURE 5.8. Requested Goods

Notes: The plot shows the average probability of a petition being preferred by low patrons. The estimates are shown for profiles with traits specified on the vertical axis. Thin (thick) bars represent 95% (90%) confidence intervals. Due to forcing each respondent to choose one of the two profiles, the baseline probability of choosing a randomly drawn slum leader profile is 0.5 (depicted by the dashed line).

By contrast, petitions demanding a paved alley were selected just under forty percent (39.1%) of the time. Health camps and ration cards were selected about fifty-one and forty-seven percent (51.6% and 46.9%) of the time, respectively. The average probability of selection for community water tanks is significantly greater than that of both health and ration camps (both at the 99.9% level).[57] These findings reinforce the idea of a hierarchy among the requested goods.

In practice, the fact that patrons appeared to disfavor paving alleys does not mean such work is never undertaken. Patron evaluations collide with an actual traffic of petitions that is uneven in its distribution of goods and services

57. The difference between health and ration card camps is not significant at the 90% level (p = 0.12).

requested. Ward councilors do not decide how to spend their time and re-sources in a vacuum, but rather react to the stream of bottom-up claims made by their constituents. Indeed, our book demonstrates that slum residents ar-ticulate their demands with significant autonomy and regularity. They do not wait for elections to have things dangled over their heads. As our prior discus-sion on the problem-solving activities of ward councilors indicates, road work is a very common type of delivered local public good. This does not under-mine the credibility of our experimental findings, but rather reflects the fact that the patron preferences we measure here are ultimately refracted through the claims that ward councilors actually receive on a daily basis. This mirrors our findings in Chapters 2 and 3, where we found preferences among residents to support co-ethnic slum leaders infrequently find expression due to the fre-quent absence of available co-ethnic leaders in settlements.

We acknowledge that the four goods and services in our experiment vary along dimensions that go beyond their credit-claiming potentials. As noted, a water tank establishes an ongoing service that can be halted.[58] Once a road is paved, or a ration card or medical examination is provided during a camp, the good or service cannot be so easily taken away. The four goods and services also vary in their per capita and per square meter costs, both in terms of their immediate provision as well as their ongoing maintenance. They might further vary in their local accessibility within settlements, as well as in how vital the goods and services are seen to be, with implications for political responsive-ness. Perhaps petitions for water are interpreted by politicians as so essential and urgent that they overwhelm other claims. With these different moving parts across the goods and services, our interpretation of the experimental findings on this trait should be approached with a degree of tentativeness.

That said, there are several reasons to consider these findings as the prod-ucts of a credit-claiming logic. First, our emphasis on credit-claiming stems from our ethnographic fieldwork, where we observed countless examples of politicians across Bhopal and Jaipur "tagging" infrastructure and organizing events to ensure that residents understood that they were the providing pa-tron. Second, we spoke with a senior elected representative in Bhopal (with nearly forty years of experience as a politician) about the relative cost of the four goods and services, with reference to a specific slum settlement in that politician's constituency that houses 1,000 people, in an area of 12,000 square

58. On water and clientelism, see Herrera 2017. On the politics of water provision in urban India, see Kumar et al. 2022.

meters. He estimated that paving the alleyways of that settlement would cost Rs. 4–5 *lakhs* ($5,400–$6,700). A fully installed water tank (a 1,000-liter PVC tank) with the necessary connections and cement base would cost Rs. 10 *lakhs* ($13,500). For medical and ration card camps, the politician described these as essentially free from his perspective—politicians can place a request with specific departments to offer a community these services. Their costs are not borne by the politician's discretionary budget.

The costs of the four goods and services in our experiment, therefore, do not appear to be driving our findings. If minimizing cost was the primary factor in shaping responsiveness, we would not expect water tanks—the most expensive good or service in our experiment—to register the largest positive effect relative to paved roads. Conversely, if the lack of explicit constraints in our experiment should incentivize politicians to favor more expensive goods (given that they do not have to figure out how to pay for them within the experiment), paving roads should trump medical and ration camps.

With respect to the geography of provision, our hypothetical petitions asked for these goods and services for the *entire* settlement. The experiment was framed in a way to deliberately hold constant the intra-settlement accessibility of the goods and services. In sum, then, there are considerable reasons to interpret our experimental findings on requested goods or services using our theoretical framework. We hope these findings will encourage further studies on the credit-claiming underpinnings of political responsiveness.

Let us now turn to the results for partisanship. Prior studies of unmediated distributive politics have focused on the partisan profile of a given constituency. Recall that our emphasis on mediated claim-making anticipates the partisan profile of the broker spearheading the demand to also be of potential importance. Patrons do appear to be somewhat sensitive to shifts in the partisan profile of brokers. Shifting a petitioning broker's status from a non-partisan independent to a rival partisan reduces their probability of selection by just over five percentage points (-5.2).[59] This may reflect the fact that rival brokers have incentives to work against a patron's efforts to claim credit for a provided

---

59. We note this significant AMCE (at the 95% level) is below our MDE for a 3-level variable (7.5 pp), and so calculate the probability of a Type S (wrong sign) or Type M (exaggerated effect) error. Gelman and Carlin 2014. Using the cjpowR package (Schuessler and Frietag 2020), we find less than a negligible 0.0001% chance of a wrong sign (Type S error), and an exaggeration ratio of 1.42 (Type M error) indicating slight overestimation.

good. Such resistance could be passive, in terms of rival workers not working to spread word of the politician's assistance. The resistance could also be active, for example by spreading contrasting messages suggesting the broker alone was responsible, or even that the real credit should lie with patrons in their own party.

Switching from an independent broker to a co-partisan broker does not improve the probability of a petition being prioritized. In fact, the AMCE here is negative, although not statistically significant (-2.5 percentage points).[60] As discussed, both co-partisans and non-aligned brokers have incentives to facilitate credit-claiming. While the incentives for the former are obvious, the non-aligned brokers are motivated by the desire to show political connectivity in the absence of formal partisan ties. Independent brokers might even view such joint efforts as a way to facilitate their entry into the party. Indeed, two out of three unaligned brokers (57 out of 85) said they had "cooperatively worked" with a political party in the past. Furthermore, credit-claiming activities conducted via independent brokers might be especially attractive to patrons because such activities provide an opportunity to expand their reputations with new clientele.[61]

Within our experiment, we did not find strong evidence that shifts in a settlement's partisan profile influence patron responsiveness.[62] Shifting the partisan status of a settlement from one in which residents are uncoordinated and fragmented in their vote choice to one in which the majority are core supporters of the patron's party (-1.1 percentage points), are supporters of the rival

60. A small number of respondents in our sample (25 out of 343, 7.3%) professed no partisan affiliation. For such non-partisan patrons, we code BJP and Congress brokers as "swing" brokers. We do so because we view non-partisan patrons as unlikely to see partisan brokers as either core or rival workers, but as someone likely to cooperate and aid in credit claiming for a provided service to mutual benefit, given the absence of a clear partisan rivalry. Excluding the 25 "non-partisan" respondents from the sample does not change any of our substantive results.

61. Suggestively, we find patrons prefer petitions from independent brokers that come from rival slums at a higher rate (56.2%) than independent broker requests from core slums (49.3%). However, this 6.9 percentage point difference is not statistically significant (p = 0.22), reflecting the power limitations of our experiment in assessing these subsample differences.

62. We do not display our results for the settlement name AMCEs, which are included in all specifications, as these were included only to improve the realism of the experiment and were not attributes of theoretical interest. We estimated the AMCEs for each settlement name using each of the other names as the reference category in turn. We found only 2 of the 15 distinct dyads (Pipal-Uttar and Neem-Pipal) are significant at the 95% level.

party (2.2 percentage points), or live in coordinated swing settlements (0.2 percentage points) all register small effects that are not significant.[63]

However, we do find suggestive evidence that patron evaluations of the partisan profile of the settlement may be sensitive to the partisan profile of the petitioning broker. For example, patrons were not overall more likely to favor requests from slums identified as largely supporting their party ("core slums") compared to those from slums identified as largely supporting their partisan rival ("rival slums").[64] Yet patron evaluations of petitions from both core and rival slums do appear to be shaped by the partisan leaning of the petitioning broker.

Figure 5.9 depicts average probabilities of selection for four types of petitions: those raised by rival brokers in rival slums, "non-rival" (core and independent) brokers in rival slums, rival brokers in core slums, and non-rival brokers in core slums. Our sample size necessitates caution when examining these subsamples of our data, but the results are nonetheless instructive. In considering petitions from "rival" settlements, patrons preferred those raised by non-rival brokers (54.2%, point B) at a higher rate than those submitted by rival brokers (46.9%, point A), although this difference is not statistically significant.[65] We observe a similar difference within core slums, between petitions from non-rival brokers (50.5%, point D) and from rival brokers (42.5%, point C). Overall, these limited findings are consistent with a view of patrons as especially attentive to how the partisan profile of a broker facilitates or impedes the ability of the patron to claim credit for any help provided. More broadly, they suggest the importance of examining politician responsiveness within a framework that considers the mediated structure of urban claim-making.

In terms of ethnicity, in line with our findings in Chapter 3 on ethnic indifference in responsiveness patterns among slum leaders, there is no evidence that the distributive preferences of patrons are positively influenced by sharing

63. These results are not sensitive to choosing a different settlement category as the baseline for these comparisons.

64. The difference in going from core to rival settlements is 3.3 percentage points, and not significant ($p = 0.272$).

65. This difference misses statistical significance ($p = 0.12$, two-tailed). As noted in footnote 60, a small number of respondents (25 out of 343, 7.3% of our sample) were "non-partisan." In instances where these respondents received petitions from "BJP" or "Congress" slums (79 out of 2058 rated petitions, 3.8% of our sample), we coded such settlements as "fragmented" (for reasons detailed in footnote 94 in Chapter 4). Excluding the 25 "non-partisan" respondents from the sample does not change any of our substantive results.

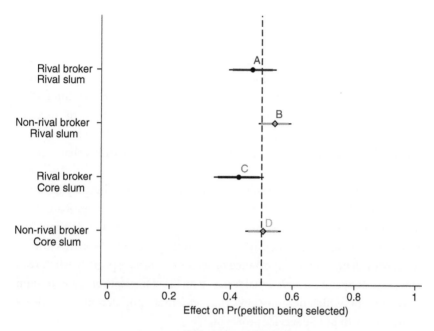

FIGURE 5.9. Partisanship and Petitioning

Notes: The plot shows the average probability of a petition being preferred by low patrons. The estimates are shown for profiles with traits specified on the vertical axis. Thin (thick) bars represent 95% (90%) confidence intervals. Due to forcing each respondent to choose one of the two profiles, the baseline probability of choosing a randomly drawn slum leader profile is 0.5 (depicted by the dashed line).

the ethnicity of the broker making the claim. Changing the petitioning broker from one who is not a co-ethnic to one who is did not significantly increase the probability of the petition being prioritized, either along the lines of caste (0.2 percentage points) or religion (1.6 percentage points). Patron responsiveness does not appear to be sensitive to the ethnic profile of the settlement, nor to the alignment between the ethnic profile of the broker and settlement along the lines seen for partisanship in Figure 5.9.[66] As argued previously, this may

66. Our petition experiment ameliorates some concerns of social desirability bias because respondents had several justifications for making a decision between two petitions and were not asked to elaborate on that decision. Moreover, we found in Chapter 4 that these same politicians expressed preferences for co-ethnics when selecting brokers to bring into their partisan networks, suggesting that they are not shy about showing biases for co-ethnics. We do note that the finding for shared caste lacks sufficient power to be conclusive and the AMCE is below the MDE for a 2-level variable.

reflect the realities of a context where ethnic groups do not present themselves as staunch vote-banks for particular parties. In such settings, the importance of the ethnic composition of neighborhoods diminishes in its usefulness as a heuristic for expected levels of support or opposition.[67] Taken together, these results cut against the assumption that responsiveness patterns within Indian machines will be dominated by ethnic considerations. If anything, the mixture of observational and experimental evidence across this book suggests a more nuanced, and sometimes muted, role for ethnicity within urban Indian machines.

Finally, let us examine the effect of settlement size. Switching a petition to come from a large settlement instead of a small one increases its probability of being prioritized by just over three percentage points (3.3). This effect just misses statistical significance at the 90% level ($p = 0.12$).[68] We view this as modest evidence of the importance of settlement size, especially when read alongside our prior observational research on the statistical correlates of slum development, which demonstrates that settlement population is positively associated with public service provision.[69]

In sum, our experimental findings shed light on how India's urban politicians prioritize among the many mediated claims that fall at their feet. These findings also, by extension, highlight important sources of exclusion in the distributive politics of India's cities. Petitions for local public goods and services that do not lend themselves to credit-claiming can fall to the bottom of pile, making it more difficult for citizens to secure them. Smaller slum settlements are less attractive locations to extend public services than larger settlements—the former exhibit a more modest number of voters through which word of a politician's patronage can spread. Finally, in sifting through petitions, politicians appear more attentive to the partisan profile of petitioning brokers than the partisan composition of the settlement per se. This

67. For this variable a co-ethnic settlement refers to cases where there is a match between the broad ethnic category of the patron and the majority of settlement residents (categories are SC, ST, OBC, upper caste, and Muslim). However, we also find no ethnic favoritism if we instead examine responsiveness towards each category of settlement ethnic makeup irrespective of the patron's ethnicity (using majority upper caste settlements as the reference category, none of the category AMCEs are larger than 2.2 pp or significant at even 90% levels).

68. We note the lack of a statistically significant AMCE here may reflect a lack of statistical power, given the MDE for our sample for a 2-level variable (6.2 pp) is higher than the AMCE for settlement size.

69. Auerbach 2020, Chapter 6.

attention aligns with quantitative evidence of the fluidity of partisan support within slums, and qualitative evidence of brokers as crucial in facilitating or impeding a patron's ability to claim credit for assistance they provide within vote-rich slums.

Conclusion

The preceding chapters have examined how residents select brokers; how brokers select which resident requests to respond to; and how politicians select brokers to bring into their parties and personal networks through the allocation of scarce party positions. This chapter engaged the final arena of competitive selection in our model of machine formation and responsiveness—how politicians prioritize among the many daily petitions they receive for local public goods. India's urban politicians do not have the resources to satisfy all of the petitions that come across their desks; they are thus forced to make tough decisions about where to spend public resources.

We observed that slum residents typically make claims for local public goods in groups, spearheaded by slum leaders. This group-based footing signals to politicians that the petition is backed by *lokshakti*, or people power. Building on these observations, we fixed our analytical focus on identifying the drivers of political responsiveness to mediated, group-based claims. In doing so, we departed from much of the experimental literature on political responsiveness, which examines individual, unmediated claims.

In assessing petitions for local public goods, we argue that India's urban politicians are driven by pressures of credit-claiming—to cut through the complex assemblage of actors and institutions involved in public service delivery to ensure that beneficiaries know that the politician is responsible for the delivered service. In India's three-tiered democracy, and in the face of a constellation of bureaucrats and departments that oversee public service delivery, many voters only know that a service is provided, in general terms, by the *sarkar* (government). Key to a politician's reputation-building efforts is to narrow such broad attribution and to take credit for delivered public services in order to maximize the electoral benefits such acts can accrue.

We also argue that, to a politician motivated by credit-claiming, certain features of a group claim should be especially influential. Credit-claiming is closely related to the extent to which the delivered good can be durably tagged by the politician. More populous neighborhoods should be more attractive places to deliver a public service than less populous neighborhoods because the former have a more expansive crowd of voters through which word of the politician's patronage can spread. Furthermore, our focus on mediated exchanges highlights the importance of considering not only the features of a community from which a request emanates, but also those of the broker spearheading the demand. Results from our petition experiment with 343 city politicians confirm the salience of several of these factors in shaping patron responsiveness, particularly the nature of the good requested and the partisan profile of the petitioning broker.

Our findings suggest that studies of political responsiveness in "mediated states" should more fully consider the role of brokers in shaping why some claims are addressed while others are dismissed.[70] Surprisingly, despite a large literature on political brokers, scholars have yet to systematically examine variation in political responsiveness to brokered claims for local public goods. This is, in part, a result of brokers frequently being studied as election-time distributors of party handouts, which precludes questions about political responsiveness to their everyday, bottom-up claim-making efforts. As we demonstrated in Chapters 2 and 3, brokers in India's slums are informal grassroots representatives in many ways, articulating resident demands to bureaucrats and political elites. This central role in spearheading community claims places the broker squarely in the cluster of petition attributes that politicians assess when making decisions about whether to respond to demands.

This chapter also builds on the importance of broadening the study of distributive targeting beyond conventional debates on ethnic favoritism or "core" versus "swing" targeting along partisan lines. With respect to ethnicity, as different parts this book illustrate, ethnic favoritism often is less pronounced than commonly assumed. With respect to partisanship, much of the literature on distributive politics focuses on contexts where the categories of core, swing, and opposition are stable and self-evident to politicians. Electoral behavior in our study cities, and many other contexts, deviates from these conditions, suggesting the need for new frameworks to understand politician responsiveness. A focus on the contextual incentives patrons face—which in our context reveals their need to claim personal credit—is a promising foundation for such future efforts.

---

70. Berenschot 2010; Berenschot 2011.

6

Conclusion

DURING ONE OF OUR VISITS to Jaipur, we sat down to speak with Amma, a resident of Ganpati Nagar *kachi basti* (slum). Amma, now in her 60s, was part of the first wave of squatters who had settled the area in the mid 1970s. Over the course of four decades, Amma witnessed the dramatic expansion of Ganpati Nagar, from a small cluster of *jhuggies* (shanties) to a crowded, three-kilometer-long settlement housing nearly 25,000 people. She also witnessed a world of local politics take shape around her, manifesting as webs of political networks connecting residents to slum leaders, and slum leaders to politicians. We asked Amma to tell us the story of the *basti's* physical and political development.

Amma and her family arrived in the *basti* in 1977. At that time, just a few dozen shanties lined the sand dunes on this eastern edge of Jaipur city. The ramshackle structures were built with sticks, tarp, thatch, and, for some, slap-dash brick siding. Without proper foundations, even a modest amount of rainfall or soil erosion threatened to topple them. The first waves of squatters also faced a total absence of infrastructure and public services—no piped water, no electricity, no paved roads, and no bathrooms or drainage. Residents had to venture out into adjacent middle-class neighborhoods each morning with buckets, searching for public taps from which to collect water. Kerosene lamps provided the only source of light at night. And without toilets, the forested area behind the slum served as an open-air bathroom for the *basti's* expanding population.

Amma and her family had moved from Jaipur's old walled city, just a few kilometers away. No longer able to afford rent in the old city, her family had heard of a large expanse of barren land on which poor people were squatting. Most of those squatters were migrant laborers who found the land attractive because of its proximity to construction and mining work. Steadily, after

Amma's family erected their shanty, more and more low-income families found their way to Ganpati Nagar.

Amma, a Muslim, found herself living beside Hindus and Muslims of different *jati* and *zat*. This religious and caste diversity intensified after the devastating 1981 floods, when displaced people from throughout eastern Rajasthan poured into Jaipur's slums looking for housing and work. Slums throughout the city swelled. Starting in the late 1980s, poor migrants also trickled into Ganpati Nagar from states like Punjab, Uttar Pradesh, Bihar, Madhya Pradesh, and even as far away as West Bengal. This multi-faith, multi-regional social environment is captured in the mosaic of temples and mosques spread throughout the settlement.

The formation of local leadership in Ganpati Nagar was rapid, a response to the need to deal with urgent threats of eviction and a complete absence of public services. The cast of slum leaders who emerged competed amongst themselves for recognition and a public following. Initially, this competition took the form of factional infighting among slum leaders linked to the Congress party. In Amma's corner of the *basti*, this involved competition between Kastor and Nanagram, two Congress-aligned slum leaders. By the early 1980s, the BJP had made inroads into the settlement. A network of BJP-affiliated slum leaders took root, and aligned with Kali Charan Saraf, a prominent BJP politician in Jaipur, adding a partisan form of competition that has lasted to this day.

Fast-forward four decades. Nearly 150 party workers affiliated with the INC or BJP currently live in Ganpati Nagar. You can hardly find an alleyway in the settlement that is not home to at least one party worker. Over the years, Amma witnessed the rise and fall of individual party workers. She was initially a staunch supporter of Ram, a Congress-affiliated slum leader with close ties to a senior Congress politician. When Ram's popularity dimmed in the early 1990s, other slum leaders took the stage and sought the support of Amma and her neighbors. Despite these changes in the faces of party workers, party networks have thrived and expanded in Ganpati Nagar, and play a key problem-solving role for residents.

The emergence of informal leadership and party networks in Ganpati Nagar represents a political process replicated countless times across India's cities. Such processes of local political organization provoke a number of crucially important, yet surprisingly understudied, questions. How is political authority crafted within the growing cities of the Global South? How, if at all, do newly urban residents have a say in who leads their local community? And once local leaders have taken on this role, how do they decide whom to help in neighborhoods marked by intense material deprivation, where intermediation is pivotal in accessing state resources?

Amma's narrative highlights other important questions. How do politicians build relationships with local political brokers—influential residents in neighborhoods they see as electorally vital? Why do politicians extend party positions to some local brokers and not others? And, as targets of petitions for public services, how do politicians prioritize among the many requests that fall at their feet?

The answers to these questions shed light on one of the most significant demographic and political changes taking place in the Global South—ballooning cities, expanding through population growth and migration and marked by widespread informality. Nearly a billion people live in slums worldwide. Understanding how residents of these precarious and pervasive neighborhoods organize, and how they develop linkages with political elites and political parties, should command substantial scholarly attention.

In their seminal work on machine politics, Stokes et al. note the "need of parties to build organizations that insinuate themselves into the lives and networks of voters."[1] That political machines seek to build organizations that penetrate poor urban neighborhoods is broadly acknowledged. Yet there has been little effort to trace *how* such insinuation occurs. Past studies document the workings of local political operatives, and occasionally the narratives of particular individuals. Such studies do not, however, provide a systematic understanding of the processes through which urban political networks form.

In large part, this neglect reflects the onerous empirical requirements of tracing such formative processes. The effort of collecting data from each layer of the networks we studied—residents, brokers, and city politicians—took us nearly a decade to complete in just two cities. While painstaking to collect, such multi-level data collection allowed us to uncover the processes through which the urban poor are incorporated into city politics. Data from residents revealed the kinds of brokers they sought to spearhead local claim-making. Data from slum leaders corroborated that these urban brokers reflected the traits that residents valued. The evidence we collected from brokers also illuminated how they decided which residents to cultivate as supporters, while data from residents showed that their patterns of received assistance often corresponded to broker preferences. And interviews and experiments involving local party patrons revealed which of the many brokers emerging within

1. Stokes et al. 2013, p. 20.

slums patrons sought to incorporate into their own party networks. The importance of these evaluations was corroborated by data showing that they aligned with the promotion patterns of actual brokers within partisan organizations. Finally, data from party patrons afforded insights into how they prioritize among the many daily petitions they receive from brokers, on behalf of larger groups of clients. In short, data from one layer of the machine could be cross-referenced against evidence from a different layer, revealing the interlocking set of competitive selections through which urban political networks form.

In this concluding chapter, we examine comparative resonances of our key arguments. We also discuss the hard limits of the party machine networks we document as key conduits of political representation and responsiveness, in terms of their ability to improve the material well-being and security of the urban poor. We then look toward the future, and discuss how the highly localized worlds we study might be affected by two current national trends in Indian politics: the centralization of political power and a rising Hindu majoritarianism. While these developments have attracted attention in high-profile debates on Indian democracy, few scholars have considered them from the vital, but often neglected, perspective of the urban poor. We conclude by offering some necessarily speculative thoughts on what the future holds for the communities we have learned so much from during the past decade.

Beyond Slums in Bhopal and Jaipur

To what extent can our findings from Bhopal and Jaipur travel within India's continent-sized political landscape? The dynamics we examined might work differently in other regions of India, which differ in their linguistic and cultural endowments. Furthermore, bipolar competition between the Congress and BJP, which defines electoral politics in our study settings, by no means extends across the country. Several states are marked by multipolar competition, which in some cases includes the BJP, the Congress, or both. In other states, especially in southern India, neither national party is a dominant player. Such differences in the structure of political competition might inform local variations in the formation of machine organizations.

At the same time, at least five key features that we argue are central to the creation of political networks in Jaipur and Bhopal are broadly, if not uniformly, observed across India: the persistent underdevelopment that leads to claim-making by low-income voters; the targeting of resident requests to local brokers rather than high-level politicians; the privileging of effective problem-solvers over solely ethnic considerations by residents; the privileging of inclusive reputations over monitoring by brokers; and the pervasive political competition across and within party organizational networks.

Our first argument, based on a decade of research, is that *citizen agency* in making everyday claims—both individually and in groups—on the state to combat persistent conditions of underdevelopment is critically important. Such bottom-up demands are crucial to catalyzing the interactions through which local brokerage networks form. While certain aspects of deprivation, notably informality in housing, are specific to slums, the conditions of underdevelopment that compel citizens to make demands on the state are shared across India.[2] A recent, large-scale survey of over 40,000 respondents by Azim Premji University (APU) and the Lokniti Programme for Comparative Democracy examined patterns of political participation between elections across twenty Indian states.[3] Respondents were asked to identify their most pressing concern. Twenty-seven percent of underprivileged (non-literate) respondents identified inadequate physical infrastructure and poverty, compared to just thirteen percent of college-educated voters. Furthermore, about half of all respondents reported difficulties with accessing public services, including garbage collection, electricity, and water. While such access varied significantly across income and education levels, these difficulties were pronounced in both urban and rural areas.[4]

Second, we argue that these requests compel citizens to seek assistance from local political actors, who relay these demands to higher-level elites.[5] Such mediated access to political elites is a key organizational feature of machine politics. Much as in Bhopal and Jaipur's slums, the APU-Lokniti study finds that inadequacies compel citizens to seek assistance from politically connected local leaders, rather than elite politicians. Only one-and-a-half percent

2. Krishna 2002; Kruks-Wisner 2018; Auerbach and Kruks-Wisner 2020.

3. Azim Premji University and Lokniti 2019. The survey had a full sample of 40,772 respondents. We thank both institutions for making this data available to us.

4. For garbage collection, 55% of rural and 40% of urban respondents reported difficulties, for electricity 46% of rural and 39% of urban respondents, and for water, 56% of rural and 44% of urban respondents.

5. As Kruks-Wisner 2018 notes, such claim-making requires a minimal capacity for local governments to deliver goods and services to residents. Our theoretical framework anticipates that the formation of machine organizations is unlikely to occur in contexts where residents perceive the state as having few resources to distribute.

(1.53%) of respondents reported that they would approach national-level MPs for assistance with a problem, and just under nine percent (8.83%) said they would approach state-level MLAs. In contrast, nearly thirty percent (28.2%) of respondents stated that they would approach local unelected leaders.[6] Importantly, these rates of approaching local leaders were comparable across urban (27%) and rural (29%) respondents, suggesting that some of the dynamics we study are not confined to urban areas.

Of course, in suggesting these broader implications of our study, we do not want to ignore contextual variations in local politics. For example, one striking difference in interactions between citizens and political authorities across rural and urban settings in India is that villagers are more likely than urban residents to approach a local elected official. The APU-Lokniti survey found that forty-one percent of rural residents had approached a village council president. In contrast, only twenty-seven percent of urban residents had approached their ward councilor directly.[7] This disparity reflects variation in the degree of decentralization between villages and cities. In the former, local elected officials are more proximate to voters than in the latter. The average ward population in Jaipur and Bhopal is 39,557 and 25,689 people, respectively. By contrast, the average population served by a village council in Rajasthan is about 5,000 people, comparable to that of a large slum in our sample.

Indeed, if we account for the fact that local village council presidents (sarpanch) operate at the scale of slum leaders, other parallels between urban and rural experiences become evident. A third key finding in our study is that slum residents prioritize effective problem-solvers when seeking assistance, and do not reflexively support members of their own castes. The value of educated local brokers echoes findings from work by Krishna in the villages of Rajasthan and Madhya Pradesh.[8] It also reflects the findings of surveys conducted in rural Rajasthan (N=10,082) and Uttar Pradesh (N=5,522), which asked villagers to name the two most important qualities in a sarpanch. "Education" was in the top two responses in both surveys, while shared ethnicity was not.[9] Moreover, in a rural survey across four southern states, Besley, Pande and Rao

6. This category includes local political leaders, caste/religious leaders, and elders outside the family.

7. A similar pattern has been noted between urban and rural residents within the state of Rajasthan. Auerbach and Kruks-Wisner 2020.

8. Krishna 2002.

9. McManus 2014.

found only eight percent of respondents stated that candidate group identity (defined along religion, caste, gender, or regional lines) was the leading reason for their vote in the *gram panchayat* election, while over thirty percent stated that the candidate's quality (reputation or policy promises) determined their vote.[10]

A fourth key argument advanced in this book is that brokers privilege building inclusive reputations over monitoring and punishing voters. One manifestation of this is the ethnic indifference brokers display in cultivating multi-ethnic clienteles. This finding is striking, especially given the widely argued role of shared ethnic networks in enabling clientelistic monitoring. Such indifference is enabled by the tremendous social diversity we observe in India's slums, which does not typify many rural communities. Yet our work resonates with other studies of political responsiveness outside of highly diverse urban slums. Dunning and Nilekani find weak evidence of ethnic favoritism among lower-level village council heads in three Indian states.[11] They also find that the need to build multi-ethnic coalitions compels politicians to favor co-partisans over co-ethnics. Additionally, Jensenius finds no evidence of Scheduled Caste politicians working more for voters from their community than for others.[12]

In contexts with lower levels of diversity than India's slums, ethnicity may play a larger role in structuring machine politics than we find here. That said, the relative diversity of cities compared to villages is hardly idiosyncratic to India.[13] Moreover, village populations themselves are far from static, and often witness considerable migratory churn that yields new patterns of inter-ethnic interaction.[14] Of course, we do not contend shared ethnic identities play no role in electoral calculations or distributive politics. Rather, read alongside the other works we mention, our work helps push back against overly

10. Besley et al. 2005, p. 18. It is important to acknowledge the limits of self-reported attitudes on direct survey questions, and indeed this is one of the reasons we largely avoid such questions in measuring the impact of shared caste or faith in this book. Yet the fact that our findings resonate broadly across these different studies and varied measures remains instructive.

11. Dunning and Nilekani 2013.

12. Jensenius 2017.

13. Nathan 2019.

14. In India, rural-rural migration for work has often placed individuals from different caste communities in proximity with each other, and has been shown to even increase "solidarity among poor, but ethnically heterogeneous people." Jenkins and Manor 2017, p. 11 as quoted in Kruks-Wisner 2018, p. 212.

simplified portrayals of Indian politics as mechanically governed by consider-ations of caste and faith.[15]

Fifth, we document how these processes of selection are undergirded by considerable political competition at every level of machine politics. Such competition is enabled by volatilities within the electoral arena: voters who often change which party they support, brokers willing to flip parties, patrons in search of upward mobility, and even party elites who switch partisan allegiances. These dynamics are observed across India. First, many, if not most, Indian voters do not hold strong partisan allegiances. A 2019 election survey of a nationally representative sample of voters found just over sixty percent (60.7%) of respondents did not report feeling close to any single party.[16] A similar survey in 2004 revealed that between thirty and forty percent of Congress and BJP supporters reported switching allegiances between the two previous parliamentary elections, a figure very comparable to reported vote-switching rates in our study slums.[17]

Competition among local political operatives is also widely apparent beyond our study setting. Accounts of village council elections in India note that they are often intensely competitive.[18] Local village operatives appear to be driven by many of the same careerist ambitions we find among brokers in urban India. A survey of village council presidents in Rajasthan found that two out of three would like to "run for political office in the future."[19] Of those wanting to run for office in the future, nearly six out of ten said they would like to run for a *higher* office. As in our study setting, such progressive ambitions are not simply wishful thinking. Chauchard notes in his study of *sarpanches* in Rajasthan, "each of the officials I interviewed had been a community-level leader before they managed to win a local-level election."[20] Such trajectories align with the interlocking competitive selections we present in this book: aspirants who successfully compete for local influence provide the pool from which successful candidates for local political positions are selected.[21]

15. See Auerbach et al. 2022 for a fuller discussion of this point.

16. Lokniti Post-poll 2019.

17. Author calculation based on Lokniti, National Election Study 2004.

18. Sharma 2001.

19. McManus 2014.

20. As quoted in Kruks-Wisner 2018, p. 104.

21. Earlier work by Bailey 1970 documented how economic changes unleashed competition between older authority figures and new entrants within a small village in the eastern Indian state of Orissa. Krishna 2002 similarly documents competition between more established

Intense competition and frequent turnover also characterize electoral politics at higher levels. An analysis of state assembly elections (1986–2007) by Jensenius and Suryanarayan recorded an average of just under eleven (10.7) candidates per constituency, with an average "effective number" of three competitive candidates per constituency.[22] These results speak to two features of our analysis: the abundant supply of political entrepreneurs and the importance of a candidate receiving major party labels to be viable. Jensenius and Suryanarayan also find evidence of considerable turnover and volatility: in only fifty-six percent of races did incumbent politicians rerun under the same party label.[23] A majority (59%) of runners-up across these races did not even run in the next election. Similar trends are apparent at both higher and lower levels of politics. In the 2019 national elections, fifty percent of BJP candidates and fifty-seven percent of Congress candidates were first-time candidates.[24] In a survey of village council presidents in Rajasthan, only fifteen percent of those who re-ran for office were re-elected, and the majority had to return to agricultural work (56.3%) or remain without work (27.1%).[25] These patterns reflect the calculations of party elites seeking to minimize penalties that voters routinely level against unpopular incumbents.[26]

Many of these volatile dynamics played out during the course of our research. Both Rajasthan and Madhya Pradesh held state assembly elections in 2018. In both provinces, the BJP was the incumbent party, and lost power to the Congress. In the run-up to these elections in Madhya Pradesh, news reports surfaced that the BJP was going to deny candidacies ("tickets" in the parlance of Indian elections) to many incumbents in a bid to quell anti-incumbency.[27] Reports indicated that the party also sought to dampen the frustrations of party workers, who were surveyed before the election and

---

authority figures and new political entrepreneurs (*naya netas*) in villages located in the same states as our study cities (Madhya Pradesh and Rajasthan).

22. Jensenius and Suryanarayan 2020.

23. In 27% of cases the incumbent did not run for re-election. In 17% of cases, the incumbent politician switched to run under a different party label.

24. 9% of Congress candidates and 5% of BJP candidates had switched their party affiliation within just the past five years. Verniers 2020.

25. McManus 2014.

26. Uppal 2009 finds evidence of a significant incumbency disadvantage of nearly 9 percentage points in state elections between 1991 and 2003. Lee 2020 finds incumbency to have a null or negative effect in national elections between 1977 and 2014.

27. *News18* 2018.

expressed displeasure with several incumbents.[28] The Congress ended up winning the election, but was immediately beset by the flaring of a long-standing factional rift between two of its major state leaders, Kamal Nath and Jyotiraditya Scindia. The dispute crested with Scindia, irked by Nath's selection as Chief Minister of the state, resigning from the Congress along with several leaders in his faction. The rift caused the Congress government to fall after just fifteen months, and put the BJP back in power.

Many of the constitutive conditions for the local politics we uncover in Jaipur and Bhopal are thus widely observed across India. Of course, we do not expect that every process will identically manifest across India's complex and continent-sized polity. Madhya Pradesh and Rajasthan are roughly comparable to Germany and Thailand, the world's nineteenth- and twentieth-most populous countries. Yet the broad similarities we outline here do lead us to expect that many of our arguments will resonate in other parts of India, especially in urbanizing areas. To date, there has been little work on how political networks form in such spaces, and we expect the importance of such work to only grow as India's urban transition proceeds.

Beyond India

In this section, we draw on a variety of secondary sources, including three cross-national surveys and a number of in-depth country studies to illustrate the broader potential of the arguments made in this book. We document how many of the forces generating machine networks within urban India are broadly present across numerous other countries of the Global South.

Cross-National Survey Evidence

Perhaps the most significant feature of machine politics we highlight in Jaipur and Bhopal is its intensive competitiveness. Machines are often conceptualized as enjoying iron-fisted political control. In this book we provide a contrasting view—that machine politics can be highly competitive, both within and between parties.

Such competitive machine politics is hardly an Indian idiosyncrasy. Take data from the Democratic Accountability and Linkages Dataset, a cross-national expert survey in which respondents were asked to evaluate political

28. Ranjan 2018.

parties in their country of expertise.[29] Respondents were asked to assess the efforts parties make to engage in the distributive strategies that are hallmarks of machines. Specifically, they were asked to assess how much effort a given party made to provide goods and services as inducements to attract voters. We examined data from all countries evaluated in Africa, Asia, and Latin America, and identified how many parties in each country were rated as exerting moderate or major effort with respect to a particular good or service. Across forty-eight cases (see Figure 6.1), we found a majority (26) in which there were *multiple* parties earning an average rating of 3 (out of 4) or higher across four different types of material benefits. These cases were distributed across all three continents.

This pervasiveness of competition is reinforced in our review of recent scholarship. We reanalyzed eighty-two major studies of clientelist exchange in the Global South, published between 2008 and 2018, and reviewed by Hicken and Nathan.[30] Across these studies, only nineteen (23%) explicitly focused on settings with a single dominant machine, with a third of these studies (8) focusing on a single country, Argentina. By contrast, thirty-four studies (41%) discussed cases where multiple machines competed against one another, and another six studied countries exhibiting a regionally varied mix of dominant and competitive machine politics. These "multilateral" cases included examples from Asia (Indonesia, India, and Taiwan), Africa (Ghana, Senegal, and Nigeria), Latin America (Brazil, Peru, and Colombia), and the Pacific.[31] Furthermore, even within canonical "unilateral machines" like the Argentine Peronists, Mexican PRI, and even the Chinese CCP, researchers found evidence of significant internal competition between local factions.[32]

These analyses make clear that the competitive machine politics we encountered in Jaipur and Bhopal are experienced by citizens across a wide range of polities. The equating of machines with uncompetitive politics is largely an artefact of a geographic focus on particular countries within the Americas. What remains striking is the lack of systematic attention to how competition shapes machine politics, especially given the prevalence of such competition across the globe. For example, our literature review found that only seventeen

---

29. Democratic Accountability and Linkages Dataset 2008–2009. Available at https://sites.duke.edu/democracylinkage/data/.

30. We thank the authors for sharing their list of references. Nathan and Hicken 2020.

31. Veenendaal and Corbett 2020.

32. Auyero 2001; Kennedy 2010; Zarazaga; 2014; Rizzo 2019.

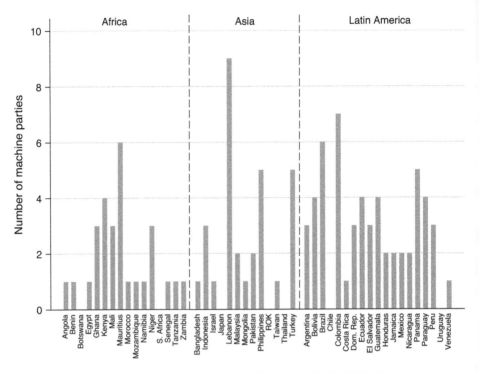

FIGURE 6.1. Competitive Machine Politics Across the Global South

Notes: Graph depicts the number of parties that country experts rate as attracting votes with the following benefits: consumer goods, preferential access to public social policies, employment in public sector or publicly regulated private sector, government contracts or procurement. Vertical axis shows number of parties averaging a 3 or higher across all four good types, on a 4-point scale [1 = negligible effort, 2 = minor effort, 3 = moderate effort, 4 = major effort]. Democratic Accountability and Linkages Dataset 2008–2009.

studies (21%) discussed how brokers are selected. Furthermore, sixteen of these seventeen investigations focused on how parties select brokers. The means by which brokers emerge within communities in competitive landscapes remains woefully understudied.

Second, many of the generative forces through which machine networks form in Jaipur and Bhopal are observed elsewhere. Specifically, our account has emphasized the importance of bottom-up demands from residents on the state. Clients select brokers best positioned to help raise these demands on their behalf, while brokers prioritize client demands when the latter are well placed to help burnish the brokers' reputations. While the importance of citizen requests within machine politics has been recently noted, these studies tend to focus on individualized requests for campaign handouts, and direct, unmediated requests to high-level politicians.[33] By contrast, our study emphasizes the importance of demands that target "low" patrons rather than elite politicians (Chapter 4), are mediated by party workers (Chapter 5), are often for local community problems rather than private benefits (Chapters 3 and 5), and, finally, are frequently raised by groups of voters rather than single individuals (Chapter 5).

Available survey evidence suggests that many of these features characterize citizen-state interactions beyond India. One example comes from the sixth round of the Afrobarometer survey, conducted in 2016, which interviewed over 50,000 respondents across thirty-six African countries. The survey asked respondents a number of questions regarding their interaction with a variety of political officials. The data indicate citizen claim-making targets local political operatives more than high-level politicians. Nearly twenty-two percent (21.85%) of respondents tried contacting a local government councilor, roughly twice the proportion (11.07%) of those who reported contacting a high-level MP. Among respondents who contacted local councilors, the majority (67%) did so for a community problem, whereas only thirty-one percent did so for a personal problem. A striking sixty-one percent of those who contacted local councilors did so in groups, while only thirty-seven percent (37.28%) reported doing so alone.

These descriptive patterns are revealing, and suggest the pervasiveness of communities coming together to raise demands of local politicians. Importantly, the survey data also suggest that many of these requests to local politicians are not raised by ordinary citizens, but rather by respondents who are embedded within partisan networks. The survey asked respondents if they had "worked for a party or candidate" in the last national election. These partisan activists comprised only ten percent of respondents who had never contacted local officials during the twelve months prior to the survey. However, they accounted for nearly a quarter of the respondents who had contacted local politicians once, and nearly half of the respondents who had contacted such officials "often" in the prior year.

The correlation between working for a party with the likelihood of raising a request persists in OLS regressions that account for a number of attitudinal

33. For individualized requests see, Nichter 2019. For unmediated requests to high-level politicians, Bussell 2019.

and demographic attributes, as well as ethnic group, region, and country fixed effects. The top panel of Figure 6.2 illustrates the results of this analysis. A respondent working for a party or candidate corresponds to a twenty-three percentage points increase in their likelihood of contacting an official at least once in the prior year.[34] This correlation persists after controlling for a respondent's level of interest in politics, and their level of political participation (voting in the past election).

We find strikingly similar results in Latin America (bottom panel of Figure 6.2). Here we draw on data from the 2013 Latinobarómetro survey, which asked a broadly comparable question about contacting government actors for assistance with "personal, family, or neighborhood problems, or problems with government officials and policies?"[35] The survey covered 20,204 respondents across eighteen Latin American countries, thirty percent (30.39%) of whom reported contacting an official "sometimes" or "often" in the past three years.[36]

The Latinobarómetro instrument also asked whether respondents worked for a political party or candidate. All respondents who reported they did such work "frequently" or "very frequently" were coded as party workers.[37] Once again, we find evidence that these politically embedded respondents were especially likely to raise demands with local political elites. While only twenty-eight percent of regular respondents reported contacting an official or politician, fifty-five percent of party workers reported doing so. The correlation between working for a party or candidate and raising demands on the state is once again robust to controlling for most of the covariates used in the Afrobarometer analysis, including ethnic group and country fixed effects.[38] In the Latin America study, a respondent being a party worker is associated with a large increase in their likelihood of making a request (21.17 percentage points). Mirroring our findings with African voters, this correlation is larger than included measures of prior electoral participation and interest in politics.

---

34. This association was significant at the 0.001 level.

35. Here we combine answers to two questions separately asking if respondents contacted a government official or elected official. Latinbarómetro 2013.

36. The survey also included 2,459 respondents from Spain, who are excluded from this analysis.

37. 8.5% of all respondents fell into these two categories.

38. Unlike the Afrobarometer survey, the Latinobarómetro survey does not ask whether respondents asked for assistance in a group or alone, or for a personal or community problem.

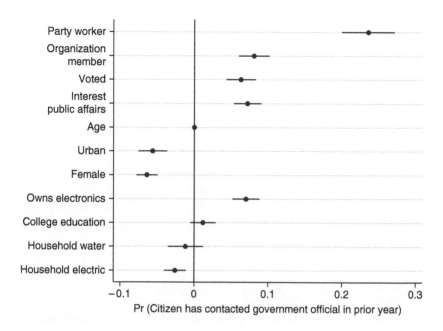

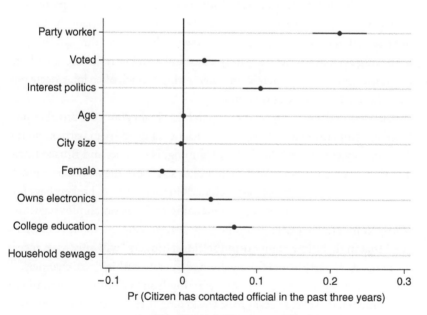

FIGURE 6.2. Who Contacts Government Officials?

Notes: The top panel uses 2016 Afrobarometer data (N = 50,564) and shows the results of OLS regressions in which the outcome is a binary indicator of respondents who had contacted a local government councilor at least once in the past year. The bottom panel uses 2013 Latinobarómetro survey data (N = 22,663). The figure shows results of OLS regressions in which the outcome is a binary indicator that identifies respondents who had contacted a government official or elected legislative representative at least once in the past three years.

Collectively, these findings suggest that bottom-up requests for assistance from politicians, often spearheaded by individuals who work for parties, are a widespread phenomenon. Our work highlights that such demands often serve to ignite processes of machine formation, and in particular the ascent of residents into positions as brokers. Such processes are likely in competitive settings, which also appear to be broadly prevalent.

At the same time, we acknowledge that these broad surveys are not well-suited to uncover more fine-grained similarities between our study and processes of machine politics elsewhere. In the next section, we shift our attention to studies that mirror our own deep focus on political machines within a specific context.

Single-Country Studies

Our book has examined competitive selection at all three layers of machine anatomy: clients selecting brokers, brokers selecting clients, and patrons selecting brokers. To our knowledge, ours is the first to simultaneously study all three selection processes, and to show how machines form through these interlocking selections. Yet our study does find striking resonances with in-depth studies of machine politics in other settings, which often interrogate one part of the set of processes we outline.

A key example is recent scholarship that has highlighted the broad importance of competition in structuring the relationship between parties and the brokers they employ. While Stokes, Dunning, Nazareno, and Brusco introduced this key question of party-led broker selection, their primary models examine a situation with a single machine.[39] In such settings, brokers have few credible exit options, allowing the machine to focus on employing those whose competence earns them the largest following. Some have even argued that in these low competition settings, brokers "will only have access to clients . . . if party leaders allow them to operate within these channels."[40] Brokers will therefore be wary of defecting from a dominant incumbent with unfettered access to resources, weakening their leverage in negotiating with elites.

39. Stokes et al. 2013. In Chapter 7 they examine a similar model, with the main difference being that the machine party now chooses between hiring brokers to enact clientelism or spending the same resources on non-clientelistic strategies to win support.

40. Novaes 2017, p. 86.

Competitive machine politics shifts the tenor of interactions between parties and brokers, along the lines we have outlined here. In Brazil, Novaes describes a system marked by many of the conditions we find in India: high levels of competition and voters routinely changing the party they support.[41] Such conditions endow brokers with exit options, incentivizing disloyalty and allowing them to drive a harder bargain for themselves and their supporters.

Competitiveness is even observed in Argentina, the setting in which Stokes and her coauthors develop their model, and a context most often portrayed as dominated by the Peronist machine. Camp documents competition within and between parties, especially in large cities like Buenos Aires and Córdoba.[42] He finds that competition requires elites to ensure that the brokers they employ do not defect to rival parties. He further shows that the threat of exit allows brokers with large followings to extract favors from party elites. This latter point aligns with the evidence we presented in Chapter 4, which demonstrates that patrons prefer brokers who display everyday competence in solving client problems, as these figures are likely to cultivate large followings.

Our findings are also echoed by recent work on competitive machine politics in Ghana. Brierley and Nathan describe the country's two major parties (the incumbent NPP and NDC) as having "hierarchical machine organizations with standing committees of internally elected executives at the national, regional, parliamentary constituency, and polling station levels."[43] This organizational structure mirrors those within the Congress and BJP. Additionally, many aspiring brokers compete for positions within these party organizations. Brierley and Nathan note that party elites select brokers from among many aspirants, much as they do in Jaipur in Bhopal. Furthermore, the elites making such decisions are constituency-level party leaders akin to our "low patrons."

The Ghana study also demonstrates that broker success in partisan organizations correlates with their efficacy at solving problems for clients, and with stronger loyalties that minimize chances of defection to another party. Their study does not survey patrons or clients, and so cannot identify whether observational patterns of broker achievement are driven by client and patron preferences. However, their findings do closely align with the efficacy and

41. Novaes 2017.

42. For example, he documents an average of 23 brokers per city councilor in Buenos Aires, and fourteen per councilor in Cordoba and San Luis. Camp 2017.

43. Brierley and Nathan 2021, p. 887.

loyalty framework outlined in Chapter 4. Brierley and Nathan also find that education and certain occupations (civil servant and small business owners) positively distinguish effective brokers, closely mirroring our findings in Chapters 2 and 3. Finally, they also show that patrons place little emphasis on a broker's monitoring capabilities.

Our work also finds parallels with scholarship that focuses on interactions between brokers and clients, rather than brokers and political parties. In Chapter 3, we argue that competition between brokers compels them to focus their efforts on building reputations for problem-solving rather than on monitoring voters. We then focus on how these concerns compel brokers to cultivate certain residents as clients. Studies of poor urban neighborhoods echo the first part of this argument.[44] Cornelius documents substantial competition among local brokers, and the need for these actors to demonstrate efficacy or risk losing their following.[45] Koster and de Vries's fieldwork in a Recife slum reveals nine community leaders competing for prominence within the same *favela* by cultivating reputations for effective problem-solving.[46] In Argentina, Zarazaga conducted a qualitative study of brokers in poor municipalities surrounding Buenos Aires. While the Peronists dominate this area, he still uncovers dueling networks of brokers associated with the incumbent and challenger parties. Furthermore, he finds that brokers are more concerned with "building reputations for accessing resources and delivering to poor people," than with monitoring voters at the polls.[47] In urban Ghana, Nathan notes that local brokers distribute benefits with full knowledge that "they do not create binding commitments ... Instead, distributing pre-election benefits is aimed more at creating reputations of performance and generosity."[48]

Beyond cities, a number of studies note competitive brokerage environments in the countryside. In Senegal, Gottlieb documents variation in the competitiveness of brokerage environments across different ethnic groups. In villages led by groups known for more competitive broker selection by

44. Suttles 1968; Gay 1994; Stokes 1995; Burgwal 1996; Auyero 2001; Dosh 2010.

45. Cornelius 1975.

46. Koster and de Vries 2012, p. 88. They note the position of community leader is "severely fought for ... one for which a reputation has to be cultivated. Community leaders are known to make efforts for the community, do personal favors for people, and thoroughly know the community's history and current problems."

47. Zarazaga 2014, p. 38, notes that "none of the brokers [he interviewed] thought it possible to check how an individual voted."

48. Nathan 2019, p. 183.

residents, she finds that brokers "are more likely to be of a good type or have interests that are aligned with those of their followers."[49] Less competitive settings are marked by brokerage that is more extractive and dependent on negative incentives to motivate followers. In Benin, Guadardo and Wantchekon find that nearly one in five of the voters they surveyed received benefits from more than one party.[50] In rural Pakistan, Shami provides evidence of competitive brokerage, especially in villages with relatively dispersed land ownership patterns.[51] Finally, a study of rural brokerage in Paraguay enumerated forty-three brokers working across ten villages.[52]

A second set of studies echo our findings in Chapter 3 regarding the kinds of residents that political machines target. For example, our finding that machines prioritize residents who are important and well-connected within their social communities resonates with other work. In the Philippines, Cruz finds that individuals with larger social networks are disproportionately targeted by machines for benefits.[53] However, it bears noting that she argues such targeting is driven by the use of social networks for monitoring voters, which diverges from our interpretation in Chapter 3. Using survey data from twenty-two Latin American countries, Schaeffer and Baker find that "social multiplier effects" can incentivize parties to privilege voters who are central within local political discussion networks.[54]

The generative conditions for political machine formation that we uncovered in Jaipur and Bhopal are thus clearly not idiosyncratic to these two cities, or even to India. We do not seek to make ad hoc claims of generalizability that go against the inductive, fieldwork-based approach we adopt. That said, several core insights from our study clearly resonate with the experiences of Indian voters outside of Jaipur and Bhopal, and indeed with electorates outside the subcontinent. Furthermore, many of the stylized facts about machine politics we challenge have emerged out of the study of particular cities, parties, and political systems. At a minimum, our findings provide a check against mechanically assuming that the findings of these studies hold globally.

49. Gottlieb 2017.
50. Guadardo and Wantchekon 2018.
51. Shami 2012.
52. Duarte et al. 2019.
53. Cruz 2019.
54. Schaeffer and Baker 2015.

The Limits of Party Machines

Our book has documented important forms of political agency, accountability, and representation in India's slums. These neighborhoods are often understood to be governed by ruthless gangs, or rendered the playthings of politicians, who dangle handouts during elections to amass support from desperate residents. Against these narratives, we find slum communities engaging in sustained, bottom-up claim-making to improve local conditions. They actively select their informal leaders through deliberative meetings, informal elections, and day-to-day decisions over whom to follow and whose door to knock on to ask for help. Slum leaders must perform or risk watching their following shift to another slum leader. As such, we find these actors submitting reams of petitions for public services. They organize protests and mobilize residents to demand development from officials. In many respects, slum leaders should be seen as informal grassroots representatives who face accountability pressures from residents with the agency to redirect their support at a moment's notice.

We have shown that slum residents' everyday political behavior aggregates to shape the form and functioning of party machines in India's cities. The urban poor are thus architects of the political networks that connect them to the state. Politicians have little choice but to engage with the slum leaders chosen by residents—and, in the allocation of party positions, to prioritize those slum leaders with attributes that will ensure their continued popularity among residents. Such attributes, we have shown, are those that boost efficacy in problem-solving—specifically, a slum leader's education. The pivotal role of residents and slum leaders in the distributive politics of India's cities challenges the notion that the urban poor are rigidly locked in clientelistic relations with politicians, and are "perversely" held accountable by the latter for their vote.

Modalities of accountability and representation in machine politics are central to the story of how poor migrants are incorporated into the politics of India's cities. These findings, however, should not obscure the limits of party machines in improving the lives of the urban poor. As we have stressed in each chapter, competitive selection in party network construction means that some residents, brokers, and communities are *not* selected, marginalizing them within the workings of machine politics.

Empirical examples of such exclusion are strewn throughout this book. We showed in Chapter 2 that Hindu residents tend to disfavor Muslims seeking to become slum leaders. In Chapter 3, we demonstrated that slum leaders are less responsive to recent arrivals because of their more limited social ties. Chapter 4 established that brokers from different caste backgrounds than patrons are less likely to be extended organizational positions. The adverse effects of such biases extend to the supporters of these brokers, who rely on the latter to extract resources from the state. In Chapter 5, we showed that goods and services that cannot be easily tagged by patrons are less attractive from a credit-claiming perspective, raising barriers to obtaining them. In prioritizing claims, politicians also consider the partisanship of brokers, and appear to disfavor requests from brokers from rival parties. Settlements lacking in leaders with attractive partisan profiles might therefore be disadvantaged in having their requests acted upon.

We further find that women are systematically underrepresented within the ranks of slum leaders. This underrepresentation reverberates upwards, given that brokers constitute the pool of slum residents from which parties pick their local operatives. It is also likely to echo downwards, given research on local government in India showing that female elected representatives often have distinct preferences over public goods and services, and are more likely to be receptive to the needs of women in their localities.[55] A lack of women in positions of informal authority within slum settlements similarly may serve to marginalize the voices and needs of female residents. Indeed, Chapter 3 documents a gender gap in residents seeking assistance from brokers, which is especially acute in settlements without any female leaders.

There are also broader limits in what party machines can deliver for the urban poor. Most households across our sampled settlements (88%), even after decades of existence on the land, have not been extended full land titles. Many of our sampled settlements (30 of 110) have not even been "notified," meaning that they are not officially acknowledged as a slum and are consequently more vulnerable to eviction.[56] Thus, while many settlements have secured a range of public services through party networks, these gains sit atop a tenuous foundation of informality. Politicians have few incentives to formalize slums, as it undermines the precarity that fuels high turnout rates at elections. Researchers have shown that persistent informality in housing is

55. On female preferences over public goods and services, see Chattopadhyay and Duflo 2004. For increased receptivity to female needs, Brulé 2020.

56. India's National Sample Survey Office (NSSO) estimated in 2014 that 59% of slums in India are not officially notified. NSSO 2014, Report 561.

detrimental to a range of human development indicators, from public health to access to credit.[57]

A lack of broad-based formalization, in part, stems from the fragmented nature of the politics we have described in this book. The formation and functioning of machine networks only reinforce the centrality of the slum, or city neighborhood, as the locus of urban distributive politics. Brokerage environments are contained and compartmentalized within each slum, with every leader being a resident of the specific settlement in which they worked. Claim-making requests through machine networks—from residents to brokers, or brokers to patrons—are similarly structured by settlement boundaries. Machine politics thus helps entrench a fractured politics in which the urban poor rarely band together to advance collective, class-based claims. We rarely find multiple settlements coordinating their mobilizing efforts to increase their *lokshakti* (people power).

A lack of wider, coordinated, class-based mobilization impedes the transformative potential of machines in urban India. What, though, is the alternative to the politics outlined in our book? Scholars of distributive politics often paint a binary between clientelistic forms of politics and programmatic politics. The latter is rule-bound, with public resources flowing from clearly specified, policy-based entitlements. This is far from the world of machine politics in India's cities. Yet we cannot assume the demise of machine politics would necessarily lead to such programmatic politics. It could instead give way to an even more elite-centric predatory politics centered around facilitating regulatory evasion and profiteering by the wealthy. Alternatively, it could be replaced by a programmatic politics that is not pro-poor, but instead advances policies favoring the city's wealthy or middle classes. The dismantling of machine networks might pave the way for programmatic politics, but equally might rob slums of the bulwark they have against even greater marginalization.

Such grim alternatives seem eminently plausible in India's current political climate. As we will describe shortly, the country exhibits trends of fiscal centralization that may weaken the strength of local machine operatives. India has also been described as experiencing its own "Gilded Age" or "Billionaire Raj," with an economic trajectory that has proven to be more pro-business than pro-market.[58] The country is marked by a declining income share of the

---

57. De Soto 2003; Field 2007; Mitlin and Satterthwaite 2013.

58. On India as being in a "Gilded Age" or "Billionaire Raj," see Crabtree 2018. On India's economic trajectory, Kohli 2012.

bottom ninety percent of the population, rising billionaire wealth in rent-thick sectors, and an overconcentration of profits in twenty large companies.[59]

This terrain does not appear fertile ground for pro-poor programmatic politics that would prove a boon for slum settlements, with widespread formalization, the blanket extension of services, and more dignity and respect afforded to residents. Programmatic politics might instead formalize the implementation of widescale evictions and displacement, making way for more lucrative uses of the land. Or an increasingly powerful business elite may join hands with an increasingly centralized political elite to entrench an oligarchic politics that renders the poor even less influential than they have been thus far. The plausibility of such scenarios fuels our ambivalence about a world where the networks described in our book are pushed aside, with little inkling of what might replace them.

The Horizon of Democracy in Urban India

Within the next three decades, India will cross an unprecedented threshold—more than half of the country's population will reside in cities and towns. Signs of this demographic transformation can be seen at every turn in India's cities, from rapid changes in the built space to the massive movement of people within and to cities. Since we started our joint research in 2014, 10 million people (roughly the entire population of Honduras, Jordan, or Sweden) have been added to India's urban population *each year*, catapulting the total urban population past 400 million.

Our book centers on an important part of this urbanization story—the emergence and modalities of political life in India's proliferating slum settlements. Like tenement housing in New York City that provided shelter to poor European migrants in the late-nineteenth and early-twentieth centuries, India's slums are catchments for low-income migrants seeking to carve out a better life in cities. And like their counterparts in Gilded Age New York, India's slums are "garrisons" of popular politics, enmeshed in political networks that connect residents and their informal leaders to political elites.[60]

---

59. According to Chancel and Piketty 2019, the top 1% of Indians captured over 20% of national income by 2015 (compared to just 10% in 1990). The share of the bottom 90% declined from roughly 65% to 43% during the same span. On rising billionaire wealth, see Gandhi and Walton 2012. Finally, just 20 companies captured nearly 70% of corporate profits in India in 2019, up from 14% just three decades prior, and compared to roughly 25% in the United States. *Economist* 2020.

60. Harriss 2007.

Our focus on the local, however, provokes an important, broader question: how does the urban politics examined in the preceding pages interact with larger developments in India's raucous democracy? Indeed, the local machine politics we examine are not isolated ecosystems, unaffected by broader sea changes in national politics. With that in mind, we conclude by considering how our book's theory and findings, centered on city politics, converse with national political trends in India.

Since the start of our joint fieldwork in 2014, the BJP under Narendra Modi has stormed the national political stage, winning outright majorities in India's lower house of parliament in the 2014 and 2019 elections—a feat ending twenty-five years of coalitional politics at the center.[61] These twin victories have left many analysts concluding that the BJP is India's new dominant party.[62] This conclusion seems especially warranted given the BJP's impressive strike rate in head-to-head battles with the Congress, the country's erstwhile dominant party.[63]

The BJP's recent supremacy in national elections is rooted in several advantages. Opinion polls highlight the consistent popularity of Narendra Modi. Seeking to harness his celebrity, party campaigns focus on Modi's personal appeal and direct rapport with voters.[64] This popularity is complemented by underlying structural advantages, notably money. In 2017, the BJP-led government introduced a set of campaign finance reforms under the guise of improving transparency. In reality, these measures enabled opaque, unlimited donations to parties through a new mechanism of electoral bonds.[65] In 2017–18, the

61. Prior to 2014, Yadav 1999 divides India's national elections into an initial era of dominance for the INC (from 1947–67); a second era marked by growing opposition to the Congress within individual states through state-specific regional parties (1967–89); and a third phase marked by high levels of fragmentation, coalition politics, and the rise of opposition forces, including many caste-based parties (1989–2014). The most significant of these forces, and the only one with credible claims to being a national rival to the INC was the BJP, which headed a coalition government from 1999–2004. Since 2014, analysts have argued we are now in a fourth phase, defined by BJP dominance at the center. Vaishnav and Hinston 2019.

62. Chhibber and Verma 2019; Vaishnav and Hintson 2019; Jaffrelot and Verniers 2020.

63. For example, when the BJP and Congress were the top-two parties in terms of vote share in a constituency, the BJP won 86% of the time in 2014, and 92% of the time in 2019. Sircar 2019.

64. Sircar 2020.

65. These reforms passed over concerns raised by the Reserve Bank of India, the Election Commission of India, and some Members of Parliament. See Sethi 2019.

BJP was reported to have secured an incredible ninety-five percent of electoral bond purchases.[66]

How might this new dominant party at the center—a party that grew out of India's Hindu nationalist movement—come to alter the mechanics of urban machine politics? The BJP's rapid ascendance has ushered in two political developments that might shift the form and functioning of machine politics in India's cities. The first is a movement toward greater political and fiscal centralization. The second is an unleashed Hindu majoritarianism—and a growing intolerance of dissent against the Modi government—that is altering the terrain of identity politics and contentious politics. We speculate on the implications of each of these developments for the future of the local worlds explored in this book.

Local Politics in a Centralizing Democracy

India's municipal governments are widely described as anemic, stuck in a morass of paltry budgets, understaffed offices, and constricted responsibilities over governance and public service delivery.[67] In most cities, urban development authorities—parastatal organizations with little direct accountability to citizens—tower over municipal governments in resources and technical capacity. This difference is often visibly conspicuous. In Jaipur, a walk around the development authority yields images of impressive computer rooms with urban planners using the latest GIS software. Jaipur's municipal office, on the other hand, is a dusty, dimly lit building with few of the resources and skilled personnel found just down the street in the development authority.

There is an urgent need for deeper decentralization in India's cities. A large literature on decentralization argues that local governments with sufficient resources, revenue-raising capacity, and administrative support are better positioned to respond to citizen needs.[68] However, scholars also argue that a key ingredient for decentralized governance is an active citizenry, ready to make demands and hold local officials to account.[69] Our book should generate considerable optimism that further decentralization will be met with robust

66. *Business Standard* 2019.
67. Ramanathan 2007; Baud and de Wit 2008; Bhan et al. 2014.
68. Manor 1999; Bardhan and Mookerjee 2006; Grindle 2009.
69. Ostrom 1996; Heller 1999; Fox 2007; Mansuri and Rao 2013.

forms of citizen participation in India's most underserved urban neighborhoods. The "active citizenship" we document should enhance a greater devolution of fiscal and political powers in cities.[70]

Yet the prospects of significant devolution of authority to municipal governments appear bleak in India's current political landscape. The BJP's electoral dominance has enabled greater fiscal and administrative centralization.[71] Institutions like the National Development Council, through which states previously negotiated with the center over budgetary allocations, have been dismantled, with decisions now largely appropriated by the national Ministry of Finance.[72] Policy reforms that were touted as centerpieces of "collaborative federalism"—notably the establishment of a new Goods and Service Tax (GST)—have ignited conflict between the center and states over how to handle shortfalls in revenue collections. In terms of administrative decisions, Aiyar and Tillin describe the "aggregation of power within the Prime Minister's Office (PMO)," and the marginalization of state governments under Modi.[73]

Additionally, the Modi government has increased the footprint of Centrally Sponsored Schemes, which are specific-purpose, monitored, central transfers to states that are often seen as tools of centralized control.[74] Welfare schemes have been renamed to include the title of Prime Minister, to burnish Modi's image with recipients. Survey data suggest that such moves have proved at least somewhat effective, with rising proportions of voters attributing credit for welfare programs to the center. These changing patterns of attribution may yield electoral dividends for the BJP, completing a cycle in which electoral dominance, fiscal centralization, and administrative control are mutually reinforcing.[75]

70. See Kruks-Wisner 2018 on active citizenship and claim-making in India.

71. The first Modi government, elected in 2014, did make some initial gestures in the direction of further decentralization. For example, in 2015, it accepted the recommendations of India's Fourteenth Finance Commission, which increased the percentage of the divisible pool of taxes shared between central and state governments that went to the latter. The government also replaced India's Planning Commission, long seen as an embodiment of centralized governance, with NITI Aayog (National Institution for Transforming India), which saw its mission as helping foster a model of "cooperative federalism."

72. Aiyar and Tillin 2020, p. 128.

73. Aiyar and Tillin 2020, p. 130.

74. Roy 2019.

75. Deshpande et al. 2019.

The centripetal political forces at play in Modi's India might come to reconfigure how the three sets of actors at the core of our book's analytical framework—voters, brokers, and patrons—look to construct political networks in the city, with implications for distributive politics. It is worth considering these implications actor by actor, and in the same sequence as the prior chapters, given the interlocking nature of their decisions.

We first consider the implications of political centralization through the eyes of poor urban voters. Slum residents already have little hope that approaching government officials will command the latter's attention. Moving the locus of political power even further above their heads—away from ward councilors and municipal bureaucrats to higher levels of government—may increasingly compel slum residents to petition higher—and less accessible—officials, where their clout as voters is diminished due to larger constituency sizes. An upward shift in the distribution of political power might weaken the ability of ward councilors to pressure service departments on behalf of residents, further restricting pathways of problem-solving for residents. Centralization, therefore, may make claim-making—the crucial way that slum residents engage a dismissive and discretionary state—even more difficult.

Deepening pessimism around expectations of state responsiveness has related implications for the quality of democracy in India's cities. A further weakening of local governance might intensify the despondency felt by many slum residents regarding their political efficacy, and thus reduce their participation in everyday forms of citizenship practice—petitioning, protesting, forming local development councils, and attending neighborhood association meetings. This has deleterious consequences for the prospects of social and political accountability in cities, for those who most need their voices heard. Centralization does not preclude the possibility of effective service delivery.[76] It does, however, make citizens dependent on central actors to effectively and fairly implement programs without the need for bottom-up accountability. The degree to which such elite benevolence manifests or sustains, and how India's urban poor politically react to this model of politics remains an important question for future study.

A greater centralization of power under a dominant party might also reorient which traits residents look for in their informal leaders. As we have

76. Analysts have spoken of the Modi government's successful pursuit of a "new welfarism" marked both by centralized delivery and a focus on the public provision of private or household level benefits (cooking gas, toilets, electricity) over local public goods (Anand et al. 2020).

shown, residents are driven in their selection of informal leaders by assessments of who is best positioned to improve the material conditions of the slum. Education and bureaucratic connectivity are two key attributes that guide such assessments. By contrast, connections to incumbents are not seen as especially valuable, given patterns of electoral volatility, and the fact that opposition party leaders retained some measure of local bureaucratic influence. Yet, under greater centralization, residents might come to increasingly understand efficacy as reduced to connectivity with the dominant national party, and hence political elites in the BJP. Partisan connectivity to New Delhi may increasingly crowd out other factors in determining who is best positioned to demand development and to gather information about increasingly important central schemes.

From the vantage point of slum leaders, the sidelining of local representatives in everyday governance thins out the number of focal points within the state around which they can make claims. Indeed, the presence of dueling party machines is enabled by robust federalism and a meaningful degree of decentralization—a party out of power at one level of government might win another, ensuring some access to the gears of the state. The centralization of power and current dominance of the BJP may push the electoral system more towards to a situation of single machine dominance, especially across the BJP's northern Indian strongholds, rendering those slum leaders without ties to the BJP less effective problem-solvers, with adverse consequences for their ability to build and maintain a popular following.

This collapsed space for claim-making, and a stronger need for connectivity to a dominant party in the center, may stifle inter-broker and inter-party competition within settlements. Those slum leaders with ties to a narrower band of centrally connected politicians will be less vulnerable to competition from entrepreneurial upstarts in the settlement, who have fewer meaningful outlets for their nascent claim-making activities. Moreover, even the most established INC (Congress) workers might recede into irrelevancy in local problem-solving efforts, and those who want to defect will face more intense competition for limited BJP organizational positions. This all serves to constrict competition and choice, thereby weakening the options of brokers seeking political careers, and, consequently, their leverage in demanding upward mobility within partisan organizations from patrons.

As the distribution of political power shifts upward and local outlets for claim-making narrow, efforts to stay in the good graces of a select group of connected party elites might come to take on greater salience in the political lives of slum leaders. At the same time, the clout of residents to pressure bro-kers diminishes. This new reality might prompt a shift in the focus of a slum leader's activities to those that signal loyalty to party and patron—taking up routine opportunities to curry favor with party elites. As a result, slum leaders may find themselves with less bandwidth or desire for spearheading bottom-up claim-making, further diminishing the ability of ordinary residents to have their problems heard and taken up.

Similarly, for "low patrons" in the city like ward councilors, signaling loyalty to co-partisan higher-ups might come to take on greater importance under centralization. Ward councilors might increasingly view their future political prospects as being tied to riding the coattails of senior party elites, diminishing incentives to build a personal base of electoral support. In turn, patron assess-ments of brokers might become untethered from the latter's ability to solve local problems, and instead rest on a broker's ability to help broadcast the patron's loyalty upward to the party.

Also relevant to low patrons, the Modi government has sought to centralize control and credit for welfare programs, potentially altering the politics of at-tribution that we find to be so important in driving the responsiveness of mu-nicipal politicians. Ward councilors in the BJP might increasingly find them-selves performing the role of local megaphone for Brand Modi, trumpeting the welfare schemes and policies of his office. This reorientation will shrink councilors' opportunities to engage in credit-claiming centered on their own initiatives, in an effort to build a personal base of popular support. We noted that power is increasingly concentrated not just in the central government, but also within the Prime Minister's Office, at the expense of the credit-claiming abilities of even state Chief Ministers. For humble ward councilors, particu-larly those not in the BJP, oxygen for credit-claiming will inevitably be sucked out of the room by such trends. This shrinking space for claiming credit, in combination with fiscal and administrative centralization, will make it more difficult for opposition politicians to directly signal to voters their own roles as benefactors in the provision of local public goods and services.

Local Politics and Hindu Majoritarianism

The success of the BJP in the last two parliamentary elections has not only heralded an electoral shift to a new dominant party. It has also entailed an ideological shift—the ascendance of Hindu nationalism, or *Hindutva*. The foundational ideology for the Sangh Parivar (family of organizations) that birthed the BJP and its predecessor, the Jana Sangh, *Hindutva* sought to standardize a set of cultural practices as the core of Hinduism and link those practices to the political form of the Indian nation-state.[77] Leaders of the Rashtriya Swayamsevak Sangh (RSS), the preeminent organization within the Sangh Parivar, have drawn on *Hindutva* ideas to structure their efforts at societal transformation through a vast network of grassroots chapters, and in articulating policy demands that would help realize this transformation.

Several major demands associated with *Hindutva*'s core agenda have been realized since the BJP came to power in 2014. Following the 2019 victory, an emboldened BJP turned more squarely to checking off items that have long been on its ideological wish list. In August 2019, the parliament abrogated Article 370, which had, since Independence, given the Muslim-majority state of Kashmir some autonomies within the Indian federation.[78] The region was stripped of statehood and converted into two union territories, whose governance is more directly controlled by the central government. That same summer, the state of Assam became a testing ground for the National Register of Citizens, culminating in a list of nearly two million people whose citizenship status is now in question. This is widely understood as a first step toward deporting Bangladeshi migrants—most of whom are Muslim.[79] By the end of 2019, the BJP government had passed the Citizenship Amendment Act, a law

77. The architect of *Hindutva*, Vinayak Damodar Savarkar, identified three pillars of national identity: a common fatherland (geographic unity), common blood (racial features), and a common culture. Only Hindus possess all three of these traits with respect to India, informing Savarkar's view that the territory of India be marked as a "Hindu Rashtra" (Hindu state). According to Savarkar, non-Hindu communities (notably Muslims and Christians) should accept what he defined as core tenets of Hindu culture in order to become part of the Indian nation. Sarvarkar 1923. Later ideologues, such as M.S. Golwalkar, emphasized the racial dimension of *Hindutva* far more than the territorial one, arguing race is "by far the most important ingredient of a nation," and that "people of a foreign origin" (which according to Savarkar's conceptualization encompassed all non-Hindus) needed to "inextricably" be fused into "the mother race" of Hinduism. As quoted in Jaffrelot 2007, p. 102.

78. Gettleman et al. 2019.

79. Assam is understood to be home to a large population of Bangladeshi Muslim migrants, many of whom came across the border to escape the violence of Bangladesh's war of independence in 1971. The state has since become a center of nativist, anti-Bangladeshi and anti-Muslim politics, and the issue of illegal migrants in Assam is used as a dog whistle by the BJP—that there are millions of undocumented Bangladeshi Muslims in India, threatening national security and benefiting from the welfare state. The citizenship register in Assam is widely understood as a way to enumerate these migrants so that they can be declared stateless and pushed out of India.

enabling religion to serve as the basis for deciding Indian citizenship in certain cases.[80] In November 2019, the Supreme Court granted a disputed piece of land in Ayodhya, Uttar Pradesh, to a government trust so that it could oversee the construction of a temple for the Hindu god Ram. The temple will be constructed on land where a mosque was destroyed by Hindu nationalists in 1992.[81] Reflecting on these events, scholars of the BJP conclude that we are seeing a shift from a "de facto Hindu majoritarian state towards a de jure Hindu majoritarian state."[82]

Underneath these high-profile policies are escalating rhetoric and quotidian forms of violence against India's Muslims, carried out by a patchwork of Hindu nationalist organizations—the Bajrang Dal, Vishwa Hindu Parishad, and RSS—and more localized groups aligned with the Hindu Right. Recent examples include attacks on Muslims and Dalits accused of eating beef, and attacks on inter-faith couples in an effort to prevent "love jihad"—a baseless conspiracy theory that India's Muslims are seeking to change religious demographics by converting Hindu women to Islam through marriage. During the coronavirus pandemic, these same groups accused Muslims of deliberately spreading the virus, leading to a spree of violence against Muslims.[83] These activities are at least implicitly sanctioned, and often explicitly encouraged, by BJP elites.[84] Respected observers of Indian politics have discussed these

---

See Shamshad 2018 on Assamese nativist politics and *New York Times* 2019 on Assam's citizenship register.

80. See Jayal 2019. Specifically, the Act paves a way to citizenship for certain migrants from adjacent countries who are Hindu, Christian, Sikh, Buddhist, and Parsi—but not Muslim. It is feared that the Citizenship Amendment Act, in combination with the National Register of Citizens, will allow the BJP government to identify and deport Muslims in India who cannot prove their citizenship. See Slater 2019.

81. While this decision was reached by the formally independent Supreme Court, it was widely anticipated. In recent years, concerns have been raised about the autonomy of the Court, which has avoided dealing with difficult and important cases featuring central government actions (including the abrogation of Article 370, which was done without consultation with the state legislature as required by the Constitution of India). See Bhatia and Parthasarathy 2019 and Khosla 2020.

82. Jaffrelot and Verniers 2020.

83. *New York Times* 2020.

84. Perrigo 2020. In November 2020, the BJP-led state government of Uttar Pradesh, India's most populous province, passed a law outlawing "unlawful religious conversions" through marriage. Chief Minister Yogi Adityanath, a hardline Hindu nationalist, said at a rally a month earlier

moves in terms of "a brute majoritarianism subordinating others" and a resolve to "show Muslims their place."[85]

How might an increasingly muscular—and less constrained—Hindu nationalism impact urban machine politics? Most immediately, it may serve to harden lines of exclusion in the construction of political networks and in the distribution of public resources. In 2019, the BJP nominated the controversial Pragya Singh Thakur to contest parliamentary elections in Bhopal. Thakur, now a Member of Parliament representing Bhopal, is a militant Hindu supremacist, who has boasted of her role in destroying the Ayodhya mosque, has valorized the man who murdered Mohandas Gandhi as a "patriot," and faces charges of partaking in a terrorist conspiracy.[86] Our own work also unearthed some seeds of an exclusionary politics centered around religious divisions. For example, we find a sizeable penalty against slum leaders who are Muslim in resident evaluations, driven by the views of Hindu residents. Moreover, we find that Muslims are numerically underrepresented in the ranks of low patrons across Jaipur and Bhopal.

Yet we also document currents that go against such exclusion, in particular the incentives of both slum leaders and urban patrons to craft cross-caste and cross-religious networks in diverse cities. We also find non-negligible levels of support for the BJP among our sampled Muslim residents, and a non-trivial proportion of Muslim slum leaders affiliated with the BJP. In combination with underlying ethnic diversity, the intensely materialist thrust of machine politics can serve to diminish the centrality of polarizing ethnic conflicts in structuring local urban politics.

Yet, a constant drum beat of *Hindutva* politics might fundamentally alter such realities. It may become increasingly difficult for slum leaders and politicians to credibly commit to assisting those of a different faith. And Muslim voters may find it harder and harder to justify supporting the BJP. Our data regarding Muslim support for the BJP came from 2015, after Modi and the BJP had come to power but well before the more recent spate of Hindu majoritarian policies just outlined. It is possible that such support has already eroded.

---

that his government would "enact a strict law to stop love jihad," and issued threats against Muslim men in interfaith relationships.

85. Mehta 2020; Guha 2020.

86. On her role in destroying the Ayodhya mosque, *India Today* 2019. On describing the murderer of Mohandas Gandhi as a "patriot," *Hindustan Times* 2020. And on her facing charges of terrorist conspiracy see, Masih 2019.

Any hardening of party-voter linkages along religious lines has concerning implications for the ability of minority groups to access public resources. Muslim majority neighborhoods in many of India's cities *already* face systematic marginalization in the distribution of public services.[87] The breakdown of multi-religious party networks may prove to deepen such marginalization. Moreover, increased religious segregation in political networks corrodes a buffer against communal conflict.[88]

Another key implication of rising majoritarianism, coupled with a centralization of power, has been shrinking room for a politics of dissent and protest. Protests against the policies of the Modi government have invited police violence and imprisonment under colonial-era sedition laws.[89] Foreign NGOs like Amnesty International and Greenpeace have been kicked out of India or forced to reduce their domestic footprint.[90] Indian NGOs are finding themselves increasingly squeezed for resources with tightening restrictions on foreign funding.[91] Journalists critical of the Modi government are harassed and intimidated.[92] In some high-profile instances, those journalists have been killed.[93] Activists and academics who are critical of the Modi government are branded as "anti-nationals" and face a deluge of harassment from the Hindu Right.[94]

These growing examples of state repression, and state-condoned citizen attacks on protestors, send a chilling message about the costs of dissent. Many have been cited as reasons for India's recent declines across several global indicators of democratic freedoms.[95] While these broad trends have been acknowledged, their local consequences for everyday politics have been less discussed.

87. Gayer and Jaffrelot 2013.

88. Varshney 2003.

89. Prasad 2020.

90. Kumar 2019.

91. Ghoshal 2020.

92. Gopalakrishnan 2018.

93. George 2020.

94. Ayyub 2020.

95. India received the largest score decline among the world's 25 largest democracies in the 2020 Freedom House ratings. In 2021, the country slipped further, from a rating of "Free" to "Partly Free." The country has also steadily declined in its V-Dem "liberal democracy" index since 2014, and in 2021 saw its status change from democracy to "electoral autocracy," with its lowest rating since the period of Emergency Rule under Indira Gandhi in 1975–77.

For the slum residents at the heart of our book, acts of contentious politics are central to their efforts to advance their material conditions. These activities range from small acts of group claim-making that assert demands for public services, to slum-wide protests involving hundreds, sometimes thousands, of residents. While scattered and localized demands for public services are unlikely to provoke the ire of the Modi government, efforts to resist national urban development programs—which, for the poor, often mean displacement—may succeed in inviting even heavier forms of state repression than in the past. The future of "world-class city making" in Modi's India may be even more intolerant of mobilizations of the poor than in the past, with troubling implications for democracy and the wellbeing of marginalized people in India's cities.[96]

In short, the twin weights of Hindu majoritarianism and political centralization in Modi's India are heavy, and they may come to disrupt some of the dynamics of urban machine politics we document in this book. Such disruptions might in turn alter the nature of citizenship practice, political representation, and distributive politics among a population of people in India's cities that already suffers from intense material deprivation and multi-faceted forms of informality. Political trends in Modi's India are poised to make it more difficult for slum residents to navigate and make claims on the state, particularly for Muslims, who now face even deeper social and political exclusion than before. The numerous and still-unfolding consequences of these political developments for local democracy in India's cities should command substantial scholarly attention.

Against this concerning backdrop, India continued to witness major waves of mass protest as we finished this book, including one spearheaded by farmers and another by a range of communities opposed to the Citizenship Amendment Act.[97] These recent collective actions underscore a key observation at the heart of this book. Ordinary citizens have substantial political agency within forms of politics that are often characterized as elite-driven. Slum

96. On the politics of "world-class city making" in India, see Ghertner 2015.

97. In late 2020, millions of farmers from across India, and especially from northwestern states like Punjab, mobilized against a set of agricultural laws. Proponents of these laws say they are necessary reforms for India's agricultural sector, while protesting farmers fear these measures will make their economic circumstances even more precarious. Gupta and Ganguly 2020. Exactly a year prior, in December 2019, protests erupted against the Citizenship Amendment Act. Jayal 2019.

residents, who live some of the most precarious lives on the planet, are not simply acted upon by urban governments. Slum residents actively shape the structures that govern them. What is even more remarkable is that they do so through processes that reflect democratic deliberation and a willingness to work across ascriptive divisions that too often result in sectarian strife. Those with the least means routinely demonstrate—from small acts of claim-making to larger, more boisterous acts of protest—the power of ordinary citizens in defending, deepening, and demanding democracy.

REFERENCES

Abadie, Alberto, Susan Athey, Guido Imbens, and Jeffrey Wooldridge. 2017. "When Should You Adjust Standard Errors for Clustering?" NBER.

Abramson, Scott, Korhan Kocak, and Asya Magazinnik. 2020. "What do We Learn About Voter Preferences from Conjoint Experiments?" Working Paper.

Accountability Initiative. 2020. *A Comprehensive Overview: Defining and Measuring Informality in India's Labour Market*. New Delhi: Centre for Policy Research.

Afrobarometer. 2016. Round 6. Available at https://afrobarometer.org/data/merged-round-6 -data-36-countries-2016.

Aiyar, Yamini and Louise Tillin. 2020. "'One nation,' BJP, and the future of Indian federalism." *India Review*. 19(2): 117–35.

Anand, Abhishek, Vikas Dimble and Arvind Subramanian. 2020. "New Welfarism of Modi government represents distinctive approach to redistribution and inclusion." *Indian Express*, December 22, 2020.

Anderson, Siwan, Patrick Francois, Ashok Kotwal. 2015. "Clientelism in Indian Villages." *American Economic Review* 105(6): 1780–1816.

Anderson, Walter and Shridhar Damle. 1987. *The Brotherhood in Saffron: The Rashtriya Swayamsevak Sangh and Hindu Revivalism*. Boulder, CO: Westview Press.

Anjaria, Jonathan Shapiro. 2016. *Slow Boil: Street Food, Rights, and Public Spaces in Mumbai*. Stanford, CA: Stanford University Press.

Arriola, Leonardo. 2012. *Multiethnic Coalitions in Africa*. New York, NY: Cambridge University Press.

Aspinall, Edward. 2014. "When Brokers Betray." *Critical Asian Studies* 46(4): 545–70.

Auerbach, Adam Michael. 2016. "Clients and Communities: The Political Economy of Party Network Organization and Development in India's Urban Slums." *World Politics* 68(1): 111–48.

———. 2017. "Neighborhood Associations and the Urban Poor: India's Slum Development Committees." *World Development* 96: 119–35.

———. 2018. "Informal Archives." *Studies in Comparative International Development* 53(3): 343–64.

———. 2020. *Demanding Development: The Politics of Public Goods Provision in India's Urban Slums*. New York, NY: Cambridge University Press.

Auerbach, Adam Michael and Gabrielle Kruks-Wisner. 2020. "The Geography of Citizenship Practice: How the Poor Engage the State in Rural and Urban India." *Perspectives on Politics* 18(4): 1118–34.

Auerbach, Adam M., Adrienne LeBas, Alison Post, and Rebecca Weitz-Shapiro. 2018. "State, Society, and Informality in Cities of the Global South." *Studies in Comparative International Development* 53: 261–80.

Auerbach, Adam Michael and Tariq Thachil. 2018. "How Clients Select Brokers: Competition and Choice in India's Slums." *American Political Science Review* 112(4): 775–91.

Auerbach, Adam Michael and Tariq Thachil. 2020. "Cultivating Clients: Reputation, Responsiveness, and Ethnic Indifference in India's Slums." *American Journal of Political Science* 64(3): 471–87.

Auerbach, Adam Michael and Tariq Thachil. 2021. "How does Covid-19 Affect Urban Slums? Evidence from Settlement Leaders in India." *World Development* 140: 1–11.

Auerbach, Adam Michael and Adam Ziegfeld. 2020. "How do Electoral Quotas Influence Political Competition? Evidence from Municipal, State, and National Elections in India." *Journal of Politics* 82(1): 397–401.

Auerbach, Adam Michael, Jennifer Bussell, Simon Chauchard, Francesca Jensenius, Gareth Nellis, Mark Schneider, Neelanjan Sircar, Pavithra Suryanarayan, Tariq Thachil, Rahul Verma, and Adam Ziegfeld. 2022. Rethinking the Study of Electoral Politics in the Developing World: Reflections on the Indian Case." *Perspectives on Politics* 20(1): 250–64.

Auyero, Javier. 2001. *Poor People's Politics: Peronist Survival Networks and the Legacy of Evita.* Durham, NC: Duke University Press.

Ayyub, Rana. 2020. "I Saw Police Stand by as Masked Men Attacked Students at a Top Delhi University." *Time.* January 8.

Azim Premji University and Lokniti. 2019. "Politics and Society between Elections Dataset (2017–2019)."

Bailey, F.G. 1970. *Politics and Social Change: Orissa in 1959.* Berkeley, CA: University of California Press.

Baland, Jean-Marie and James Robinson. 2012. "The Political Value of Land." *American Journal of Political Science* 56(3): 601–19.

Baldwin, Kate. 2013. "Why Vote with the Chief? Political Connections and Public Goods Provision in Zambia." *American Journal of Political Science* 57(4): 794–809.

———. 2016. *The Paradox of Traditional Chiefs in Democratic Africa.* Cambridge: Cambridge University Press.

Banfield, Edward C. and James Q. Wilson. 1963. *City Politics.* Cambridge, MA: Harvard University Press and the M.I.T. Press.

Bansak, Kirk, Jens Hainmueller, Daniel Hopkins, and Teppei Yamamoto. 2020. "Using Conjoint Experiments to Analyze Elections: The Essential Role of the Average Marginal Component Effect (AMCE)." Working Paper.

Bardhan, Pranab and Dilip Mookherjee. 2006. *Decentralization and Local Governance in Developing Countries.* Cambridge, MA: MIT Press.

Baud, Isa and Joop de Wit. 2008. *New Forms of Urban Governance in India.* New Delhi: Sage.

Bayart, Jean-Francois. 1993. *The State in Africa: The Politics of the Belly.* London: Polity.

Bayat, Asef. 1997. *Street Politics: Poor People's Movements in Iran.* New York, NY: Columbia University Press.

Bedi, Tarini. 2017. *The Dashing Ladies of the Shiv Sena: Political Matronage in Urbanizing India.* Albany, NY: SUNY Press.

Berenschot, Ward. 2010. "Everyday Mediation: The Politics of Public Service Delivery in Gujarat, India." *Development and Change* 41(5): 883–905.

———. 2011. *Riot Politics: Hindu-Muslim Violence and the Indian State*. New York, NY: Columbia University Press.

———. 2014. "Political Fixers in India's Patronage Democracy." In *Patronage as Politics in South Asia*. Edited by Anastasia Piliavsky. 392–401. New York, NY: Cambridge University Press.

———. 2018. "The Political Economy of Clientelism: A Comparative Study of Indonesia's Patronage Democracy." *Comparative Political Studies* 51(12): 1563–93.

Besley, Timothy, Stephen Coate, and Glenn Loury. 1993. "The Economics of Rotating Saving and Credit Associations." *American Economic Review*, 83(4): 792–810.

Besley, Timothy, Rohini Pande, and Vijayendra Rao. 2005. "Participatory Democracy in Action: Survey Evidence from South India." *Journal of the European Economic Association* 3(2–3): 648–57.

Besley, Timothy, Jose Montalvo, and Marta Reynal-Querol. 2011. "Do Educated Leaders Matter?" *The Economic Journal* 121(554): 205–27.

Bhan, Gautam. 2016. *In the Public's Interest: Evictions, Citizenship, and Inequality in Contemporary India*. Athens, GA: University of Georgia Press.

Bhan, Gautam, Amlanjyoti Goswami, and Aromar Revi. 2014. "The Intent to Reside." *State of the Urban Poor Report*. Delhi: Oxford University Press.

Bhatia, Gautam and Suhrith Parthasarathy. 2019. "Peace Bought by an Unequal Compromise." *The Hindu*. November 25.

Bhavnani, Rikhil. 2009. "Do Electoral Quotas Work After They are Withdrawn? Evidence from a Natural Experiment in India." *American Political Science Review* 103(1): 23–35.

Bhavnani, Rikhil and Bethany Lacina. 2019. *Nativism and Economic Integration Across the Developing World: Collision and Accomodation*. New York, NY: Cambridge University Press.

Björkman, Lisa. 2014. "You Can't Buy a Vote: Meanings of Money in a Mumbai Election." *American Ethnologist* 41(4): 617–34.

———. 2014. "'Vote Banking' as Politics in Mumbai." In *Patronage as Politics in South Asia*. Edited by Anastasia Piliavsky. 176–95. New York, NY: Cambridge University Press.

Bradley, Donald S. and Mayer Zald. 1965. "From Commercial Elite to Political Administrator: The Recruitment of the Mayors of Chicago." *American Journal of Sociology*, 71(2): 153–67.

Brass, Paul. 1965. *Factional Politics in an Indian State: The Congress Party in Uttar Pradesh*. Berkeley, CA: University of California Press.

Brierley, Sarah and Noah Nathan. 2021. "The Connections of Party Brokers." *Journal of Politics* 83(3): 884–901.

Brulé, Rachel. 2020. *Women, Power, and Property: The Paradox of Gender Equality Laws in India*. New York, NY: Cambridge University Press.

Burgwal, Gerrit. 1996. *Struggle of the Poor: Neighborhood Organization and Clientelist Practice in a Quito Squatter Settlement*. Amsterdam: CEDLA.

Business Standard. 2019. "Ruling BJP Got 95% of Funds: Why There's an Uproar over Electoral Bonds." https://www.business-standard.com/article/current-affairs/ruling-bjp-bags-95-of-funds-why-there-s-an-uproar-over-electoral-bonds-119040500309_1.html.

Bussell, Jennifer. 2019. *Clients and Constituents*. New York, NY: Oxford University Press.

Butler, Daniel and David Broockman. 2011. "Do Politicians Racially Discriminate Against Constituents? A Field Experiment on State Legislators." *American Journal of Political Science* 55(3): 463–77.

Caldeira, Teresa. 2017. "Peripheral Urbanization." *Environment and Planning D: Society and Space* 35(1): 3–20.

Calvo, Ernesto and Maria Victoria Murillo. 2004. "Who Delivers? Partisan Clients in the Argentine Electoral Market." *American Journal of Political Science* 48(4): 742–57.

———. 2012. "When Parties Meet Voters." *Comparative Political Studies* 46(7): 851–82.

Camp, Edwin. 2017. "Cultivating Effective Brokers: A Party Leader's Dilemma." *British Journal of Political Science* 47: 521–43.

Carlson, Elizabeth. 2015. "Ethnic Voting and Accountability in Africa." *World Politics* 67(2): 353–85.

Carnes, Nicholas and Noam Lupu. 2016. "Do Voters Dislike Working-Class Candidates? Voter Biases and the Descriptive Underrepresentation of the Working Class." *American Political Science Review* 110(4): 832–44.

Census of India. 2011. New Delhi: Ministry of Home Affairs. Available at https://censusindia .gov.in/2011-common/censusdata2011.html.

Chancel, Lucas and Thomas Piketty. 2019. "Indian Income Inequality, 1922–2015: From British Raj to Billionaire Raj?" *The Review of Income and Wealth* 65(S1): S33–S62.

Chandra, Kanchan. 2004. *Why Ethnic Parties Succeed*. Cambridge: Cambridge University Press.

———. 2006. "What is Ethnic Identity and Does it Matter?" *Annual Review of Political Science* 9: 397–424.

———. 2017. *Democratic Dynasties: State, Party, and Family in Contemporary Indian Politics*. New York, NY: Cambridge University Press.

Chandra, Kanchan and Chandrika Parmar. 1997. "Party Strategies in the Uttar Pradesh Assembly Elections, 1996." *Economic and Political Weekly* 32(5): 214–22.

Chattopadhyay, Raghabendra and Esther Duflo. 2004. "Women as Policy Makers: Evidence from a Randomized Policy Experiment in India." *Econometrica* 72(5): 1409–43.

Chauchard, Simon. 2016. "Unpacking Ethnic Preferences." *Comparative Political Studies* 49(2): 253–84.

———. 2018. "Electoral Handouts in Mumbai Elections: The Cost of Political Competition." *Asian Survey* 58(2): 341–364.

Chatterjee, Partha. 2004. *The Politics of the Governed*. New York, NY: Columbia University Press.

Chhibber, Pradeep, Francesca Jensenius, and Pavithra Suryanarayan. 2014. "Party Organization and Party Proliferation in India." *Party Politics* 20(4): 489–505.

Chhibber, Pradeep and Rahul Verma. 2019. *Ideology and Identity: The Changing Party Systems of India*. New York, NY: Oxford University Press.

Chubb, Judith. 1982. *Patronage, Power, and Poverty in Southern Italy: A Tale of Two Cities*. New York, NY: Cambridge University Press.

Colburn, David R. and George E. Pozzetta. 1976. "Bosses and Machines: Changing Interpretations in American History." *The History Teacher* 9(3): 445–63.

Collier, David. 1976. *Squatters and Oligarchs: Authoritarian Rule and Policy Change in Peru*. Baltimore, MD: Johns Hopkins University Press.

Cornelius, Wayne. 1975. *Politics and the Migrant Poor in Mexico City*. Stanford, CA: Stanford University Press.

Corstange, Daniel. 2016. *The Price of a Vote in the Middle East*. Cambridge: Cambridge University Press.

Cox, Gary and Matthew McCubbins. 1986. "Electoral Politics as a Redistributive Game." *Journal of Politics* 48(2): 370–89.

Crabtree, James, 2018. *The Billionaire Raj*. New York, NY: Tim Duggan Books.

Cruz, Cesi. 2019. "Social Networks and the Targeting of Vote Buying." *Comparative Political Studies* 52(3): 382–411.

Daby, Mariela. 2021. "The Gender Gap in Political Clientelism: Problem-Solving Networks and the Division of Political Work in Argentina." *Comparative Political Studies* 54(2): 215–44.

Dal Bó, Ernesto, Frederico Finan, Olle Folke, Torsten Persson, and Johanna Rickne. 2017. "Who Becomes a Politician?" *The Quarterly Journal of Economics* 132(4): 1877–1914.

Das, Veena and Michael Walton. 2015. "Political Leadership and the Urban Poor." *Current Anthropology* 56, Supplement 11: S44–S54.

Dash, Bharatee Bhusana and J. Stephen Ferris. 2020. "Economic Performance and Electoral Volatility: Testing the Economic Voting Hypothesis on Indian States, 1957–2013." *Party Politics* 27(6): 1105–1119.

Davis, Mike. 2006. *Planet of Slums*. New York, NY: Verso.

de Soto, Herando. 2003. *The Mystery of Capital*. New York, NY: Basic Books.

de Wit, Joop. 1997. *Poverty, Policy and Politics in Madras Slums*. Delhi: Sage.

Democratic Accountability and Linkages Project. 2009. Duke University https://sites.duke.edu /democracylinkage/data/.

Deshpande, Rajeshwari, Louise Tillin, and K.K. Kailash. 2019. "The BJP's Welfare Scheme: Did they Make a Difference in the 2019 Elections?" *Studies in Indian Politics* 7(2): 219–33.

Diaz-Cayeros, Alberto, Federico Estévez, and Beatriz Magaloni. 2016. *The Political Logic of Poverty Relief: Electoral Strategies and Social Policy in Mexico*. New York, NY: Cambridge University Press.

Dixit, Avinash and John Londregan. 1996. "Redistributive Politics and Economic Efficiency." *American Political Science Review* 89(4): 856–66.

Dosh, Paul. 2010. *Demanding the Land: Urban Popular Movements in Peru and Ecuador, 1990–2005*. University Park, PA: Penn State Press.

Duarte, Raul, Frederico Finan, Horacio Larreguy and Laura Schechter. 2019. "Brokering Votes with Information Spread via Social Networks." NBER Working Paper 26241.

Dunning, Thad and Janhavi Nilekani. 2013. "Ethnic Quotas and Political Mobilization." *American Political Science Review* 107(1): 35–56.

Durkheim, Émile. 1933 [1893]. *The Division of Labor in Society*. Translated by George Simpson. Émile Durkheim on the Division of Labor in Society. Thomas Y. Crowell.

Economist. 2020. "India Inc's profits increasingly belong to a tiny clutch of companies." May 23. https://www.economist.com/business/2020/05/21/india-incs-profits-increasingly-belong -to-a-tiny-clutch-of-companies.

Erie, Steven. 1988. *Rainbow's End: Irish-Americans and the Dilemmas of Urban Machine Politics, 1840–1985*. Berkeley, CA: University of California Press.

Fearon, James D. 1999. "What Is Identity (as We Now Use the Word)?" Unpublished manuscript. Stanford, CA: Stanford University.

Fershtman, Chaim and Uri Gneezy. 2001. "Discrimination in a Segmented Society." *Quarterly Journal of Economics* 116(1): 351–77.

Field, Erica. 2007. "Entitled to Work: Urban Property Rights and Labor Supply in Peru." *Quarterly Journal of Economics* 122(4): 1561–1602.

Fox, Jonathan. 1994. "The Difficult Transition from Clientelism to Citizenship: Lessons from Mexico." *World Politics* 46(2): 151–184.

———. 2007. *Accountability Politics: Power and Voice in Rural Mexico*. New York, NY: Oxford University Press.

Frye, Timothy, Ora John Reuter, and David Szakonyi. 2014. "Political Machines at Work: Voter Mobilization and Electoral Subversion in the Workplace." *World Politics* 66(2): 195–228.

Gaikwad, Nikhar and Gareth Nellis. 2017. "The Majority-Minority Divide in Attitudes Toward Internal Migration: Evidence from Mumbai." *American Journal of Political Science* 61(2): 456–72.

———. 2021. "Do Politicians Discriminate Against Internal Migrants? Evidence from Nationwide Field Experiments in India." *American Journal of Political Science* 65(4): 790–806.

Gandhi, Aditi and Michael Walton. 2012. "Where do India's Billionaires Get Their Wealth?" *Economic and Political Weekly* 47(40): 10–14.

Gans-Morse, Jordan, Sebastian Mazzuca, and Simeon Nichter. 2014. "Varieties of Clientelism." *American Journal of Political Science* 58(2): 415–32.

Gay, Robert. 1990. "Community Organization and Clientelist Politics in Contemporary Brazil." *International Journal of Urban and Regional Research* 14(4): 648–66.

———. 1994. *Popular Organization and Democracy in Rio de Janeiro*. Philadelphia, PA: Temple University Press.

Gayer, Laurent and Christophe Jaffrelot. 2013. *Muslims in Indian Cities*. New York, NY: Oxford University Press.

Gelman, Andrew. 2007. "Scaling Regression Inputs by Dividing by Two Standard Deviations." *Statistics in Medicine* 27(15): 2865–73.

Gelman, Andrew and John Carlin. 2014. "Beyond Power Calculations: Assessing Type S (Sign) and Type M (Magnitude) Errors." *Perspectives on Psychological Science* 9(6): 641–51.

George, Nina. 2020. "Gauri Murder Case Awaits Closure." *Deccan Herald*. September 3.

Gettleman, Jeffrey, Suhasini Raj, Kai Schultz, and Hari Kumar. 2019. "India Revokes Kashmir's Special Status, Raising Fears of Unrest." *New York Times*. August 5.

Ghertner, Asher. 2015. *Rule by Aesthetics*. New York, NY: Oxford University Press.

Ghoshal, Devjyot. 2020. "NGOs Say India's New Rules on Foreign Funding Will Hit Operations." *Reuters*. October 1.

Gilbert. Alan. 1998. *The Latin American City*. 2nd Edition. London: Latin America Bureau.

Gill, Kaveri. 2012. *Of Poverty and Plastic: Scavenging and Scrap Trading Entrepreneurs in India's Urban Informal Economy*. New Delhi: Oxford University Press.

Gingerich, Daniel and Luis Medina. 2013. "The Endurance and Eclipse of the Controlled Vote." *Economics and Politics* 25(3): 453–80.

Glaeser, Edward. 2011. *Triumph of the City*. New York, NY: Penguin Books.

Gonzalez-Ocantos, Ezequiel, Chad Kiewiet de Jonge, Carlos Melendez, Javier Osorio, and David Nickerson. 2012. "Vote-Buying and Social Desirability Bias." *American Journal of Political Science* 56(1): 202–17.

Gopalakrishnan, Raju. 2018. "Indian Journalists Say They Intimidated, Ostracized if They Criticize Modi and the BJP." *Reuters*. April 26.

Gosnell, Harold. 1933. "The Political Party versus the Political Machine." *Annals of the American Academy of Political and Social Science* 169(1): 21–8.

———. 1937. *Machine Politics: Chicago Model*. Chicago, IL: Chicago University Press.

Gottlieb, Jessica. 2017. "Explaining Variation in Broker Strategies: A Lab-in-the-Field Experiment in Senegal." *Comparative Political Studies* 50(11): 1556–92.

Government of India. 2015. *Slums in India: A Statistical Compendium*. New Delhi: Ministry of Housing and Urban Poverty Alleviation.

Goyal, Tanushree. 2022. "How Women Mobilize Women into Politics: A Natural Experiment in India." Working Paper, Princeton University.

Greene, Kenneth. 2007. *Why Dominant Parties Lose: Mexico's Democratization in Comparative Perspective*. Cambridge: Cambridge University Press.

Grindle, Merilee. 2009. *Going Local: Decentralization, Democratization, and the Promise of Good Governance*. Princeton, NJ: Princeton University Press.

Grossman, Shelby. 2021. *The Politics of Order in Informal Markets*. New York, NY: Cambridge University Press.

Guardado, Jenny and Leonard Wantchekon. 2018. "Do Electoral Handouts Affect Voting Behavior?" *Electoral Studies* 53: 139–49.

Guha, Ramachandra. 2020. "Gandhi Said RSS was 'Communal with a Totalitarian Outlook'— and That's Still True." *Scroll*. December 20.

Gupta, Akhil. 2012. *Red Tape: Bureaucracy, Structural Violence, and Poverty in India*. Durham, NC: Duke University Press.

Gupta, Surupa and Sumit Ganguly. 2020. "Why India's Farmers Won't Stop Protesting." *Foreign Policy*. December 18.

Habyarimana, James, Macartan Humphreys, Daniel Posner, and Jeremy Weinstein. 2007. "Why does Ethnic Diversity Undermine Public Goods Provision?" *American Political Science Review* 101(4): 709–25.

Hainmueller, Jens and Daniel Hopkins. 2015. "The Hidden American Immigration Consensus." *American Journal of Political Science* 59(3): 529–48.

Hainmueller, Jens, Daniel Hopkins, and Teppei Yamamoto. 2014. "Causal Inference in Conjoint Analysis." *Political Analysis* 22(1): 1–30.

Hansen, Thomas Blom. 2001. *Wages of Violence: Naming and Identity in Postcolonial Bombay*. Princeton, NJ: Princeton University Press.

Harding, Robin. 2015. "Attribution and Accountability: Voting for Roads in Ghana." *World Politics* 67(4): 656–89.

Harding, Robin and David Stasavage. 2014. "What Democracy Does (and Doesn't Do) for Basic Services: School Fees, School Inputs, and African Elections." *Journal of Politics* 76(1): 229–45.

Harriss, John. 2005. "Political Participation, Representation, and the Urban Poor." *Economic and Political Weekly* 40(11, March 12–18): 1041–54.

———. 2007. "Antinomies of Empowerment: Observations on Civil Society, Politics, and Urban Governance in India." *Economic and Political Weekly* 42(26): 2716–24.

Hart, Keith. 1973. "Informal Income Opportunities and Urban Employment in Ghana." *The Journal of Modern African Studies* 11(1): 61–89.

Heller, Patrick. 1999. *The Labor of Development: Workers and the Transformation of Capitalism in Kerala, India.* Ithaca, NY: Cornell University Press.

Heller, Patrick, Partha Mukhopadhyay, Subhadra Banda, and Shahana Sheikh. 2015. "Exclusion, Informality, and Predation in the Cities of Delhi." New Delhi: Centre for Policy Research.

Herrera, Veronica. 2017. *Water and Politics: Clientelism and Reform in Urban Mexico.* Ann Arbor, MI: University of Michigan Press.

Hicken, Allen. 2011. "Clientelism." *Annual Review of Political Science* 14: 289–310.

Hicken, Allen and Noah Nathan. 2020. "Clientelism's Red Herrings." *Annual Review of Political Science* 23: 277–94.

Hidalgo, F. Daniel and Simeon Nichter. 2016. "Voter Buying: Shaping the Electorate through Clientelism." *American Journal of Political Science* 60(2): 436–55.

Hiddleston, Sarah. 2011. "Cash for Votes a Way of Political Life in South India." *The Hindu.* March 16, 2011.

Hilgers, Tina. 2012. *Clientelism in Everyday Latin American Politics.* New York, NY: Palgrave Macmillan.

Hindustan Times. 2020. "'Nathuram Godse was a Patriot,' says BJP's Pragya Thakur; Sparks Outrage." May 13.

Hirschman, Albert. 1970. *Exit, Voice, and Loyalty: Responses to Decline in Firms, Organizations, and States.* Cambridge, MA: Harvard University Press.

Holston, James. 2008. *Insurgent Citizenship: Disjunctions of Democracy and Modernity in Brazil.* Princeton, NJ: Princeton University Press.

Holzner, Claudio. 2004. "The End of Clientelism? Strong and Weak Networks in a Mexican Squatter Movement." *Mobilization* 9(3): 223–40.

Hossain, Naomi. 2009. "Rude Accountability: Informal Pressures on Frontline Bureaucrats in Bangladesh." *Development and Change* 41(5): 907–28.

Hull, Matthew. 2012. *Government of Paper: The Materiality of Bureaucracy in Urban Pakistan.* Berkeley, CA: University of California Press.

Ichino, Nahomi and Noah Nathan. 2013. "Crossing the Line: Local Ethnic Geography and Voting in Ghana." *American Political Science Review* 107(2): 344–61.

India Today. 2019. "I'm Proud of Demolishing Babri Masjid, Says Sadhvi Pragya, EC Slams Notice." April 21.

Jaffrelot, Christophe. 1998. *The Hindu Nationalist Movement in India.* New York, NY: Columbia University Press.

———. 2000. "The Rise of the Other Backward Classes in the Hindi Belt." *The Journal of Asian Studies* 59(1): 86–108.

———. 2007. *Hindu Nationalism: A Reader.* Princeton, NJ: Princeton University Press.

———. 2019a. *Majoritarian State: How Hindu Nationalism is Changing India.* New Delhi: Harper Collins.

———. 2019b. "BJP's Rise Has Meant a Shrinking Number of Muslim Lawmakers in India." *The Wire.* March 26.

Jaffrelot, Christophe and Gilles Verniers. 2020. "A New Party System or a New Political System?" *Contemporary South Asia* 28(2): 141–54.

Jayal, Niraja Gopal. 2019. "Citizenship Amendment Act." *Indian Express*. December 24.

Jeffrey, Craig and Stephen Young. 2014. "*Jugad*: Youth and Enterprise in India." *Annals of the American Association of Geographers* 104(1): 182–95.

Jenkins, Rob and James Manor. 2017. *Politics and the Right to Work*. New York, NY: Oxford University Press.

Jensenius, Francesca. 2017. *Social Justice through Inclusion: The Consequences of Electoral Quotas in India*. New York, NY: Oxford University Press.

Jensenius, Francesca and Pavithra Suryanarayan. 2020. "Electoral Switching in Indian Elections." Working Paper.

Jha, Saumitra, Vijayendra Rao and Michael Woolcock. 2007. "Governance in the Gullies." *World Development* 35(2): 230–46.

Jones, Rodney. 1974. *Urban Politics in India: Area, Power, and Policy in a Penetrated System*. Berkeley, CA: University of California Press.

Kapur, Devesh and Milan Vaishnav. 2018. *Costs of Democracy: Political Finance in India*. New York, NY: Oxford University Press.

Kasara, Kimuli. 2007. "Tax Me if You Can: Ethnic Geography, Democracy, and Taxation of Agriculture in Africa." *American Political Science Review* 101(1): 159–72.

Kennedy, John James. 2010. "The Price of Democracy: Vote-Buying and Village Elections in China." *Asian Politics and Policy* 2(4): 617–31.

Khan Mohmand, Shandana. 2019. *Crafty Oligarchs, Savvy Voters: Democracy Under Inequality in Rural Pakistan*. New York, NY: Cambridge University Press.

Khosla, Madhav. 2020. "With Freedom at Stake, Courts are Collapsing." *New York Times*. September 9.

Kitschelt, Herbert and Steven Wilkinson. 2007. *Patrons, Clients, and Policies*. New York, NY: Cambridge University Press.

Kohli, Atul. 1990. *Democracy and Discontent: India's Growing Crisis of Governability*. Cambridge: Cambridge University Press.

———. 2012. *Poverty Amid Plenty in the New India*. New York, NY: Cambridge University Press.

Koster, Martijn. 2012. "Mediating and Getting 'Burnt' in the Gap: Politics and Brokerage in a Recife Slum, Brazil." *Critique of Anthropology* 32: 479–97.

Koster, Martijn and Pieter de Vries. 2012. "Slum Politics: Community Leaders, Everyday Needs, and Utopian Aspirations in Recife, Brazil." *Focaal* 62: 83–98.

Koter, Dominika. 2013. "King Makers." *World Politics* 65(2): 187–232.

Kothari, Rajni. 1964. "The Congress 'System' in India." *Asian Survey* 4(12): 1161–1173.

Kothari, Rajni and Rushikesh Maru. 1970. "Federating for Political Interests: The Kshatriyas of Gujarat." in *Caste in Indian Politics*. Edited by Rajni Kothari. Chapter 3. New Delhi: Orient Longman.

Krishna, Anirudh. 2002. *Active Social Capital*. New York, NY: Columbia University Press.

———. 2003. "What is Happening to Caste? A View from Some North Indian Villages." *Journal of Asian Studies* 62(4): 1171–1193.

———. 2007. "Politics in the Middle: Mediating Relationships Between the Citizens and the State in Rural North India." In *Patrons, Clients, and Policies*. Edited by Herbert Kitschelt and Steven Wilkinson. Chapter 6. New York, NY: Cambridge University Press.

———. 2010. *One Illness Away*. Oxford: Oxford University Press.

———. 2013. "Stuck in Place: Investigating Social Mobility in 14 Bangalore Slums." *The Journal of Development Studies* 49(7): 1010–28.

Krishna, Anirudh, Emily Rains, and Erik Wibbels. 2020. "Negotiating Informality: Ambiguity, Intermediation, and a Patchwork of Outcomes in Slums of Bengaluru." *Journal of Development Studies* 56(11): 1983–99.

Kruks-Wisner, Gabrielle. 2018. *Claiming the State*. New York, NY: Cambridge University Press.

Kumar, Sujeet. 2019. "India has been Hostile to NGOs for Decades. Modi made it Worse." *Quartz India*. May 3.

Kumar, Tanu, Alison Post, Isha Ray, Megan Otsuka, and Francesc Pardo-Bosch. 2022. "From Public Service Access to Service Quality: The Distributive Politics of Piped Water in Bangalore." *World Development* 151: 1–14.

La Porta, Rafael and Andrei Shleifer. 2014. "Informality and Development." *Journal of Economic Perspectives* 28(3): 109–26.

Larreguy, Horacio, John Marshall, and Pablo Querubin. 2016. "Parties, Brokers, and Voter Mobilization." *American Political Science Review* 110(1): 160–79.

Larsen, Lawrence and Nancy Hulston. 1997. *Pendergast!* Columbia, MO: University of Missouri Press.

Latinobarómetro Survey. 2013. Corporación Latinobarómetro, Santiago. Available at https://www.latinobarometro.org/latContents.jsp.

Lee, Alexander. 2020. "Incumbency, Parties and Legislatures: Theory and Evidence from India." *Comparative Politics*. 52(2): 311–31.

Leeper, Thomas, Sara Hobolt, and James Tilley. 2020. "Measuring Subgroup Preferences in Conjoint Experiments." *Political Analysis* 28(2): 207–21.

Lessing, Benjamin. 2020. "Conceptualizing Criminal Governance." *Perspectives on Politics* 19(3): 854–73.

Levitsky, Steven. 2003. *Transforming Labor-Based Parties in Latin American*. New York, NY: Cambridge University Press.

Lokniti. 2004. National Election Study. National Election Studies Database. New Delhi: Centre for the Study of Developing Societies. Available https://www.lokniti.org/national-election-studies.

Lokniti. 2019. "All India Post-Poll NES 2019-Survey Findings." Available at https://www.lokniti.org/media/PDF-upload/1579771857_30685900_download_report.pdf.

Luconi, Stefano. 1997. "Italian Americans and Machine Politics: A Case-Study Reassessment from the Bottom Up." *Italian Americana* 15(2): 123–42.

Magaloni, Beatriz. 2008. *Voting for Autocracy: Hegemonic Party Survival and its Demise in Mexico*. New York, NY: Cambridge University Press.

Manor, James. 1999. *The Political Economy of Democratic Decentralization*. Washington, DC: World Bank.

———. 2000. "Small-Time Fixers in India's States." *Asian Survey* 40(5): 816–35.

———. 2010. "What do they Know of India Who Only India Know?" *Commonwealth and Comparative Politics* 48(4): 505–16.

Mansuri, Ghazala and Vijayendra Rao. 2013. *Localizing Development: Does Participation Work?* Washington DC: World Bank.

Mares, Isabela and Lauren Young. 2019. *Conditionality and Coercion: Electoral Clientelism in Eastern Europe.* New York, NY: Oxford University Press.

Masih, Niha. 2019. "Meet One of India's Most Divisive New Legislators: A Hindu Nun Charged with Terrorism." *Washington Post.* June 13.

McCaffery, Peter. 1992. "Style, Structure, and Institutionalization of Machine Politics: Philadelphia, 1867–1933." *Journal of Interdisciplinary History* 22(3): 435–52.

McClendon, Gwyneth. 2016. "Race and Responsiveness: A Field Experiment with South African Politicians." *The Journal of Experimental Political Science* 3(1): 60–74.

McManus, Jeffery. 2014. "Educational Qualifications of Village Leaders in North India." MA Thesis, Harvard Kennedy School.

Medina, Luis Fernando and Susan Stokes. 2007. "Monopoly and Monitoring: An Approach to Political Clientelism." In *Patrons, Clients, and Policies.* Edited by Herbert Kitschelt and Steven Wilkinson. 68–83. Cambridge: Cambridge University Press.

Mehta, Pratap Bhanu. 2020. "Ayodhya's Ram Temple is First Real Colonization of Hinduism by Political Power." *Indian Express.* August 5.

Michelutti, Lucia, Ashraf Hoque, Nicholas Martin, David Picherit, Paul Rollier, Arild Ruud, and Clarinda Still. 2018. *Mafia Raj: The Rule of Bosses in South Asia.* Stanford, CA: Stanford University Press.

Mitlin, Diana and David Satterthwaite. 2013. *Urban Poverty in the Global South.* London: Routledge.

Mitra, Arup. 2003. *Occupational Choices, Networks, and Transfers.* New Delhi: Manohar Publishers.

Montgomery, Mark. 2008. "The Urban Transformation of the Developing World." *Science* 319(5864): 761–64.

Morton, Rebecca and Kenneth Williams. 2010. *Experimental Political Science and the Study of Causality.* Cambridge: Cambridge University Press.

Murillo, Maria Victoria, Virginia Oliveros and Rodrigo Zarazaga. 2021. "The Most Vulnerable Poor: Clientelism Among Slum Dwellers." *Studies in Comparative International Development.* 56 (April): 343–63.

Nathan, Noah. 2019. *Electoral Politics and Africa's Urban Transition.* Cambridge: Cambridge University Press.

National Sample Survey Office. 2014. "Urban Slums in India, 2012." Report 561. New Delhi: Ministry of Statistics and Programme Implementation.

Nellis, Gareth. 2015. "The Fight Within." Working paper.

Nelson, Joan. 1970. "The Urban Poor." *World Politics* 22(3): 393–414.

New York Times. 2019. "A Mass Citizenship Check in India Leaves 2 Million People in Limbo." September 1. https://www.nytimes.com/2019/08/31/world/asia/india-muslim-citizen-list.html.

New York Times. 2020. "In India, Coronavirus Fans Religious Hatred." April 12. https://www.nytimes.com/2020/04/12/world/asia/india-coronavirus-muslims-bigotry.html.

News18. 2020. "BJP May Deny Tickets to Many MLAs in Rajasthan, MP To Stave Off Anti-Incumbency." October 27. https://www.news18.com/news/politics/bjp-may-deny-tickets-to-many-mlas-in-rajasthan-mp-to-stave-off-anti-incumbency-1916451.html.

Nichter, Simeon. 2008. "Vote Buying or Turnout Buying?" *American Political Science Review* 102(1): 19–31.

———. 2019. *Votes for Survival: Relational Clientelism in Latin America.* Cambridge: Cambridge University Press.

Nichter, Simeon and Michael Peress. 2017. "Request Fulfilling: When Citizens Demand Clientelist Benefits." *Comparative Political Studies* 50: 1086–1117.

Nooruddin, Irfan and Pradeep Chhibber. 2008. "Unstable Politics: Fiscal Space and Electoral Volatility in the Indian States." *Comparative Political Studies* 41(8): 1069–91.

Novaes, Lucas. 2017. "Disloyal Brokers and Weak Parties." *American Journal of Political Science* 62(1): 84–98.

Oldenburg, Philip. 1976. *Big City Government in India.* Tucson, AZ: University of Arizona Press.

Oliveros, Virginia. 2021. "Working for the Machine: Patronage Jobs and Political Services in Argentina." *Comparative Politics* 53(3): 381–402.

Ostrogorski, Moisei. 1902. *Democracy and the Organization of Political Parties.* New York, NY: Macmillan.

Ostrom, Elinor. 1996. "Crossing the Great Divide: Coproduction, Synergy, and Development." *World Development* 24(6): 1073–87.

Peattie, Lisa. 1978. *The View from the Barrio.* Ann Arbor, MI: University of Michigan Press.

Perlman, Janice. 1976. *The Myth of Marginality: Urban Poverty and Politics in Rio de Janeiro.* Berkeley, CA: University of California Press.

Perrigo, Billy. 2020. "Why India's Most Populous State Just Passed a Law Inspired by an Anti-Muslim Conspiracy Theory." *Time.* November 25.

Posner, Daniel. 2005. *Institutions and Ethnic Politics in Africa.* New York, NY: Cambridge University Press.

Post, Alison. 2018. "Cities and Politics in the Developing World." *Annual Review of Political Science* 21: 115–33.

Prasad, Shubha Kamala. 2020. "India is Cracking Down on University Protests. Here's What You Need to Know." *Washington Post.* January 10.

Pur, Kripa Ananth and Mick Moore. 2010. "Ambiguous Institutions: Traditional Governance and Local Democracy in Rural South India." *Journal of Development Studies* 46(4): 603–23.

Rains, Emily and Anirudh Krishna. 2020. "Precarious Gains: Social Mobility and Volatility in Urban Slums." *World Development* 132: 1–13.

Ramanathan, Ramesh. 2007. "Federalism, Urban Decentralisation, and Citizen Participation." *Economic and Political Weekly.* February 24.

Ravanilla, Nico, Michael Davidson, and Allen Hicken. 2022. "Voting in Clientelistic Social Networks: Evidence from the Philippines." *Comparative Political Studies*, FirstView.

Ray, Talton. 1969. *Politics of the Barrios of Venezuela.* Berkeley, CA: University of California Press.

Resnick, Danielle. 2012. "Opposition Parties and the Urban Poor in African Democracies." *Comparative Political Studies* 45(11): 1351–78.

Rizzo, Tesalia. 2019. "When Clients Exit: Breaking the Clientelist Feedback Loop." Working Paper.

Robinson, James and Thierry Verdier. 2013. "The Political Economy of Clientelism." *Scandinavian Journal of Economics* 115(2): 260–91.

Rodden, Jonathan. 2019. *Why Cities Lose.* New York, NY: Basic Books.

Roy, Ananya. 2011. "Slumdog Cities: Rethinking Subaltern Urbanism." *International Journal of Urban and Regional Research* 35(2): 223–38.

Roy, Rathin. 2019. "Changing Fiscal Dynamics." *Seminar*. http://wwav.india-seminar.com/2019 /717/717_rathin_roy.htm.

Rudolph, Lloyd and Susanne Hoeber Rudolph. 1960. "The Political Role of India's Caste Associations." *Pacific Affairs* 33(1): 5–22.

Rueda, Miguel. 2015. "Buying Votes with Imperfect Local Knowledge and a Secret Ballot." *Journal of Theoretical Politics* 27(3): 428–56.

Ruparelia, Sanjay. 2015. *Divided We Govern*. Oxford: Oxford University Press.

Sachar Committee. 2006. "Social, Economic, and Educational Status of the Muslim Community in India." Government of India.

Savarkar, Vinayak Damodar. 1923. *Hindutva: Who is a Hindu?* New Delhi: Bharatiya Sahitya Sadan.

Schaffer, Frederic Charles. 2007. *Elections for Sale*. Boulder, CO: Lynne Rienner.

Schaffer, Joby and Andy Baker. 2015. "Clientelism as Persuasion-Buying." *Comparative Political Studies* 48(9): 1093–1126.

Schlesinger, Joseph. 1966. *Ambition and Politics: Political Careers in the United States*. Chicago, IL: Rand McNally and Co.

Schneider, Mark. 2019. "Do Local Leaders know Their Voters? A Test of Guessability in India." *Electoral Studies* 61: 1–12.

Schuessler, Julian and Markus Freitag. 2020. "Power Analysis for Conjoint Experiments." Working Paper.

Scott, James C. 1969. "Corruption, Machine Politics, and Political Change." *American Political Science Review* 63(4): 1142–1158.

———. 1972. *Comparative Political Corruption*. Englewood Cliffs, NJ: Prentice-Hall.

Sethi, Nitin. 2019. "Electoral Bonds: Seeking Secretive Funds, Modi Government Overruled RBI." *Huffington Post*. November 17. https://www.huffpost.com/archive/in/entry/rbi -warned-electoral-bonds-arun-jaitley-black-money-modi-government_in_5dcbde68e4b0d 43931ccd200.

Shami, Mahvish. 2012. "Collective Action, Clientelism, and Connectivity." *The American Political Science Review* 106(3): 588–606.

Shamshad, Rizwana. 2018. *Bangladeshi Migrants in India*. New York, NY: Oxford University Press.

Shankar, B.V. Shiva. 2018. "Eye on Votes, Ticket Aspirants Offer Sops to Migrant Communities, Slum-Dwellers." *Times of India*. February 20.

Sharma, Mukul. 2001. "Bihar: Making of a Panchayat Election." *Economic and Political Weekly* 36(19): 1577–81.

Sharma, Ravi. 2008. "Coupons for Liquor." *Frontline* 25(12), June 7–20.

Shefter, Martin. 1978. "The Electoral Foundations of the Political Machine: New York City, 1884–1897." In *The History of American Electoral Behavior*. Edited by Joel Silbey et al. 263–98. Princeton, NJ: Princeton University Press.

Sircar, Neelanjan. 2018. "How Political Parties Choose their Candidates to Win Elections." *Hindustan Times*. March 28.

———. 2019. "Lok Sabha Results 2019: BJP's Win Margins Rose in 2019." *Hindustan Times*. May 25.

———. 2020. "The Politics of Vishwas." *Contemporary South Asia* 28(2): 178–94.

Slater, Joanna. 2019. "Why Protests are Erupting Over India's New Citizenship Law." *Washington Post*. December 19.

Spater, Jeremy and Erik Wibbels. 2020. "Social Density, Clientelism, and Targeted Pork." Working Paper, Duke University.

Srinivas, M.N. 1955. *India's Villages*. Bombay: Asia Publishing House.

Srinivas, M.N and A.M. Shah. 2007. *Grassroots of Democracy*. New Delhi: Permanent Black.

Srivastava, Ranjan. 2018. "BJP does Some Math for Plan to Buck Anti-Incumbency in Madhya Pradesh." *Hindustan Times*. November 1.

Stevens, Mark. 2009. "The Enigma of Meyer Lissner." *The Journal of the Gilded Age and Progressive Era* 8(1): 111–36.

Stokes, Susan. 1995. *Cultures in Conflict*. Berkeley, CA: University of California Press.

———. 2005. "Perverse Accountability." *American Political Science Review* 9: 315–25.

———. 2011. "Political Clientelism." In *The Oxford Handbook of Political Science*. Edited by Robert Goodin. 648–74. New York, NY: Oxford University Press.

Stokes, Susan, Thad Dunning, Marcelo Nazareno, and Valeria Brusco. 2013. *Brokers, Voters, and Clientelism*. Cambridge: Cambridge University Press.

Suttles, Gerald. 1968. *The Social Order of the Slum: Ethnicity and Territory in the Inner City*. Chicago, IL: Chicago University Press.

Szwarcberg, Mariela. 2015. *Mobilizing Poor Voters*. New York, NY: Cambridge University Press.

Tarlo, Emma. 2003. *Unsettling Memories: Narratives of the Emergency in Delhi*. Berkeley, CA: University of California Press.

Thachil, Tariq. 2014. *Elite Parties, Poor Voters: How Social Services Win Votes in India*. New York, NY: Cambridge University Press.

———. 2017. "Do Rural Migrants Divide Ethnically in the City? Evidence from an Ethnographic Experiment in India." *American Journal of Political Science* 61(4): 908–26.

———. 2018. "Improving Surveys Through Ethnography: Insights from India's Urban Periphery." *Studies in Comparative International Development* 53(3): 281–99.

———. 2020. "Does Police Repression Unite or Divide Poor Migrants? Evidence from Urban India." *Journal of Politics* 82(4): 1474–89.

Trounstine, Jessica. 2008. *Political Monopolies in American Cities: The Rise and Fall of Bosses and Reformers*. Chicago, IL: University of Chicago Press.

United Nations. 2018. "68% of the World Population Projected to Live in Urban Areas by 2050, Says UN." https://www.un.org/development/desa/en/news/population/2018-revision-of-world-urbanization-prospects.html.

United Nations (UN)-Habitat. 1982. *Survey of Slum and Squatter Settlements*. Dublin: Tycooly International.

———. 2013. *State of the World's Cities, 2012/2013*. New York, NY: Earthscan from Routledge.

Uppal, Yogesh. 2009. "The Disadvantaged Incumbents: Estimating Incumbency Effects in Indian State Legislatures." *Public Choice* 138(1–2): 9–27.

Vaishnav, Milan. 2017. *When Crime Pays: Money and Muscle in Indian Politics*. New Haven, CT: Yale University Press.

Vaishnav, Milan and Jamie Hintson. 2019. "India's Emerging Crisis of Representation." Washington, DC: Carnegie Endowment for International Peace.

Vaishnav, Milan, Saksham Khosla, Aidan Milliff, and Rachel Osnos. 2019. "Digital India? An Email Experiment with Indian Legislators." *India Review* 18(3): 243–63.

Van Houten, Pieter. 2009. "Multi-Level Relations in Political Parties." *Party Politics* 15(2): 137–56.

Varshney, Ashutosh. 2003. *Ethnic Conflict and Civic Life*. New Haven, CT: Yale University Press.

Veenendaal, Wouter. 2019. "How Smallness Fosters Clientelism: A Case Study of Malta." *Political Studies* 67(4): 1034–52.

Veenendaal, Wouter and Jack Corbett. 2020. "Clientelism in Small States: How Smallness Influences Patron-Client Networks in the Caribbean and the Pacific." *Democratization* 27(1): 61–80.

Verniers, Gilles. 2020. "What Candidate Selection Tells Us About BJP, Congress Strategies." *Hindustan Times*. May 14.

Wade, Robert. 1988. *Village Republics: Economic Conditions for Collective Action in South India*. New York, NY: Cambridge University Press.

Weiner, Myron. 1978. *Sons of the Soil*. Princeton, NJ: Princeton University Press.

Weitz-Shapiro, Rebecca. 2014. *Curbing Clientelism in Argentina: Politics, Poverty, and Social Policy*. New York, NY: Cambridge University Press.

White, Ariel, Noah Nathan, and Julie Faller. 2015. "What do I Need to Vote? Bureaucratic Discretion and Discrimination by Local Election Officials." *American Political Science Review* 109(1): 129–42.

Wiebe, Paul. 1975. *Social Life in an Indian Slum*. Delhi: Vikas Publishing.

Wilkinson, Steven. 2004. *Votes and Violence*. New York, NY: Cambridge University Press.

Wirth, Louis. 1938. "Urbanism as a Way of Life." *American Journal of Sociology* 44(1): 1–24.

Witsoe, Jeffrey. 2015. *Democracy Against Development: Lower-Caste Politics and Political Modernity in Postcolonial India*. Chicago, IL: University of Chicago Press.

World Bank. 2015. Development Indicators Database. https://data.worldbank.org/indicator /NY.GDP.PCAP.CD.

Yadav, Yogendra. 1999. "Electoral Politics in the Time of Change: India's Third Electoral System, 1989–99." *Economic and Political Weekly*. 34(34): 2393–9.

Zarazaga, Rodrigo. 2014. "Brokers Beyond Clientelism." *Latin American Politics and Society*. 56(3): 23–44.

Ziegfeld, Adam. 2016. *Why Regional Parties? Clientelism, Elites, and the Indian Party System*. New York, NY: Cambridge University Press.

INDEX

Boldface numbers refer to figures and tables.

pervasiveness in machine politics of the
Global South, 226–28, **228**; roots of: ethnic diversity in new urban spaces, 29–31;
roots of: limits of muscle power, 33–35;
roots of: multi-level electoral environment, 31–33; single-country studies highlighting the importance of, 232–35; slum
leadership and, 47
competitive brokerage environments, 63n67
credit-claiming: centralization and, 245;
neighborhood size and, 191, 193; partisanship in brokered exchanges and, 195–96;
responsiveness to petitions/brokered requests and, 16, 180, 206–10; type of good
and, 190–91, **192**; by ward councilors,
185–86
Curley, James, 18

education: importance of in urban slums,
69; as an indicator of leader competence,
70n89; levels of in India, 70n90; patron
assessment of brokers based on, 156; patron selection of brokers and, 159–60,
164–66; of residents, brokers, and patrons, **148**; as a trait of slum leaders, 68–70,
75–76, 79n108, 92, **93**, 222, 236
efficacy: electoral (*see* electoral efficacy);
everyday, 155–56, 166–68 (*see also* education, patron selection of brokers and);
loyalty and, patron choice in evaluating
brokers, 172–74; patron assessment of
broker, 155–57
elected government, three-tiered system of,
31–33
electoral behavior: ability of brokers to assess, 125–26; fluidity in vote choice, 32;
phases of Indian national, 240n61; turnout, 125; vote-buying, 60, 101, 134. *See also*
Bharatiya Janata Party (BJP); Indian National Congress (INC)
electoral efficacy, 155–57; patron selection of
brokers and, 159, 164, 167
elite responsiveness. *See* patron responsiveness to brokered requests

ethnicity: broker responsiveness and, 114,
118, 120, 123–24; caste identity/regional
identity as, 66–67; competition and ethnic diversity, 29–31; distributive concerns
and, 59–60; efficacy and, evaluation of
slum leaders based on, 76–78; ethnic diversity in sampled slums, **106**; ethnic indifference, building of inclusive reputations and, 223; limits of as explanation for
the emergence of a broker, 47–48; patron
selection of brokers and, 159, 162–63; political machines and, 24–26, 223–24; political responsiveness in brokered exchanges
and, 196–99, 212–14; reputation-seeking
and, 104–6; responsiveness to petitions/
brokered requests and, 181; simplified
portrayals of Indian politics based on,
pushing back against, 223–24. *See also*
caste identity
experiments in broker responsiveness, 15;
alternative interpretations of findings,
124–26; assistance received, resident
traits and, 120–23, **122**; clients and neighbors, evaluation of, 117–19, **119**; findings,
112–17, 124; impact of resident traits on
broker responsiveness, **113**; measuring
broker responsiveness, 108–12; multi-
ethnic support bases and, 123–24; questions about, 117; social desirability bias,
potential for and checks on, 117–24
experiments in leadership selection, 13, 64–66;
comparing brokers and neighbors, **81**;
correspondence to actual broker characteristics, 91–98; education as a trait of slum
leaders, 68–70, 75–76, 79n108; effects of
broker attributes on preferences for slum
leaders, **74**; efficacy and ethnicity, 76–77,
78; ethnicity (caste and regional identity)
as a trait of slum leaders, 66–67, 73–75;
findings, 72–80; interpretation of results,
77, 79; occupation as a trait of slum leaders, 70–72, 76; partisan identity as a trait
of slum leaders, 68, 75; as a political preference, test for, 80–82

claims by, 187–89; group claims by, dearth of studies on, 178–79; Hindu majoritarianism/nationalism and, 250; petitions from (*see* petitions); responsiveness of brokers to (*see* brokers, cultivation of and responsiveness to clients by); selection of brokers by, 52–58; slum leader involvement in claims by, 189–90; time in settlement, broker responsiveness and, 111–12, 115, 120–21, 125. *See also* urban poor

Saraf, Kali Charan, 238
Saraswati: emergence of a political leader in, 44–48; population and setting of, 44; slum leader election rules in, **45**
Savarkar, Vinayak Damodar, 246n77
Scindia, Jyotiraditya, 226
selection framework, 20; "active clients," 21–22; "ambitious brokers," 22–24; "multi-ethnic machines," 24–26; "politics beyond elections," 26–27
Senegal, competitive machine politics in, 234–35
settlements. *See* slums
slum leaders. *See* brokers
slums, 48; as context for study of political machines, 27–29; ethnic composition of, responsiveness to brokered requests and, 201; ethnic diversity in, 29–31 (*see also* ethnicity); minimal violence in the politics of, 33–35; partisan composition of, patron selection of brokers and, 160–61, 165; partisan composition of, responsiveness to brokered requests and, 201; population

size of, patron selection of brokers and, 160, 165; population size of, responsiveness to brokered requests and, 200, 214; portion of the population housed in, 4; transformation into epicenters of urban elections, 3; usage of the term, 12n35; worldwide population of, 219. *See also* squatter settlements
squatter settlements, 12, 48. *See also* slums

Thakur, Pragya Singh, 248
Tweed, William, 18

United States: local ward committees in Chicago, 143; party machines in, 8–9; Republican machine in Philadelphia, 140n22
urbanization: formation of political networks during, 11–18; in India, 4, 239. *See also* cities
urban political networks. *See* political machines
urban poor: advancing scholarship on the politics of the, 18–27; agency of (*see* agency); as architects of the political networks connecting them to the state, 236; city politics, incorporation into, 7–11; conventional portrayals of, 43–44; political organization of (*see* political machines); selection framework for (*see* selection framework). *See also* residents

violence, slum leadership and, 33–35
Vishwa Hindu Parishad, 247
vote-buying, 60, 101, 134

www.ingramcontent.com/pod-product-compliance
Ingram Content Group UK Ltd.
Pitfield, Milton Keynes, MK11 3LW, UK
UKHW030706020325
455718UK00002B/12

9 780691 236087